REACHING CLOUD VELOCITY

Illustrations by authors, or by kind permission from the original authors with credit provided.

Second Edition 2024.

www.reachingcloudvelocity.com

REACHING CLOUD VELOCITY
SECOND EDITION

A Leader's Guide to
Success in the AWS Cloud

Jonathan Allen & Thomas Blood
With forewords by Werner Vogels,
Mark Schwartz, & Adrian Cockcroft

FOREWORD

Dr. Werner Vogels, CTO and VP at Amazon.com

Innovation has always been part of Amazon's DNA, but about twenty years ago, we went through a radical transformation to make our iterative process (invent, launch, reinvent, relaunch, start over, rinse, repeat, again and again[1]) even faster. The changes we made affected how we built applications and organized our company.

Back then we had only a small fraction of the customers that Amazon serves today. But we knew that if we wanted to expand the products and services we offered, we had to change how we approached application architecture.

The giant, monolithic "bookstore" application and giant database that we used to power Amazon.com limited our speed and agility. Whenever we wanted to add a new feature or product for our customers, we had to edit and rewrite vast amounts of code on an application we'd designed specifically for our first product—the bookstore. This was a long, unwieldy process requiring complicated coordination, and it limited our ability to innovate fast and at scale. And then, if we wanted to enter a new country, we had to replicate all our infrastructure and keep all our code base in sync across multiple countries.

With that in mind, we created a blueprint for change with our "Distributed Computing Manifesto." This was an internal document describing a new architecture. We used this manifesto to begin restructuring our application into smaller pieces called "services" that enabled us to scale Amazon dramatically.

But changing our application architecture was only half the story. Back in 1998 every Amazon development team worked on the same application, and every release of that application had to be coordinated across every team.

To support this new approach to architecture, we broke down our functional hierarchies and restructured our organization into small, autonomous teams—small enough to feed each team with only two pizzas. We focused each of these "two-pizza teams" on a specific product, service, or feature set, giving them more authority over a specific portion of the app. This turned our developers into product owners who could quickly make decisions that affected their individual products.

Breaking down our organization and application structures was a bold idea, but it worked. We were able to innovate for our customers much faster, and we've gone from deploying dozens to millions of feature deployments each year as Amazon has grown. Perhaps more dramatically, our success in building highly scalable infrastructure ultimately led to the development of new core competencies and resulted in the founding of AWS in 2006.

And we continue to work in two-pizza teams today.

We're not alone in our quest to innovate quickly. Companies must increase their agility to continually uncover new opportunities and create better products to remain competitive. This is why more and more AWS customers are embarking on similar journeys.

Today millions of AWS customers in more than 190 countries around the world have made the AWS Cloud an important part of the way they do business—paying only for the cloud resources they need when they need them. They have greatly benefited from the performance, availability, security, reliability, scalability, and low cost it provides.

We have had the privilege of traveling the world and speaking to thousands of AWS customers. Executives always want to hear how other companies benefit from the cloud and how they made the change. One executive who successfully moved his business to AWS was then CIO of Dow Jones, Stephen Orban. Stephen loved sharing what he had learned so much that he joined AWS in 2014 as our first AWS Enterprise Strategist. He has traveled the globe as I have, speaking with AWS customers and sharing the lessons he learned as a leader who moved to the cloud.

Since then the Enterprise Strategy team has grown. Companies still look to learn lessons from other AWS customers. Although there is no compression algorithm for experience, guidance that offers an empathetic narrative to the leader who wants an experiential and prescriptive approach to the AWS Cloud can be a powerful accelerant.

Jonathan and Thomas, the authors of this book, joined Stephen's team in 2016, bringing their own experience as executives who led cloud transformations. They have subsequently worked with over one thousand AWS customers, which has given them a unique perspective on what it takes to fully unlock the cloud's benefits for your business.

Reaching Cloud Velocity is a guide to AWS Cloud adoption for decision-makers and leaders and points a way to use the cloud as part of your digital transformation. In its pages you will learn how the cloud can improve your business operations; how to develop a cloud strategy; how to structure and build your cloud leadership team; the nuts and bolts of people, process, architecture, and migrations; cloud databases; machine learning; security and governance; and much more. There is no other book I know of that so completely details everything executives and other decision-makers need to know to make the journey to the cloud.

Take, for example, one of the most powerful methods to unlock agility: serverless. Thousands of customers, from iRobot to National Australia Bank, use it. To quote Jonathan and Thomas's chapter on compute, containers, and serverless:

> Today's Agile software development teams are a heterogeneous mix of skill types and include software development engineers, security engineers, software quality engineers, and data scientists. The tools they use to deliver solutions, even with microservices, can be incredibly diverse. It's not just the application code you must consider; it's the surrounding elements. Identity management, telemetry tracking, logs, security groups, databases, management information systems—the list goes on. The time engineers and developers spend maintaining these tools… could be spent pulling forward and solving user problems by applying logic, data, or a better UX experience. Removing the work (and continuing to abstract higher and more efficiently) is where serverless comes in. It has a profound impact on development.

The book is full of practical advice you can use on your journey to the cloud. We are fortunate to have Jonathan and Thomas share their experiences, those of their AWS colleagues, and most importantly, the experiences of hundreds of AWS customers they have worked with as part of the Enterprise Strategy team.

I hope that as you read this book, you gain a better understanding of how to successfully make the journey to the AWS Cloud and the many advantages your organization will accrue when you do. Every day at Amazon is Day 1, and every one of us at AWS stands ready to support you in your journey. The book you now hold in your hands is the first step.

—WERNER

FOREWORD

Adrian Cockcroft, Former VP of Cloud Architecture Strategy at AWS

The pace of innovation has changed radically. It's no longer possible to stay competitive on an annual cycle of product or service updates, as the underlying technology capabilities change every day, and today's winners have figured out how to continuously adopt and drive new technology. Netflix is globally recognized as one of *the* most successful and innovative companies, and part of that success comes from a focus on working with AWS to maximize its cloud velocity. I've spent the last decade talking to a wide variety of organizations from around the world and trying to distill and share the lessons that can be learned from Netflix. The partnership between AWS and Netflix is an excellent example of long-term benefit to both sides. Netflix likes to be a very early adopter of new technologies so it has great leverage to guide and match the technology to its needs with minimal upfront investment. Netflix was one of the first customers to use many AWS services and features that exactly fit its requirements. We've also seen many other companies use a deep partnership with AWS and gain cloud velocity to lead their markets, including Goldman Sachs, Intuit, Cerna, Verizon, and Volkswagen.

The competition question comes up often. Netflix competes with Amazon Prime Video, and there are two points to consider. The first is that by using AWS—the most scalable, feature-rich, and reliable cloud provider—Netflix is running on the same platform, which neutralizes any technology advantage that Amazon Prime Video could have. The second is that Netflix set out to be a strategically important and highly visible customer of AWS from the early days and, with a decade of success, ended up as one of the largest AWS customers. It turns out that the customer obsession AWS talks about a lot is not limited to the biggest and most strategic companies. I see examples every day of AWS catering to its entire customer base. Amazon Prime, Netflix, Hulu, Disney, Fox, Warner, HBO, and most of the other streaming video platforms around the world run on AWS.

The other big lesson from Netflix originates from Amazon. Netflix has many small autonomous teams with clear ownership and responsibility and freedom to move quickly (Amazon calls these "two-pizza teams"). In 2006 Werner Vogels published an ACM Paper that included the idea that developers should "run what they wrote." Netflix made this part of its cloud transition, and each team stopped building components of a monolith deployed by a central operations team and turned those components into microservices with self-service automated continuous deployment into production. This approach to DevOps "teaches the developers to operate" on an automated cloud platform, encourages the shortest time to value possible, and is the best approach to getting out of the way of innovation. The most universal metric for innovation is actually time to value (think of it as innovation latency"), as it doesn't matter how big the organization is. If you can have an idea and see it running later that day, you lower the barriers to innovation for everyone.

Innovation velocity should scale up with size, but many organizations slow down so much as they get bigger that they don't see the velocity gains. One of the amazing things about a distributed organization is that velocity can increase faster than the growth rate as each new generation of innovative services builds on top of the previous capabilities.

Finally, I'm very happy to see a section of this book dedicated to the strategic planning technique known as Wardley mapping using some examples I came up with to help map the evolution of technologies from custom to products to services to utilities. These maps are a very useful approach to facilitate discussion and consider make-versus-buy decisions as data center-based applications migrate to the cloud.

This book contains a lot of great examples and advice, written by authors who've been there and done that, on how to innovate quickly and leverage the cloud.

—ADRIAN

FOREWORD

Mark Schwartz, Director of Enterprise Strategy at AWS

The cloud is changing not just IT but how business itself is conducted. More than that, it is deeply changing the world in which we live. Consider the work of the International Center for Missing and Exploited Children, which now uses AWS's facial recognition technology to scan social media to locate missing children and pass leads to law enforcement. The International Rice Research Institute has provisioned thirty-seven thousand cores of computing power in the cloud to sequence the genomes of three thousand rice varieties from eighty-nine countries to find the most drought-resistant and productive strains of this grain, which is a staple in the diets of over half the world's population. When a company moves workloads from its own data center to the cloud, carbon emissions are reduced by 88 percent. The cloud is drastically reducing humanity's negative impacts on our environment.

In the business world, enterprises can innovate, get products quickly to market, earn the fruits of their creativity, and then innovate again when competitors catch up. McDonald's developed and launched its food delivery mobile application in just four months and then scaled it globally.[2] 3M assembled 600 of its employees, conducted a three-day hackathon to experiment with new cloud technologies like machine learning and IoT, tried out seventy or so new ideas, then chose the ones that seemed most promising for future investment.[3]

This new, fast pace of development improves stability, quality, resilience, compliance, and security—perhaps the opposite of what you would expect. With the cloud, an enterprise can use speed to manage risk, respond quickly to attacks and failures, and automate repeated functions to make them more reliable and predictable. GE Oil and Gas reduced its P0 and P1 production issues (Priority 0 and Priority 1) by 98 percent when it moved to the cloud. This correlation between speed and stability was confirmed by studies reported in the book *Accelerate: The Science of Lean Software and DevOps*[4] and the annual *State of DevOps* reports.[5]

Even better: the cloud enables new software delivery techniques like DevOps and new architectures like microservices, which can further increase systems' speed, quality, and resilience. The combination of the cloud, new architectures, and new delivery processes is driving the competitive dynamics of the digital age, giving companies new ways to grow revenue, reduce costs, and reduce risks.

And it's easy.

Anyone can go home from work, take out their credit card, and spin up some new virtual machines in the cloud. (Their credit card might not even be charged since AWS has a generous free tier.) Compare that to yesterday's need to buy hardware, set it up, and operate and maintain it.

So what's the problem?

The AWS Enterprise Strategy team meets with more than a thousand large enterprise customers every year—enterprises filled with bright, creative people leading their industries with their ability to execute innovative ideas that create and drive their market categories forward. Cloud technology may be straightforward for them, but gaining all the benefits the cloud offers is hard. To take advantage of all those wonders of modern technology described in the paragraphs above, enterprises need to shift their cultures, develop new ways of evaluating IT investments, rethink their processes, devise new operating models, and evolve new skills. Those things are hard.

In the Enterprise Strategy team's meetings with enterprise executives across all industries and geographies, I find that similar obstacles and challenges recur. Yes, every enterprise is different—challenges manifest themselves in unique ways, and solutions have different elements. But any large organization looking to make a large transformation faces the same impediments at its roots.

These are the challenges of an organization that was successful and has devised ways of working based on that past success. Its employees possess the skills they needed in the past, and the corporate culture reinforces the norms that previously worked. But this organization realizes that what made them successful in the past will no longer make them successful in the new digital age of rapid change, uncertainty, and complexity. It needs to unlearn much of what it has learned and develop a nimbleness that will allow it to face the uncertain future.

And that is hard.

So this organization turns to the Enterprise Strategy team for prescriptive guidance. What have we seen that works? How did we lead our own companies' transformations before we joined AWS? What worked and what didn't work in those enterprises? How did we deal with cultural change, employee skill gaps, and changing security models?

Jonathan Allen and Thomas Blood wrote this book to answer those questions for a wider audience. They bring their experience, skills, and ability to formulate and articulate effective strategies and tactics. They lay out topic-by-topic and chapter-by-chapter how an enterprise can and must adapt to the cloud-enabled world. The approaches they describe are well-tested and aimed at the key questions that enterprise leaders face as they transform their organizations. Just like in person, Jonathan and Thomas are witty, empathetic, and creative in presenting the critical techniques an enterprise can use to thrive in the digital cloud-enabled future.

Consider this excerpt from their chapter on culture:

> Management is not about enforcing control in a hierarchy of functional responsibilities. It is about gaining the power that a team-oriented approach offers by amplifying the team's ideas, creating clarity around goals, removing impediments, and devising and allocating resources to support the team's activities. You need to engage the middle manager's ingenuity in accomplishing new goals where impact can be tied to business success and which, collectively with other goals, supports new ways of working. An important task for leaders today is to find ways to creatively redefine their middle managers' goals and incentives, aligning them with transformation.

In just a paragraph, Jonathan and Thomas give us the key to overcoming the supposedly "frozen middle," the layer of management that appears to be resisting change. Later in the book, they introduce the notion of "seductive adoption"—the technique of making new ideas so compelling that they drive their own adoption. These are the techniques we see working for enterprises as they do the hard work of transforming to face the digital age.

As an example of a more nuts-and-bolts challenge that many AWS customers face, Jonathan and Thomas devote a chapter to the tactics of migrating into the cloud—safely, yet with determination and impact. It is essential reading for the many organizations stymied by this challenge.

This book is the guide that IT leaders have been waiting for—the opinionated, no-fooling-around handbook for those serious about setting their companies up for future success by taking advantage of the cloud. Read it and enjoy.

—MARK

CONTENTS

Preface to the Second Edition

We published the first edition of *Reaching Cloud Velocity* in March 2020. It was not an ideal time to launch anything. The world was focused on the pandemic. The book's planned launch events and speaking ops were rightly curtailed; we wrote one modest LinkedIn post each and left it there. Then a rewarding but surprising thing occurred. The community appreciated our no-nonsense, down-to-earth, and easy-to-digest language on best practices for transforming your business to leverage the cloud. Thousands of Amazon Kindle and paperback versions of the book (Amazon still sells books, right?) were sold, significantly exceeding our expectations.

Some things have changed with the journey to the cloud. Many things haven't. The tone and content of our discussions with leaders have evolved. Today's conversations focus on *how* and *why*, and topics have become much deeper. Leaders have learned from their mistakes just like we did: On-premises infrastructure is hard to scale and comes with a bucketload of technical debt and "fun" new operational risks. (Only now it's tough to get support at 3:00 a.m.; tech talent has their pick of jobs with flexible hours).

Leaders who thought they needed multiple cloud providers (and learned that all clouds are not created equal) needed to hire redundant expert talent for multiple clouds while having the right governance guardrails in place. Trying to get to economies of scale with discounts across multiple providers is hard (and maybe not worth it).

Leaders have learned that recruiting new folks and offering more money is not enough to retain them; organizations must adopt an operating model and culture that empowers employees operationally. And some leaders have rightly learned that the cloud is a means to an end, not an end in itself. What matters is business outcomes, actionable steps to reach those outcomes, and how the cloud can fundamentally enable them.

So what's changed?

> ***Part 1.*** We've rewritten "AWS Cloud" from the ground up, focusing on the fundamentals and differentiators and providing an abridged grounding of the cloud.
>
> ***Part 2.*** We've adapted "Building the Business Case" into "The CFO Matters," reflecting on the crucial engagement that needs to occur in that role. We also transformed "Measuring Business Agility" into "Measuring the Success of Your Journey," as this question comes up time and time again.
>
> ***Part 3***. The chapter titles have stayed the same, but the content has been refreshed. Of particular note is "The Cloud Center of Excellence (CCoE)," which we've updated with lessons learned over the last five years, including how to operate multiple CCoEs in a very large enterprise.

Part 4. We've completely rewritten "Enterprise DevOps" and "Your Evolving Target Operating Model" into "Your Interim Operating Model" and "Your Target Operating Model—DevOps."

Part 5. We've largely left this section alone because it primarily describes immutable architecture—but we've updated data points as needed.

Part 6. We've added two new chapters to unlock data value at scale using "Data and Data Mesh" and (of course) "Generative Artificial Intelligence."

Part 7. We've added two more chapters: "Sustainability in the Cloud" and (drum roll) "The Multicloud Question."

We sincerely hope you enjoy the second edition. Please leave a review on Amazom.com. At AWS feedback is a gift—and who doesn't like gifts?

Thank you for all your support.

Acknowledgments

The difference between saying "I want to write a book" and the reality of publishing one is so utterly vast that calling it chalk and cheese doesn't do it justice. Writing this book has been a two-year journey of compressing experiential lessons and ensuring the content is appropriate and accurate (despite AWS's relentless innovation).

Fellow authors we've spoken to acknowledge that it is many times harder than they initially presumed. We are humbled by the sheer amount we've had to learn not only in writing and publishing but also in understanding the resources, support, and goodwill from others needed to bring a book to life.

And for that we have many people to thank.

First, we need to thank the leaders who have supported us in creating this book: Ishit Vachhrajani, Kamini Aisola, former manager Philip Potloff, former CMO Rachel Thornton, and former manager Stephen Orban. (Special thanks to Stephen for hiring us in the first place.) And thanks to all our colleagues in the AWS Enterprise Strategy team for their thought leadership—we learn from you every day.

Second, we want to thank our AWS mentor, Miguel Alava, for his unwavering advice, support, and curiosity for what we were doing and Darren Mowry for his ever-infectious support. Thanks to Dr. Werner Vogels—not only for kindly writing his foreword but also for sharing stories of Amazon's early days with us; Adrian Cockcroft for writing his foreword and helping us look around corners we didn't know existed; and Mark Schwartz for writing his foreword, answering our unending stream of questions about authorship and how things work, and providing extremely valuable (and at times difficult-to-hear) feedback.

Third, we want to pay special thanks to those Amazonians who unselfishly gave us their time helping, writing, editing, or lending us their intellectual archives: Jeff Barr, Joe Chung, Clarke Rodgers, Adrian Hornsby, Danilo Poccia, Julian Simon, John Enoch, Zehra Syeda-Sarwat, Mark Ryland, Bill Shinn, Matt Walburn, Jonathan Jenkyn, Michael South, John McDonald, Phil de Valance, Doug Vanderpool, Stephanie Lavocat, Christie Gifrin, Shiri Blatt, Rachel Richardson, Monica Benjamin, Matt Lambert, Emily Neumann, and Anand Pillai.

Finally, we would like to thank those folks outside of AWS who helped: everyone who helped at Silverfox, Simon Wardley from Leading Edge Forum, Peter Hinssen from nexxworks, Drew Firment from A Cloud Guru, and a special thanks to our second edition copy editor, Lauren Keleher.

Jonathan would like to thank his wife, Mandy, for her patience, support, love and understanding as his role often takes him away from home. He gives a special shout-out to his children, Jessica, Matthew, and Emilia, who keep him young at heart. Thanks to his coach, James Caplin (*lux ex tenebris*).

Thomas would like to thank Mike Kilander for his friendship, loyalty, support, and inspiration for more than two decades. Thomas has learned from many over the years, but wants to especially thank Frank Hespe for his friendship and for understanding the importance of asking the right question; James Isom for his friendship and for convincing Thomas to pursue a career in IT; Ed Gerck for his wisdom in system design and cryptography and for introducing him to the theories of Claude Shannon; Joe LoPiccolo for his insights on thinking about customers, procurement, and operations; and Eric Tao for teaching him about teaching, software, and architecture. Thomas is most grateful to his family and Barbara for putting up with his crazy travel schedule.

Introduction

According to Darwin's *Origin of Species*, it is not the most intellectual of the species that survives; it is not the strongest that survives; but the species that survives is the one that is able best to adapt and adjust to the changing environment in which it finds itself.

—LEON C. MEGGINSON, PROFESSOR AND AUTHOR[6]

Finding the right title for this book took nearly as long as writing it. How do you find a succinct, prescriptive, memorable title for a leadership guide to AWS Cloud that expresses the sheer breadth of the subject and meets one of the reader's greatest needs: finding a faster speed in business? When we finally thought of *Reaching Cloud Velocity*, it fit the bill perfectly (and the website address was available!).

Working with thousands of AWS customers over the last seven years, combined with our own leadership experience as executives, has given us a privileged perspective on enterprise change in the cloud. The tech world's current inflection point is a once-in-a-lifetime event, and we are humbled to be part of it. It is so exciting to help AWS customers suddenly see improvements across their businesses. Costs become understandable. Security is simplified. Flexibility improves. Enterprises can focus more on their customer outcomes. This is immensely rewarding.

Executives love to learn from fellow executives what works and, more importantly, what doesn't. The catalyst behind the book's creation was the desire to Think Big and share these combined learnings with as many enterprise leaders as possible. Engaging with countless Amazonians along the way has been genuinely fascinating. They have all unselfishly offered their experience in a customer-obsessed way to help this book's creation. We thank them all.

One of the mechanisms intrinsic to AWS is its effective use of tenets (or principles, if you like). You will hear more about them in virtually every chapter throughout the book. We think it's essential for you, the reader, to understand the tenets we established to write this book together.

All good tenets start with the words "We believe that."

We believe that:

- ***Prescriptive guidance matters.*** Leaders are looking for cloud guidance they can copy and paste and, crucially, amend to fit the context of their business.
- ***There is no compression algorithm for experience.*** But we will share the best practices from our experience and the hundreds of customers we have worked with. If we have seen something fail time and again, we will say so.
- ***This book should be referenceable.*** The table of contents is your friend.
- ***This is for all leaders.*** Irrespective of your role or level.

- ***Enabling people to upskill quickly and safely is critical.*** Let's focus on the people change while being cognizant of the technical possibilities that are constantly evolving.
- ***This should not be a textbook.*** Make this book easy to read and digest, not a cerebral challenge (yes, Amazon does this with its Narrative process). It should be 320 pages at most. (Darn it; we tried.)
- ***Durable strategies persist, but tactical details change.*** We strive to provide immutable best practices but recognize that details can be ephemeral.
- ***Speed matters.*** You don't have to experience every mistake yourself to learn; this book aims to accelerate your velocity.
- ***We are Amazonians; we are peculiar.*** AWS embraces diversity and thrives on uniqueness; our peculiar passion percolates prodigiously throughout.

Enjoy!

JONATHAN AND THOMAS

PART I
AWS CLOUD

1.1 Getting Started

There is no compression algorithm for experience.

—ANDY JASSY, PRESIDENT AND CEO AT AMAZON

Our experience has taught us (usually the hard way) that technology is the easiest part of transformation because engineers love to build things and know how to solve technical problems. We have found that most enterprises struggle with the cultural, procedural, and business transformations necessary to maximize the results of adopting the cloud. This often includes remembering how to do IT well after decades of outsourcing and how to apply Agile and DevOps in the enterprise. It also includes the impact on other stakeholders, such as HR, Finance, Legal, etc.

We are often amazed at how large companies with brilliant, talented employees who have brought fantastic innovations to the market need help articulating their vision or measurable goals. They worry about the disruption swirling around them and how companies can seemingly bring powerfully innovative products to market in ninety days with just a handful of people.

They have forgotten the early years when they were lean and hungry, when they had a clear goal to conquer the world. Now many companies, including well-known enterprises, are fiddling around the edges, making small but unimaginative product changes. They somehow have enough marginal success for the investors to remain calm.

Such companies are ripe for disruption. Don't be one of them!

When we meet with AWS customers, we start with the "Voice of the Customer." Where are you going? What are your goals for this year, next year, and the foreseeable future? What are three things you are struggling with right now? Some executives have brilliant, cogent answers to those questions, and some don't. It starts with a vision. Once you can clearly articulate the *raison d'être*—the reason you exist or your mission—you can rally your employees and motivate them for the next big thing. And more likely than not, that next big thing will require new ways of doing business and will probably benefit from going to the cloud. It will likely need significant changes to your people, process, technology, and, ultimately, your corporate culture.

Good leaders know that their vision drives everything. The question is this: How do you make the vision a reality?

The vision is likely based on meeting your customer's needs, and each department or functional unit needs to figure out how to align its purpose to the overarching vision. The product team must determine what new feature or service best meets that need, and marketing must figure out how to communicate with the customers about the latest product, feature, or service. HR must understand what positions to fill to create and support the business and its vision. And IT must figure out how best to support the entire business in its efforts to realize the vision.

Being an IT leader in today's world is one of the most challenging jobs on the planet. Imagine having a $100 million system go live at 4:00 a.m., with a thousand tasks to do, a high likelihood of something going very wrong, and the literal success of your company in your hands. The IT leader's job is to maintain existing systems cost-effectively while simultaneously creating new capabilities, minimizing risk, protecting corporate assets, and securing customer data. All too often, however, IT becomes the department of "Not so fast" while other departments perceive it as a cost center and necessary evil. The reality is that IT is essential to the success of nearly every organization on the planet. In a world where time to market (TTM), business agility, and innovation are on every executive's mind, IT must enable the company to go faster, be more agile, and innovate—all while meeting their traditional cost control and risk management roles.

This is where the cloud comes in.

Enterprises come to AWS for many reasons. They often try to understand how Amazon can innovate into so many adjacent businesses. Sometimes the executive team has created a slide with phrases like *cloud strategy, all-in, cloud-first,* etc., and IT feels compelled to explore what the cloud has to offer. Sometimes there is a compelling event, such as the three-day, on-premises database outage Netflix suffered more than a decade ago; the imminent expiration of a data center lease; the possibility of selling off part of the business; or the need to drive down operational costs more aggressively.[7] Markets are desperate for cost savings and the accompanying desires to increase time to value (TTV) and ship features faster while being secure and resilient. Whatever the initial impetus, once companies decide to explore AWS, they quickly realize that the benefits are far greater than they initially expected.

Early in Amazon's history, teams spent far too long building infrastructure rather than bringing unique new ideas to life. They had to remove what Amazon CTO and VP Dr. Werner Vogels calls "undifferentiated heavy lifting"[8] and create reusable building blocks instead. This was the catalyst that led to the creation and launch of the very first AWS service, which has now grown to over 200 services that are just a click or an API call away. To emphasize this point, we often ask leaders if they would ever consider building their own email service. Invariably when we ask that question, they look at us incredulously. But that is what many companies have been doing all along—they have built and maintained systems that are essential to business operations but don't drive differentiating value today. They certainly don't differentiate their business from the competition. Or as our AWS Enterprise Strategist Miriam McLemore (former Corporate CIO of Coca-Cola), once said, "You may love your data center, but it doesn't love you!"

So why do businesses persist in maintaining systems that they could consume as a service? "Why?" is a great question when encountering anything routine or bureaucratic. If something does not differentiate you from your competition and drive business value creation, see if there is a building block that can take care of it for you. There probably is. Use that building block instead of wasting time and effort recreating a utility.

This is easy to say but can be quite challenging when you have decades of legacy technology and processes. But rest assured, every question you could ask has almost certainly been asked before. The goal of this book is to condense some of the very best leadership guidance we can offer into actionable steps.

Now let's get started!

1.2 AWS Cloud

Invention comes in many forms and at many scales. The most radical and often transformative of inventions are often those that empower others to unleash their creativity—to pursue their dreams.

—JEFF BEZOS

When Charles Phillips, the CEO of Infor, stood on stage at the AWS San Francisco Summit in 2014, he made an assertion that resonated with us: "Friends don't let friends build data centers."

2014 was also an inflection year for our cloud journeys—when we started building on AWS. We remember hearing this exact quote repeated at AWS re:Invent (the annual global AWS conference) in Las Vegas later that year and reflecting on its intent. Why *are* we building our own data centers? Is building data centers the business we are in?

No, it's not.

In the tech industry, there are always passionate debates about the pros and cons of one solution over another. Here's a perennial adage: Ask a software engineer to give you an answer about using one technology versus another and you'll get the answer "It depends." Whatever tech we are passionate about, it's always interesting to see which ideas survive the white-hot crucible of business.

AWS Cloud is one case that has survived the crucible of debate and dramatically impacted businesses of every size and industry, from Netflix and Disney to Coca-Cola, McDonald's, Goldman Sachs, Capital One, and Airbnb —the list goes on and on. There are now millions of AWS customers around the planet. So how does the cloud so significantly and positively impact these customers?

From our experience and travels, we find a vast number of ways the cloud can positively impact a business. As Mark Schwartz writes in his book A Seat at the Table, "build vs. buy" is finally an achievable reality. Schwartz writes, "Software development has changed...there are supporting APIs, platforms, frameworks, and tools that take care of much of the grunt work of development." AWS calls this grunt work "undifferentiated heavy lifting." Removing swathes of this undifferentiated heavy lifting from customers lies at the crux of the cloud reality, which has and continues to change the world. This is tremendously liberating; it upends decades of pent-up frustration between IT departments and their business colleagues and powers the reality of Agile development and operations. Before we dive deeper into how to do this and the best practices, it's worth taking a few pages to help level set and explore the global infrastructure of AWS.

What Is Cloud Computing?

Cloud computing refers to the on-demand delivery of IT resources via the internet with pay-as-you-go pricing. Instead of buying, owning, and maintaining their own data centers and servers, organizations can acquire technology such as compute power, storage, databases, and other services as needed. It's similar to utilities: consumers flip a switch to turn on the lights in their home, and the power company sends electricity along with a monthly bill for each kilowatt-hour used. In cloud computing, AWS manages and maintains technology infrastructure in a secure environment, and businesses can access these resources via the internet to develop and run their applications. Capacity can grow or shrink instantly, and companies only pay for what they use.

Now we want to pause here and address a few painful misconceptions we see early in cloud journeys. First, many leaders initially believe that "all clouds are created equal" and that they are a commodity.

Public clouds are not created equal and are, therefore, not a commodity.

Each public cloud provider is radically different. We encourage you to delve deeper into the profound reasons why, especially security and operational resilience. Like most things in life, it's only when you test drive and use something under load that you learn the critical importance of its capabilities.

Second, folks often double down on their first misconception, believing they can spread their workloads and "get the best of everything" or worse—put their workloads in one place and their data in another to "get the best price." Both misconceptions lead to bad places with massive amounts of wasted time, blood, sweat, and tears. When you speak to those who have run hundreds or thousands of workloads, they will tell you why this thinking is flawed. We will share more on why.

Let's explore eight critical differentiating elements to maintain a high standard when choosing a cloud provider.

Security. There is a profound reason why "Security is job zero" (AWS is a geeky company, so we start counting at zero) at AWS. Unless trust is earned by constantly putting security first, everything else is redundant.

When companies choose to host their data and applications with AWS, they want the best security they can get. Many enterprises are drawn to AWS because of its obsession with security. Its leverage of computer science techniques, such as using automated reasoning to help answer critical security questions about their infrastructure and detect misconfigurations, is just one small example of this. We are happiest when AWS customers hold their data as encrypted cipher text with encryption keys they manage and own. Of the hundreds of leadership teams we've worked with, we've yet to meet an enterprise venturing to the cloud that doesn't have security as its number one operational element. We explore security much deeper in Chapter 7.1 Security Is Always Job Zero.

Availability. What AWS calls a Region differs greatly from what others call a region. Each AWS Region is fully isolated from the rest and comprises at least three Availability Zones (AZs). Each AZ is physically independent of the others in the Region and far enough apart to minimize the risk that an AZ-level event would impact business continuity. The AZs within a Region are connected by encrypted high-bandwidth, low-latency network connections over dedicated, fully redundant fiber. Each AZ has one or more AWS data centers within it. The unique benefit we found when we were AWS customers is running applications across the three AZs concurrently with Elastic Load Balancing (ELB) routing traffic and leveraging the relevant data services that the application may need, even when the application needs data with strong consistency across those AZs.

Strong consistency is a crucial model in the world of data replication. After Process A updates a data item, it always needs to access the updated value and never the old one. The different data consistency you may need for your application depends entirely on your business needs. Always speak to your AWS Solutions Architect about which services can best achieve your replication and consistency needs.

And if one of those data centers within one of those AZs suffers an outage, your workloads, when properly architected, can run within the remaining AZs. This thoughtful infrastructure availability design and its consistent global implementation across 33 Regions and 105 AZs (at the time of publishing) radically changes what uptime can be achieved. AWS takes the time to do this because of the many painful lessons learned as Amazon.com scaled to handle immense volumes while remaining online. The approach is very effective. In 2022, The Hackett Group conducted its global study, *The Business Value of Migration to Amazon Web Services,* on more than one thousand organizations that had migrated applications to AWS for at least twelve months. Those organizations saw a 50 percent reduction in critical infrastructure-related incidents per month in a twelve-month period.[9]

Durability. For those of us who ever had to recover data from on-premises systems, the rigamarole of hereditary tape strategies sent to offsite storage still sends shivers down our spines. Seriously. Cataloging tapes and dealing with lost tapes, agents installed on servers, and replication of storage arrays can keep you awake at night (even if on-premises cross-network replication strategies have matured tremendously). Outages are one thing, but being unable to recover data after an incident is really the stuff of nightmares. And that's why following hot on the heels of availability, durability is crucial when considering service creation. Again—not all providers are created equal.

One of the most dramatic examples is Amazon Simple Storage Service (Amazon S3), which was the very first generally available service launched all the way back on March 14, 2006.[10] (We love Jeff Barr's incredibly short, to-the-point blog for launching a service that many folks call a superpower in itself). Amazon S3 now stores over 200 trillion (2e+14) objects, which is a number that is hard to wrap your head around, so let's break it down into something a little easier. That's almost twenty-nine thousand objects for each resident of Earth. Amazon S3 is designed to provide 99.999999999 percent (that's eleven nines) data durability per year. This durability level corresponds to an average annual expected loss of 0.000000001 percent. For example, if you store ten million objects with Amazon S3, you can expect to lose a single object once every ten thousand years on average. So yes, durability matters. Be sure to ask uncomfortable and direct questions to anybody attempting to sell you a similar service in this regard.

Performance. The performance standard for computing is always evolving; we demand and expect things to improve. We can all look back with fondness on very early examples of technology not remotely comparable to what we use every day. We personally started programming back in the 1980s on the 8-bit Commodore 64 (hey, 64 KB was a lot of memory back then!). The AWS customers we have worked for rightly demand performance levels keep increasing while costs go down. We could wax lyrical on this topic for some time, but the point is: you have performance choice. The bar is raised every year. With over 750 Amazon Elastic Compute Cloud (Amazon EC2) instance types (covering Mac, AMD, Intel, and AWS's own Arm processors); network bandwidth up to 1600 Gbps; custom high performance computing (HPC) adapters; graphics processing units (GPUs); and near-infinite exabyte levels of storage, you have a lot of choices. AWS continues to innovate on behalf of customers relentlessly; it is never done with performance. It's also one of the reasons AWS has been named a Leader in the 2023 Magic Quadrant for Strategic Cloud Platform Services.[11] Expect and demand unrelenting, cost-effective performance choices.

Scalability. The horizontal scaling (often called scale-out) of servers, database capacity, file storage, and bandwidth on on-premises data centers is hard. We mean really hard. We've both managed and run data centers for years, spent many a budget cycle guessing who/what/

when can occur in a forlorn game of "guess the capacity needed," and—you guessed it—failed. You can dramatically overbuy capacity and never use it or, even worse, not have enough capacity when business needs jump. The ability for your server performance to shrink or grow near-infinitely, dynamically, or predictively while only paying for what you need is required. Amazon S3 file storage has this ability, and Amazon EC2 Auto Scaling provides this feature for Amazon EC2 instances across AZs. Want to dive deeper? Then read Chapter 5.1 Compute, Containers, and Serverless, for more. Many companies had challenges scaling during the COVID-19 pandemic, but not AWS.[12]

Services. There are over 200 full-feature services now available from AWS. This can feel like a daunting number. No one is an expert in all of them, and you don't have to try to be either. The critical thing is that you know what you want to achieve as a business and can leverage services; that means you don't have to build anything that will create undifferentiated heavy lifting to achieve the business outcome. The AWS services provide a global standardized set of building blocks you can use to run your business and operate globally. AWS offers a broad set of global cloud-based products, including compute, storage, database, analytics, networking, machine learning and AI, mobile, developer tools, IoT, security, enterprise applications, and much more. The general policy of AWS is to deliver AWS services, features, and instance types to all AWS Regions within twelve months of general availability based on various factors such as customer demand, latency, data sovereignty, and other factors.

Cost and sustainability. These go hand in hand. Only pay for what you use and ensure the service types you get give you the right performance/cost price point. For example, AWS Graviton4, AWS's latest and most power-efficient processor, provides up to 30 percent better compute performance, 50 percent more cores, and 75 percent more memory bandwidth than Graviton3 processors, delivering the best price performance and energy efficiency for a broad range of workloads running on Amazon EC2. AWS offers more than 150 different Graviton-powered Amazon EC2 instance types globally at scale and has built more than two million Graviton processors. Cost and sustainability benefits matter at scale. Research has shown that AWS's infrastructure is 3.6 times more energy efficient than the median of US enterprise data centers and up to five times more energy efficient than the average in Europe.[13] That said, simply migrating to AWS isn't enough to meet the sustainability and cloud financial management goals that today's enterprises are setting. To make conscious use of our planet's resources, applications running on the cloud must be built with efficiency in mind. See Chapter 7.3 Sustainability in the Cloud to dive deeper on this topic.

Ecosystem. Buyers and builders want choice. Many just want a working solution off the shelf that they can implement quickly without much hassle. They want prepackaged, hardened, and vendor-supported software, and they would like to leverage the licenses they already own. AWS Marketplace has more than twelve thousand offerings, including independent software vendors (ISVs) and partner solutions. When we first moved to the cloud, vendors often packaged software with hardware—this model is increasingly redundant. Creating and maintaining an Amazon Machine Image (AMI) is a lot easier for the ISV. Vendors pick one or two places to run their software, so using the cloud provider with the most software vendors running on it saves you massive amounts of time. It removes undifferentiated heavy lifting when using their software.

So what do these differentiated capabilities do for you? Moving to the cloud typically offers five primary benefits.

The first benefit is agility. AWS lets customers quickly spin up resources as needed, deploying hundreds or even thousands of servers in minutes. Customers can develop and roll out new applications quickly, and teams can experiment and innovate more quickly and frequently. If an experiment fails, you can always deprovision those resources without risk.

The second benefit is cost savings. If you look at how people move to the cloud, it almost always begins with cost. AWS allows customers to trade capital expenses for variable expenses and only pay for IT as they consume it. And the variable fee is much lower than what customers can do for themselves because of AWS's large economies of scale. For example, Dow Jones has estimated global infrastructure cost savings of $100 million by migrating its data centers to AWS.[14]

The third benefit is elasticity. Before we migrated to AWS, we over-provisioned to ensure we had enough capacity to handle our business operations at the peak activity level. Once we became AWS customers, we could provision the number of resources that we needed, knowing we could instantly scale up or down along with our business needs.

The fourth benefit is that the cloud allows you to innovate faster. You can focus your precious human resources on developing applications that differentiate your business and transform your customers' experiences. You no longer need to spend time and money building and maintaining things already available as a service that don't add value.

The fifth benefit is that AWS enables you to deploy globally in minutes. You can take an idea that works in one location, test it in another, and quickly deliver it to customers worldwide.

If you would like to explore this abridged introduction to the cloud in more depth, look at one of our favorite videos. In 2016 James Hamilton spoke at AWS re:Invent[15] about the depth and breadth of decisions and thoughtfulness that go into the infrastructure. It's a fascinating glimpse into the long-term thinking typical of AWS. Search YouTube for "AWS re:Invent 2016: Amazon Global Network Overview with James Hamilton" to dive deeper; it stands the test of time.

1.3 Orientation

Absorb what is useful, discard what is useless, and add what is specifically your own.

—BRUCE LEE, MARTIAL ARTIST AND ACTOR

You know precisely where you are. You are juggling eighty-five tasks and reading or listening to this book in a carved-out precious moment of reflection.

We know this because we have been there.

As the leader, you are attempting to run everything in harmony. You're working flat out to give yourself just a little more wriggle room to focus on those things that matter—like growing the company through innovation or ensuring you can get to the gym today.

But of those eighty-five tasks you are juggling, some weigh more than others.

We have all been on the receiving end of *that* phone call—the one at 3:00 a.m. notifying you that a critical company system just had a significant problem.

"Hey, we are escalating it to you as the leader."

Forewarned is forearmed. Except now your sleep is broken, your adrenaline has just spiked your heart rate, and there is only a forlorn hope of getting back to proper rest. Ready yourself for battle tomorrow.

For those who have read *The Phoenix Project*,[16] Brent's adventures feel uncomfortably familiar as he battles to deliver a Big Complex Project with impossible timelines, moving targets, and decreasing morale while simultaneously trying to improve efficiency and handle customer challenges. This is all while trying to grow revenue in an increasingly hostile environment with the added sweetener of a morphing and threatening security landscape. We read this book when it was first published in 2013, and we found it uncomfortably hilarious as we related it to our own professional and personal experiences.

Every leader continuously orients themselves, maintains situational awareness, and ensures their next step is the most impactful action to take. You will find "Call to Action" steps in many chapters, which provide direct suggestions for the next most powerful action you can take. We know change is challenging and exhausting, and change fatigue is real. We want our efforts to deliver results. We obsess about the perceived risk of fundamental change, but in our hearts, we know continuous change is required. We want to make a profound difference across cost efficiency, TTM, security, and employee morale to grow our business and delight our customers.

There is no right or wrong approach for structuring technology decision-making across an organization, but there are trade-offs between centralization (efficiency, standardization) and autonomy (TTM, innovation). Most of the executives we talk to increasingly favor the latter. This diversity makes it hard to predict what every organization's cloud journey will look like, but we have organized the rest of the book into parts to allow you to read cover-to-cover or cherry-pick as you like.

In Part 2 we focus on the fundamental challenges of aligning business and IT intent, gaining buy-in, and understanding the key business dynamics that have changed since the cloud enabled new business execution models. These models allow businesses to break down desired outcomes into items that can be built and delivered while minimizing the interdependencies that previously meant limited outcomes and teams working at the pace of the slowest component.

In Part 3 we give a brief overview of the culture and team dynamics involved in digital transformation and the importance of getting executives, early cloud teams, and a business office established. We also cover the often-overlooked importance of principles in this regard.

In Part 4 we go into detail about the importance of helping your teams adjust on the reskilling journey, working through the interim, and moving into an ever-evolving target operating model.

In Part 5 we lead you on a deeper journey into the technical fundamentals of how the cloud operates and how you can leverage tooling and techniques to enable your migration.

In Part 6 we begin with the goal—the data-driven enterprise everyone aspires to—and work backward.

And in Part 7 we stroll through security, governance, sustainability, and multicloud.

PART II
BUSINESS OUTCOMES

2.1 The Future of Enterprise IT

In the future all the code you ever write will be business logic.

—DR. WERNER VOGELS

What will the future look like? This is a frequent question we and many others at AWS get asked often. When Jeff Bezos answers this question, he says it is far better to ask, "What's not going to change in the next ten years?" As customers, we won't want slower delivery times, more expensive items, or less choice. So focus your energy on innovating to improve these things because any improvements will be significant. What will the future look like in enterprise IT?

We will still want things that are delivered quickly, cost-effective, reliable, and secure. That is straightforward. But beneath this highly loaded question is a painful truth: what enterprise leaders are dealing with today are the challenges they created for themselves or inherited from yesteryear. As leaders, we know the amount of time we have to spend imagining and enabling the future is directly constrained by the operational needs of our incumbent systems.

This "yesterday challenge" is encapsulated in the book, The Day After Tomorrow: How to Survive in Times of Radical Innovation, by nexx-works founder Peter Hinssen.

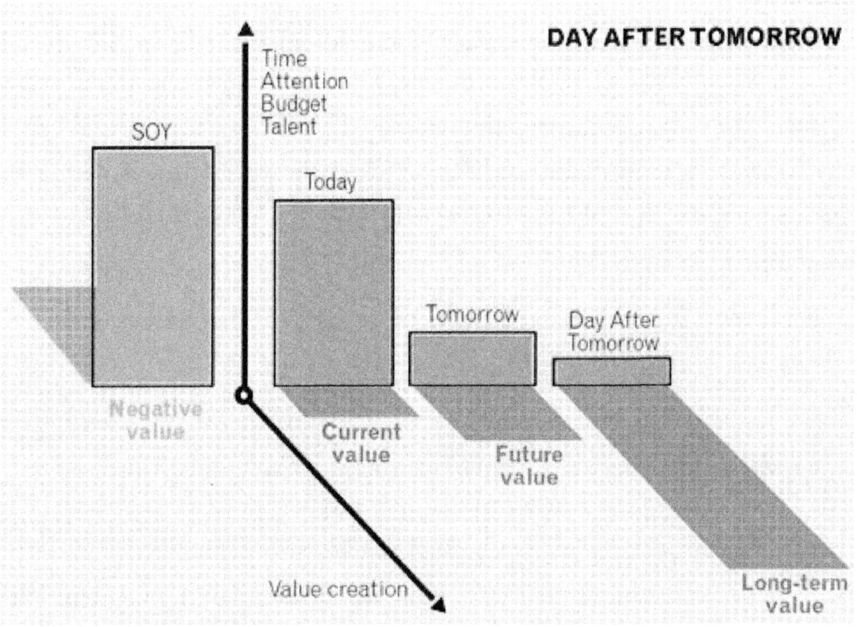

Figure 1 Ship of yesterday *(The Day After Tomorrow)*

We focus the lion's share of our time and effort on maintaining the current book of business since we cannot jeopardize our current revenue or contractual obligations. We also spend a great deal of time and money (and often blood, sweat, and tears) on the effects of decisions we (or our predecessors) made long ago. This "ship of yesterday," as Peter calls it (you can replace "ship" with another word if you prefer), is the source of much unplanned work and requires painful workarounds, duct tape, and baling wires to keep it running (how many COBOL engineers do you have on staff?). Very little time or resources remain to prepare for tomorrow and create future value. And many of us have no time to work on the "day after tomorrow" for long-term value, putting us at risk of future disruption by nimble competitors without all this baggage.

Getting Future Ready

Leaders want to hear from other leaders about what has worked and what has not. Thus the AWS Enterprise Strategy team was born. AWS recruited tenured executives who have driven transformations and experienced the extreme highs and lows that come with it. As a team, we dedicate a great deal of time to meeting with AWS customer executives. It is one of the most requested sessions we have.

Engagements address many aspects of enterprise IT depending on the customer's needs. But there are some incredibly consistent enterprise issues that we hear from executives:

- We're stuck between Agile and waterfall (WAgile).
- We're held hostage by software licensing.
- Security posture keeps me awake at night.
- We're stuck between two worlds (digital and nondigital channels) without enough funding to do either well.
- Talent focuses on the wrong things.
- There are too many box checkers and not enough engineers or developers.
- We're unable to attract and retain talent.
- There's intransigent middle management ("We can do it, but only if we can control it").
- There's technical pet projects (Squirrel!).
- We want to innovate, but we're scared to fail.
- The standalone innovation team is doing something weird.
- Mainframe—please help me modernize.
- WebLogic—please, please help me modernize.
- Exadata—please help me escape!

- How do I continually reskill my workforce?
- How do I deal with a workforce that is about to retire?
- Too many choices, argh!
- Oh no. I built an abstraction layer, and it isn't working.
- We are too slow.
- Where are you going? Where are we going?
- Stuck on the CAPEX-intensive hardware upgrade train—please help.
- Stuck on the never-ending OS upgrade—please help.
- The data center lease is expiring; how do we move everything by this date?

This list goes on and on. We can engage in these conversations with experiential empathy. We believe passionately that having the correct business mission, goals (aligned to solving customers' problems), and agreed principles (leadership and technology) in place can dramatically improve the situation of every one of these pain points.

We also spend time with enterprises that are (rightly) worried about disruption. But they have advantages that startups greatly covet: deep knowledge of their markets, skilled and committed employees, financial resources, customer base and brand equity, operational processes, compliance certifications, and deep pockets of data.

Using these strengths to fight disruptors in your industry is how you outmaneuver them. It's not the startups disrupting your organization; it's your customers' expectations!

These sessions typically lead to some exciting inflection points. First, Software-as-a-Service (SaaS) has been increasingly adopted by enterprises for its ability to allow greater focus on the business. The cloud's service offerings enable you to double down on this strategy, using standard building blocks to remove a ton of heavy lifting and, in effect, level up your human resources to perform far more valuable work.

Second, there is an essential distinction between rapid idea failure (which is to be encouraged) and failure in production (which is never okay). How often are you, as a leader, faced with a tsunami of well-intentioned business ideas from colleagues but lacking the capacity to add in "one more project or epic?" It's far better to have a team sprint for two weeks to test the hypothesis and either eliminate or double down on an idea with data. Having building blocks that you can either turn off or turn into production is the game-changing enabler here.

Third, not everything has to be Agile. If what you offer your customers as a business is highly commoditized and needs a Six Sigma methodology, that is absolutely fine. If you are innovating at the edge, then a different operating model is fine. Agile works exceptionally well for us. Six Sigma originates from terminology associated with the statistical modeling of manufacturing processes. The maturity of a manufacturing process can be described by a sigma rating indicating its yield or the percentage of defect-free products it creates—specifically, within how many standard deviations of a normal distribution the fraction of defect-free outcomes corresponds to.

Finally, bringing IT and business together is crucial. As IT executives, we may arm ourselves with new knowledge, but unless our business colleagues go on the journey with us, we cannot execute. The delivery gold is found in overlapping and mutually beneficial goals. Executive teams understanding what is required is one of the hardest changes of all. For an excellent deep dive into this topic, we strongly recommend the book *War and Peace and IT* by Mark Schwartz, published by IT Revolution.[17] Our teammate goes deep on bridging the gaps between

IT and "the business" and executing Agile at scale as part of your target operating model.

Moving to a High Frequency That Focuses on the Right Things

We want enterprise IT to be future ready, deliver quickly, be cost-effective, and be reliable and secure. What distinguishes enterprises that achieve this from those that don't?

You can typically compare the modern enterprise IT environment to an oscilloscope. At one end, you have:

Low-frequency IT. At this low tempo, change is infrequent. Any movement involves risk, instability, and lots of effort. This is typified by releasing three or four times a year in a high-pressure cauldron of business system analysis, architecture, infrastructure building, application, logic, data, and UX development. Automation and trust are low, resulting in high documentation overhead. Handoffs are controlled events—most human resources are devoted to planning and coordinating "the process." Command and control is the norm.

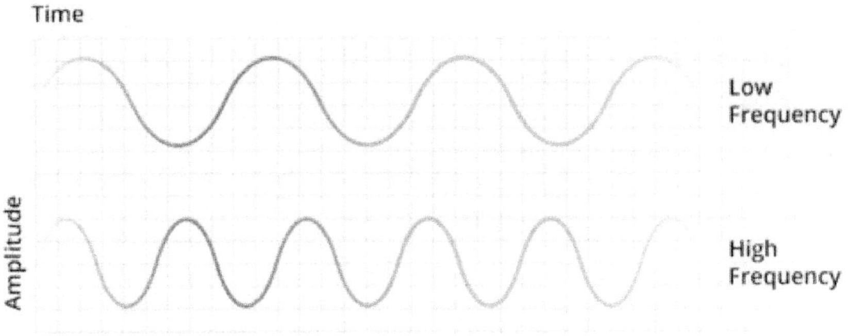

Figure 2 Low vs. high frequency

High-frequency IT. At this high tempo, change is constant. A flywheel of frequent value delivery limits risk and focuses on customer benefit over preventing operational disruption caused by change. Teams are guided by consistent principles and are rewarded for high automation and a focus on logic, data, user experience, resiliency, and security. Shifting technology right when a managed service is available is par for the course. (Easy, right? Of course it's not!)

Over the years we have seen catalytic events or difficult people drive a kneejerk reaction that becomes ingrained as bureaucratic behavior and part of the shared unspoken values. The trigger might be a catastrophic event such as a failed launch, security event, audit failure, or critical system outage that leads the enterprise to a low-frequency cadence with fewer releases, more planning, reviews, and signoffs ad nauseam. These events cause scar tissue. We love how Paul Graham puts it on X, formerly known as Twitter: "If you think people have scar tissue, you should see organizations. Each time there's a disaster, they create a process to prevent future disasters of that type. Eventually, they accrete a thick layer of these processes, preventing them from moving. Then they die" (@paulg, August 22, 2022).

Accompanying this newly ingrained behavior is normally a complex customer and technical support pyramid that accumulates layers of technical debt, reducing the velocity of creative activities. An attempt to focus on a big vision without learning and practicing how to execute a small one exacerbates the situation.

The Death Star Program (We'll Get It Right This Time—No, Really)

Enterprises are often focused on a big vision rather than practicing small executions. So projects are *big*—with bigger ambitions and a focus on lots of upfront planning. They create vast scopes of work. And even if they work in Agile sprints, releasing every sprint is not the focus. Instead the focus is on assembling lots of work for a big bang release that requires more coordination and integration before anything is deployed. The ever-squeezed testing cycle becomes more and more frantic as the midnight go-live countdown ticks. This is typical because:

- Big visions mean big projects culminating in one big release (one long wavelength is the project's scope), so everybody tries to get their pet project scoped in.
- Before anyone can start, the enterprise writes extensive requirements documents, preplanning every phase of the initiative.
- Without data to support the vision, the scope of the big idea is further bloated.
- As the risk operating zone increases, enterprises try to plan risk away and impose gatekeepers and gatekeeping processes to limit risk and ensure projects are delivered as planned.
- Security, testing, and integration signoffs are manual processes.
- Launch heroines and heroes are required to put the puzzle together, meet deadlines, and salvage failing expectations of the big vision. This leads to a symbolic and surreal death march to the finish line.

Moving from Low-Frequency to High-Frequency

The goal is to move from the old matrixed and siloed resources laden with technical debt, outsourced resources, and waterfall project delivery—which is mismatched to today's digital world—to high-frequency value creation. So how do you move from a low-frequency world, where vast, risky projects are birthed every two years, to a high-frequency world, where you iterate quickly to identify customer problems, test ideas have validity, and use data to decide whether to pivot or persevere and solve customer problems.

Call to Action

Step 1. Reduce the scope. Move from big bets languishing in development for extended periods to smaller batch size releases. Think about frequent value delivery, find what blocks this from happening, and remove the blocker.

Step 2. Move from HiPPO- to data-driven decisions. HiPPO is an acronym for "Highest Paid Person's Opinion" or "Highest Paid Person in the Office." HiPPOs are leaders who are so self-assured that they don't need other ideas or data to affirm their correctness. Relying on their experience and smarts, they quickly shoot down contradictory positions and dismiss the underling's input. Move from HiPPO-based decision-making to data-driven decisions where ideas and requirements are considered hypotheses to be tested and measured.

Step 3. Break down the silos. Break down the silos between IT and the business and then look to reduce the siloed technology teams. Bring teams together to focus on product or outcome.

Step 4. Maximize work not done. Carefully select when you will build, buy, or use technology. Don't waste time building something that is already a solved problem. See Chapter 2.3 Mapping Your Way Through.

Step 5. Build in security from the start. Don't bolt on security. If you need to, reduce the scope of the business outcome to ensure security is built into every sprint or stage. Plan for the best case rather than unknowns. Don't rely on emergency responses to self-remediating embedding checks that assume attacks, failures, and flaws will happen. See Chapter 7.1 Security Is Always Job Zero.

Step 6. Invest in your workforce. This is covered in detail in Chapter 4.1 Becoming Cloud-Fluent at Scale.

Step 7. Build in reliability and sustainability from the start. This is covered in detail in Chapter 5.3 Resilience and Reliability and Chapter 7.3 Sustainability in the Cloud.

Step 8. Pack the "ship of yesterday." Migrate then refactor your incumbent workloads over time. This is covered in detail in Chapter 5.4 Completing a Large-Scale Migration and Modernization.

Final Thought

The building blocks to fundamentally transform enterprises, differentiate their business from the competition, and improve the products and services they deliver to customers are available. But using them requires letting go of the decisions of yesterday that consume so much of your time, money, and other resources. For some IT executives, this is a challenging thing to do; change brings some amount of risk. But the risk that comes with doing nothing is typically far greater.

2.2 Your Business Strategy and Principles Matter

Hope is not a strategy.

—ANONYMOUS

As we discussed in the previous chapter, the tempo of IT delivery is changing to a high-frequency model. So the IT team can now go and change the world and drive innovation, right? Not so fast. There is no such thing as a technology strategy without a business strategy. But surely we know how to set strategies and run organizations? An organizational playback was produced early in the twentieth century! Let's take a quick look.

Shocking? Yes! Have you seen some of these things in your place of work? Yes, we have too. This is a declassified copy of a document that the Office of Strategic Studies (the forerunner to the CIA) produced to give partisans in occupied territories during World War II to sabotage the enemy. Yes, it was sabotage via bureaucracy!

Being a witness or, heaven forbid, involuntary party to one of these behaviors for years is an uncomfortable thought. How we are introduced to the workforce and what we learn early on have a disproportional stake in how we behave. In the same way it affects toddlers, nurture can profoundly impact what we believe is "right way." But there is another way of thinking that reflects how the workplace is shaped—explicitly or implicitly established tenets or principles. There

(a) Organizations and Conferences

(1) Insist on doing everything through "channels." Never permit short-cuts to be taken in order to expedite decisions.

(2) Make "speeches." Talk as frequently as possible and at great length. Illustrate your "points" by long anecdotes and accounts of personal experiences. Never hesitate to make a few appropriate "patriotic" comments.

(3) When possible, refer all matters to committees, for "further study and consideration." Attempt to make the committees as large as possible — never less than five.

(4) Bring up irrelevant issues as frequently as possible.

(5) Haggle over precise wordings of communications, minutes, resolutions.

(6) Refer back to matters decided upon at the last meeting and attempt to re-open the question of the advisability of that decision.

(7) Advocate "caution." Be "reasonable" and urge your fellow-conferees to be "reasonable" and avoid haste which might result in embarrassments or difficulties later on.

(8) Be worried about the propriety of any decision — raise the question of whether such action as is contemplated lies within the jurisdiction of the group or whether it might conflict with the policy of some higher echelon.

Figure 3 Simple Sabotage Field Manual (OSS, 1944)

are whole books on what makes a good tenet or principle, such as Ray Dalio's *Principles: Life and Work*.[18] While our book doesn't dive that deeply into the subject, we at AWS hold tenets close to our hearts. They guide our decision-making to the lowest level possible in what is now a very large business. It's how reversible decisions are made; at AWS we call them two-way door decisions. If we walk through this door and don't like the outcome, we turn back around and undo it. A one-way door decision can't be undone. These two-way door decisions can be made quickly, perpetually.

If you look at how many business schools over the last one hundred years have used principles to teach business graduates (and we have), some of the "Uh-oh" moments become clear.

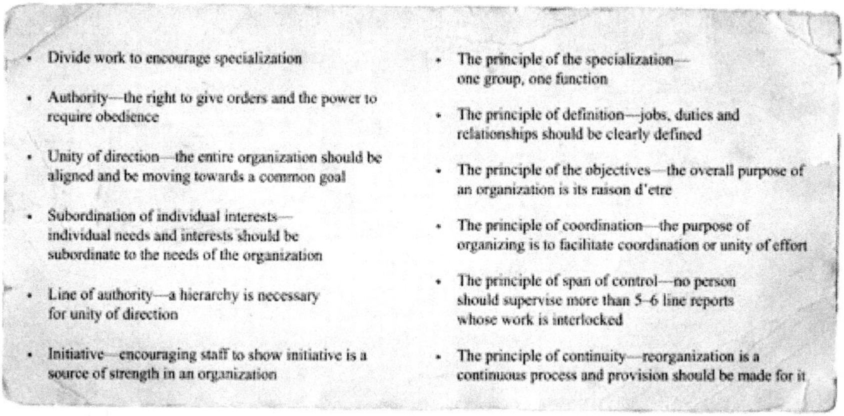

- Divide work to encourage specialization
- Authority—the right to give orders and the power to require obedience
- Unity of direction—the entire organization should be aligned and be moving towards a common goal
- Subordination of individual interests—individual needs and interests should be subordinate to the needs of the organization
- Line of authority—a hierarchy is necessary for unity of direction
- Initiative—encouraging staff to show initiative is a source of strength in an organization
- The principle of the specialization—one group, one function
- The principle of definition—jobs, duties and relationships should be clearly defined
- The principle of the objectives—the overall purpose of an organization is its raison d'etre
- The principle of coordination—the purpose of organizing is to facilitate coordination or unity of effort
- The principle of span of control—no person should supervise more than 5–6 line reports whose work is interlocked
- The principle of continuity—reorganization is a continuous process and provision should be made for it

Figure 4 Abridged Fayol and Urwick principles

Yes, many things that shape our organizations are stuck in the past. Henry Fayol (*General and Industrial Management*) and Lyndall Urwick (*The Elements of Business Administration*) did much of the pioneering work on business principles in the early twentieth century. It's an understatement to say that business has changed between then and now.

The book *No Rules, Rules* by Reed Hastings (CEO and founder of Netflix) and Erin Meyer puts it best: "The Industrial Revolution has powered most of the world's successful economies for the past 300 years... management paradigms from high-volume, low-error manufacturing have come to dominate business organizational practices."[19]

What has this got to do with strategy and bold goals? Everything.

In our meetings with AWS customers, we often discover that business executives recognize the need to change and believe leveraging the cloud can be a fundamental enabler of agility and growth. They believe leveling up and removing work they don't need to do allows them to focus on what makes their business, their business. But they often struggle when articulating the precise way to do it. They are stuck using playbooks, principles, and methods that influence their organizational design. Unfortunately the default reaction is often to start using new methods. This is a mistake. Just because Jane and Johnny New Startup is growing their business and threatening yours, and you hear through the grapevine that they are using BizDevFinSecGenAIOps, does not mean you should start using that new method without considering how you want your organization to operate, make decisions, and execute.

Harrington Emerson, the great efficiency engineer and business theorist, puts it best: "As to methods, there may be a million and then some, but principles are few. The person who grasps principles can successfully select their own methods. The person who tries methods, ignoring principles, is sure to have trouble."[20]

This is why changing your organization by implementing Agile, Scrum, Kanban, DevOps, DevSecOps, FinOps, MLOps, Lean, Six Sigma, site reliability engineering, and the new flavor of the month—platform engineering—is tragically, probably doomed to fail.

If you have not provided a framework of principles that allow your employees to make reasoned and empowered decisions, then guess what? Employees will wait for someone else to make decisions, make ill-considered decisions, or make no decisions at all.

Bridging the Gap

Most executives we speak with acknowledge that their IT and business strategies must be aligned. They should be the same! There can only be a business strategy—all other considerations should be details of how you execute against that strategy.

Creating your unique business strategy (assuming you are a commercial organization) is beyond the scope of this book and, sadly, beyond the scope of our team. It is utterly context-specific and unique to the landscape you operate within. If you are a public sector organization, you will be mission-focused instead of commercially oriented—a very different strategy composition.

Of the countless strategy books out there (we have read and sadly discounted many), one book that can be useful is *Good Strategy/Bad Strategy: The Difference and Why It Matters* by Richard Rumelt.[21]

Richard covers the uncomfortable truths. First, simply having a strategy is a strategy. Most organizations operate reactively to daily challenges with only a fuzzy outline of long-term goals that they mistakenly call "strategy." Leaders often struggle to articulate their organization's strategy beyond vague plans like "make alliances" or "set strategic goals." Second, a good strategy, above all else, leverages your strengths against your competitor's weaknesses. It is often most effective when it harnesses the element of surprise to leverage unexpected strengths against known weaknesses. When a good strategy reveals previously hidden strengths, the competition does not have prepared defenses against it, and the strengths become even more compelling. We explore this more in Chapter 2.3 Mapping Your Way Through.

Leaders can resolve this dilemma by providing precise and concise direction. Providing clarity of purpose separates great leaders from merely good ones.

Some executives of the thousands of enterprises our team members have met have focused on minor, incremental improvements. While this is right, strictly speaking, incrementalism does not create disruptive opportunities for your business. Creative destruction does not come from investing in safe bets or incremental change. Transformations are fueled by passion and a strong belief in a better future. This is where bold leadership goals can be beneficial. Be careful when using them—goals are not a strategy in themselves—but clearly stated, they can be a catalyst (and rallying target) for profound change.

While working at Capital One, Jonathan witnessed Global CIO Rob Alexander stand on stage at AWS re:Invent 2015 and declare to forty-two thousand people (with many more on live stream) that Capital One would close eight data centers by 2020. The goal was stated publicly, backed up with significant and unrelenting support from the entire executive team, and supported with effective feedback mechanisms. Capital One not only met but exceeded its goal, closing all its data centers by 2020.

Another example is Enel, an Italian multinational power company and leading integrated player in the world's power and gas markets. In 2015 Enel decided to migrate 5,500 of its 9,500 servers to AWS and close all but one data center. They were able to execute this ambitious goal in just nine months! Such accomplishments are not possible with an incrementalistic mindset. Enel's executive leadership created a seemingly impossible goal. Then it galvanized the entire organization with partners' help, to move most of its IT systems to the cloud in record time. This was not just another cloud migration. Fabio Veronese, Head of ICT Solution Center Infrastructure & Networks, says the move was "massive and fast." Veronese said it was successful because Enel saw it as a business move instead of an IT move.

In early 2022, as Ukrainians watched Russian tanks and troops amass at its borders, the government began physical preparations to defend its country and people. Less noticeable were the digital fortifications also underway—plans to secure the data that serves as an essential record of Ukraine and those who call it home.

Before the Russian invasion, Ukrainian law required certain government data and select private sector data to be stored in servers physically located in Ukraine. A week before the Russian military invaded the country, Ukraine's parliament passed legislation to allow government and private sector data to move to the cloud. Ukrainian leadership put out a public call for help, and AWS was among the first organizations to respond. Because of AWS's previous experience in disaster response and efforts to help Ukrainian organizations build cybersecurity defenses in the conflict lead-up, AWS technical experts (including solutions architects) quickly established secure communications with officials in Kyiv's government ministries and Ukrainian representatives across Europe.

On February 24, 2022, the day of the invasion, members of the AWS public sector team met with members of the Ukrainian government. The discussion focused on bringing AWS Snowball devices—ruggedized compute and storage hardware—into Ukraine to help secure, store, and transfer data to the cloud. That conversation took place on a Thursday. By Saturday morning, a set of Snowballs arrived in Kraków, Poland. Late that night and early into Sunday, they reached their destinations in Ukraine. These Snowball devices became the foundation for preserving Ukraine's data. Working across time zones and language barriers, AWS solutions architects partnered with their technical counterparts in Ukraine to begin the process of moving critical Ukrainian government data to the cloud quickly and securely. They moved huge swaths of information from local servers to AWS data centers.

As the war unfolded, Ukraine's largest private bank, PrivatBank, which serves 40 percent of the Ukrainian population, moved all its operations to the cloud. The bank's technical team worked with AWS to securely migrate 270 applications and 4 petabytes of client data residing on 3,500 Ukraine-based servers in less than 45 days. According to PrivatBank's head of IT, Mariusz Kaczmarek, the reason for the move was "to limit our dependence on hardware located in different regions across Ukraine from being destroyed during the war." But Kaczmarek doesn't see a reason to go back when the war is over. "We intend to continue operating in this mode further on," he said in a LinkedIn post. PrivatBank's customers can now access their funds and the bank's services online. While not precisely "business as usual," they are conducting business— and the same is true for the Ukrainian government.

TTM is critical. Focus matters. Speed matters. Speed is an executive choice, and the cost of delay is a good metric to consider in this case. Had Enel or Capital One dallied in executing their ambitious goals, they would have incurred extra costs in operations and staff. These businesses would've needed to contend with the opportunity cost of missed revenue generation.

Too many organizations fall into the trap of allowing well-meaning managers to defer action or kick the can down the road. We're always shocked when we hear of companies that decide to build their own data center. Time, effort, and inherent limitations are no longer justified. Bold leaders who choose to close their data centers and embrace future opportunities are now required.

Our friend Stephen Orban (former CIO for Down Jones and former VP at AWS) once wrote that today's technology executives should consider themselves Chief Change Management Officers (CCMO) when leading their organization's journey to the cloud.[22] In addition to handling the merger of business and technology, the CCMO is also responsible for providing clarity of purpose. That means staying determined and patient and articulating your strategy, how your team fits into that strategy, and where there is and isn't flexibility. Above all, lead the change. Stephen explains:

> "Early in my leadership tenure, I thought—naively—that just because I was the boss everyone would do what I said. I learned the hard way that this is, of course, not how leadership works. It wasn't until I started to clearly articulate what was important about our strategy that the behavior of my team started to change. Before presenting a new idea or goal to my team, I had to consider how everyone fits into this strategy and how it tied back to the business and everyone's careers. Then, I had to capitalize on every opportunity to reinforce these points."[23]

Call to Action

Step 1. Remove ambiguity by defining your business strategy. Netflix declared a bold goal. Netflix Chief Product Officer Neil Hunt said, "Our long-term goal is to let AWS do all the infrastructure work, especially where it isn't Netflix-specific. Our development team can focus on the features that are unique to Netflix so we can deliver the most compelling services to our members."[24]

Step 2. Remove inertia by establishing your principles. Everyone in the organization needs to make thousands, if not tens of thousands, of decisions. Clear principles and using a few well-considered bold goals clarify the direction. Decisions not aligned with the overarching goal are probably unimportant and should be deferred or eliminated.

Step 3. Remove the excuses by removing roadblocks. People are naturally uncomfortable with change; left to their own devices, they prefer the devil they know over the unknown and uncertain path toward a bold goal. Valid concerns must be addressed (including funding and training, if necessary). Everything else presented as reason or evidence not to proceed is likely an excuse to maintain the status quo. Excuses come in all shapes and forms, including cost, security, compliance, lack of experience, and many more. Answer each excuse once and move on. In the words of Inmarsat Cloud and Infrastructure Director Tim Brown at the 2019 AWS Executive Leaders event in London: "The biggest thing we fight every day is reversion."

Step 4. Measure progress through a few critical measures tied to your goals. Define what the goal's successful outcomes look like. Make the results known and measurable. Clearly articulate your motivations and goals to your team and stakeholders and hold everyone accountable for moving the needle in the right direction.

Step 5. Reward progress. Reward the behavior that drives goal attainment. Recognize victories along the way. Use a standup or all-hands meeting to recognize positive progress.

Final Thought

Make sure your business strategy includes technology. Avoid cheap mission statements and copy-and-paste "values." Work out your strengths and how to use them to offset your weaknesses. Establish a few bold goals and drive at them relentlessly.

2.3 Mapping Your Way Through

You cross the river by feeling the stones.

—SIMON WARDLEY

You may understand your strengths and weaknesses, but where should you invest? What parts of your business outcomes are becoming a utility (stop doing them), and which are becoming strategic (invest in them)?

In business you are constantly called upon to create strategies—plans for future initiatives that are important to long-term success. This is certainly the case when taking your company to the cloud. A major migration effort requires planning, coordination, resources, and effort to get it right. It requires a strategy. You can't wave a magic wand one afternoon and declare your initiative done when you're just getting started.

The problem is that many business strategies never actually deliver their intended results. Nearly a decade ago, a study of 163 CEOs and other top execs by Forbes Insights and Financial Dynamics revealed that almost one-third of all business strategies don't achieve their stated goals.[25] Based on our observations of the increasingly fluid business landscape, we suspect that number is even lower now. According to the study, the top five reasons for failure include:

- Unforeseen external circumstances (24 percent).
- Lack of understanding among those involved in developing the strategy and what they need to do to make it successful (19 percent).
- The strategy itself is flawed. (18 percent).
- Poor match between the strategy and core competencies of the organization (16 percent).
- Lack of accountability or of holding the team responsible (13 percent).

These points of failure indicate whoever crafted the strategies significantly lacked situational awareness. They lacked clarity about the environments in which they were doing business. The people tasked with executing the strategies were uncertain how to achieve them, and serious mismatches existed between the strategies and purpose of the companies that deployed them.

Every great journey has a beginning and an end—the destination. You start on the busy streets of New York City and end up in a quiet lodge overlooking the Grand Canyon on holiday. Or you graduate college with a degree in art history, and twenty years later, you're the COO of a fast-growing tech company with people and offices scattered around the globe.

The same is true in business. You begin with a consumer desire to solve a long-standing problem and deliver a new product or feature that fulfills that consumer desire (and perhaps sells millions of copies in the process). Or your business's growth requires building out, opening, and staffing new offices in Atlanta, Nairobi, and London.

How do you find your desired destination as quickly and efficiently as possible, with minimal wrong turns, crashes, and dead ends?

You use a map.

We are big fans of Simon Wardley and his approach to mapping strategies. For four years Simon served as CEO of a company called Fotango, a UK-based photo-sharing service. He developed the idea for mapping strategies when he needed to figure out whether the strategy he and his team created would work.

Of more significant concern, Fotango was growing, profitable, and healthy, and Simon could not explain why. Was it because of the company's remarkably well-crafted, insightful strategies (doubtful) or simply dumb luck (more likely)?

Simon explains the roots of his concern:

> "I was the most senior of executives. The company would live or die by my strategic choices, or so I thought. I wrote the strategy, or at least variations were presented to me, and I would decide. But something had gone terribly wrong in my journey. Somehow along the path to becoming a CEO, I had missed those all-important lessons that told me how to evaluate a strategy. I still had no means to understand what a good strategy was and it was no longer enough for me to think it "seems fine." I needed more than that as I was the experienced executive that the less experienced took guidance from."[26]

Simon did what many other CEOs at the time did: He read lots of books about business strategy, learned how to use SWOT analysis and two-by-two matrices, and hired a consulting firm to improve communication within his team—hoping he would see the light and the right strategies would emerge as a result.

They didn't.

Plagued with self-doubt (and deathly afraid that he would soon be revealed as an impostor—a "fake CEO" not worthy of helming Fotango), Simon happened to read Sun Tzu's *The Art of War*. This book was the key inspiration for his approach to mapping.

Sun Tzu says that when two opponents compete, five factors matter: purpose, landscape, climate, doctrine, and leadership. As Simon considered this idea, he realized that maps—specifically topographical intelligence—were one of the most important keys to developing successful military strategies.

What if maps could be successfully applied to business development and supporting IT strategies? What then?

Planning

Tools commonly employed in business and IT strategy are flow charts, two-by-two matrices, balanced scorecards, complex operating models, IT roadmaps, dependency diagrams, and the list goes on and on. While these tools may help answer important questions or planning, they often amount to mere handwaving—the equivalent of expensive, consultant-developed PowerPoint presentations and spreadsheet models that look impressive at first glance only to gather dust on the corporate bookshelf.

You need a map. Something to help you get from point A to point B. Imagine you are a strategic adviser to the commander of Leonidas's forces at Thermopylae. Which tool would you use to advise the king?[27]

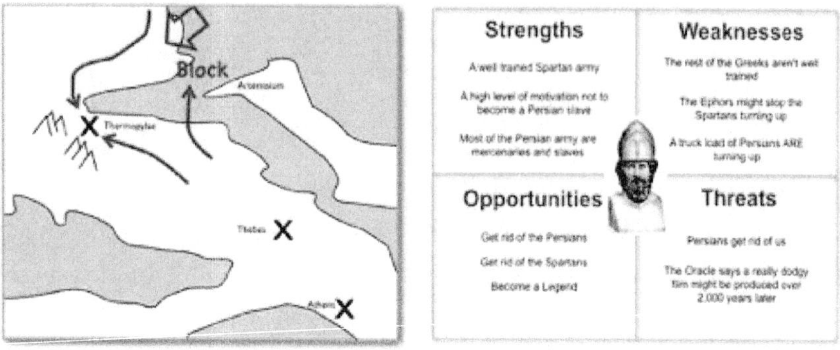

Figure 5 Wardley mapping—Map vs. SWOT

That's what we thought. The map is intuitive and conveys a great deal of information in a single glance. It would be best if you had a clear understanding of distance, time, space, and terrain factors that dictate avenues of approach and reveal insurmountable obstacles.

What is needed is a mechanism known in mapping as wayfinding: a system that guides people through a physical environment and enhances their understanding and experience of the space in which they operate. Wardley maps provide this wayfinding system. They depict activities needed to fulfill user needs (i.e., the value chain) and an evolutionary axis. Visible things are located at the top of the map, and invisible things, such as back-office components, are placed toward the bottom. The system requires a sense of how things evolve. Most successful companies started as innovators in their space—they create a unique and valuable solution for a particular problem set. This is what Wardley calls the pioneer period. As companies build on their initial success, they optimize and refine their initial solution—the settler period. Over time the solution or product, often under competitive pressure, evolves into a utility. This period is managed by the "town planners."

The challenge is that many organizations have neither a clear sense of evolutionary time nor an idea of the strategic environment in which they operate.

When a corporate board tells the CIO to be more innovative, but the company has been operating in the settler or town planner mindset for a decade or two, it's a small wonder that innovation is relegated to a lab. Here it might create something useful that will never emerge in the marketplace because the COO does not know how to operationalize it.

Wardley maps are an excellent tool to visualize where your business is at a given moment and the path forward. Wardley maps show value chains versus evolution. They are organized with a time dimension along the x-axis, starting with Genesis on the left and then traversing the evolutionary path from Custom Built, through Product (or Rental) and finally Utility. If you think about a product or service you offer today, it is generally between an original idea and a fully commoditized offering.

Technology leaders decide whether to build, buy, or use and understand available technology. Why would you build something already available as a secure, scalable, and cost-effective service?

Using the discipline of a map allows you to figure out what you need to focus on and what is already a utility you can leverage to remove work. It's incredible to us how many people continue to miss this step.

To build a Wardley map, place the user need at the top and then add everything that supports it. The most visible things are also at the top, and you dive deeper and deeper until, at the bottom of the map, you have commodities or utilities like data centers, electricity, buildings, and so forth. At the top, you might have a mobile app or an interface—something that supports a customer. Then there are all the bits in between.

Simon likes to point out that you start with something novel that you had to create from scratch and was hard to build. Think back twenty years—a data center was a custom thing to build from scratch. If you had a better data center than your competitor, you had a better product because your data center was faster. The *idea* of building a data center is in the Genesis phase (on the left side of a Wardley map). Actually building one moves the data center to the Custom Built phase. Then you buy a cage in a colocation center and prebuild it with some standard racks, which moves the data center to the Product phase. Data centers finally become a Utility—the fastest way to open a state-of-the-art data center today is to open an AWS account.

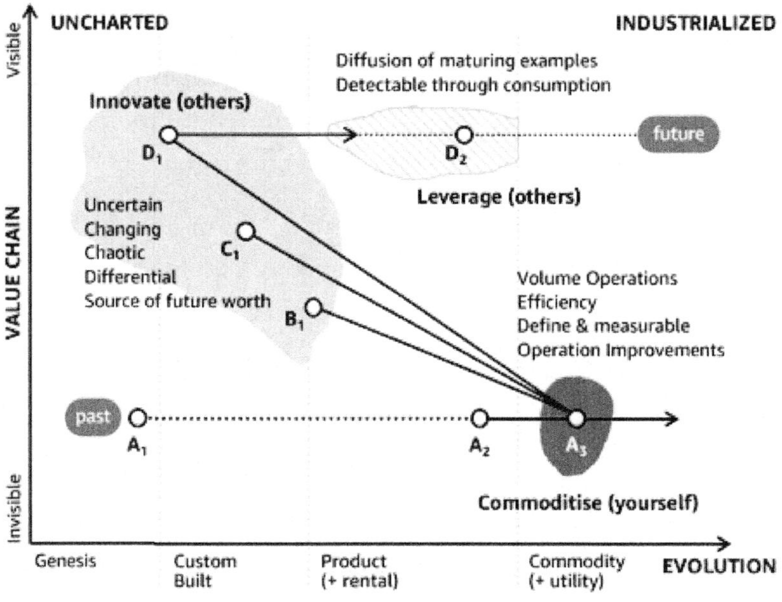

Figure 6 Wardley mapping—Value chain with evolution

Since everyone now has access to leading-edge data center technology via AWS, you must build something on top of that. So the innovation moves up a level—to the upper left of a Wardley map, closer to the customer—while things that are lower in the value chain move to the bottom right.

On the left-hand side, you are consciously experimenting. You've never built it before—no one's ever built it before—it's startup land, a brand-new feature. You're experimenting, A/B testing, iterating rapidly, and throwing ideas against the wall to see if they stick.

On the right-hand side, it's essential to fine-tune everything. It's Six Sigma—getting out all the variation—and cost optimization. People are familiar with this thing—it's a standard interface like electricity. But a lot of innovation is happening in generating electricity from renewable sources.

A Wardley map visualizes not only where you are (your current technology stack) but where you're going (its evolution over time). It shows position and movement.

This map can be used to drive toward meeting a strategic goal, imagine the future, or think about how you might create that future.

In a presentation at AWS Palo Alto, Adrian Cockcroft, former VP of Cloud Architecture Strategy at AWS, gave an example of applying a Wardley map to the development of a travel search product—using Simon Wardley himself as the subject.[28]

Simon Wardley hates to fly coach—the cramped seats cause him significant discomfort and back pain. So he wanted to create a mobile search app to find comfy flight options.

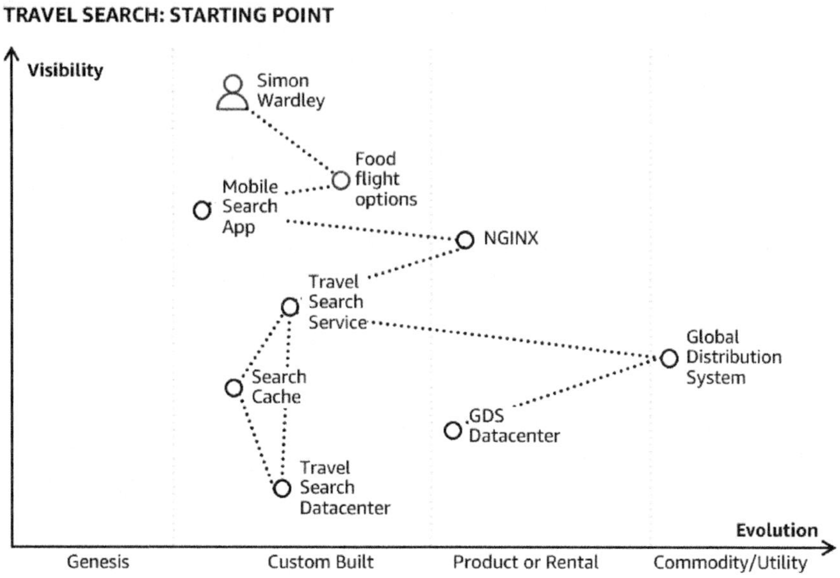

Figure 7 Wardley mapping example

When you create a map, the first question is: What problem are you trying to solve? Let's say that users want faster, more personalized search. The business wants faster feature releases and lower costs. The next question is: What does the value chain look like? You've got the user need at the top, followed by a search interface, some sort of travel data store, and compute and storage. See Figure 7 for a map of Wardley's travel search product.

Wardley's user need—to find flight options—is at the top. He has a custom-built mobile search app that talks to NGINX (an API service farther to the right on the map). Then there's a travel search service, a search cache for caching all the recent searches to make it more efficient, and a travel search data center—all Custom Built. Finally, a global distribution system (GDS), like Sabre or Amadeus, runs in its own data center.

As this app runs, it catches a lot more data. Costs are rising, and it's taking longer to complete searches. So look at the Wardley map to see how you can make the stack more efficient and cost less.

Rewrite NGINX using Amazon API Gateway, rewrite the travel search service using AWS Lambda, and run the search cache on Amazon ElastiCache for Redis. All those things move to the right, which in the cloud is a Utility. You no longer run these functions in a custom data center, making everything faster, cheaper, more reliable, etc.

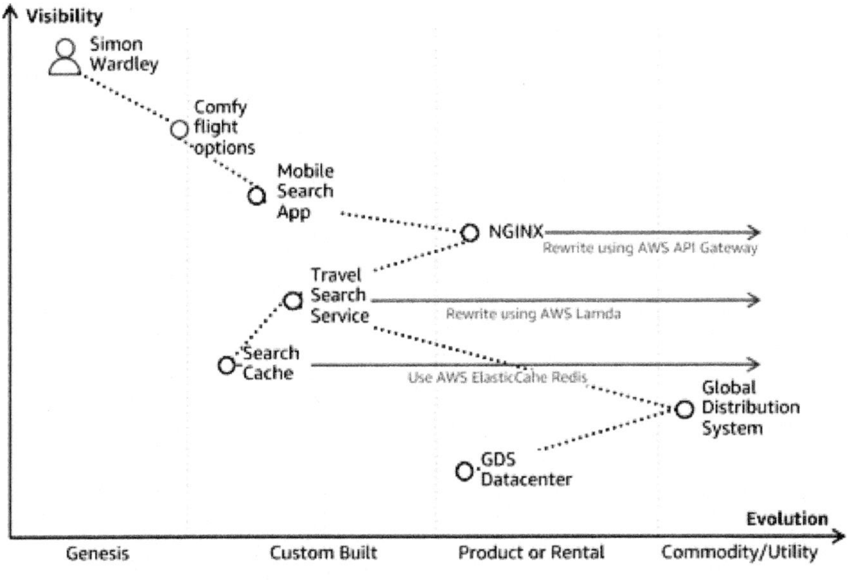

Figure 8 Wardley mapping with change(s)

Finally, you can work with the GDS supplier to migrate its service to the same AWS Region as the rest of the application, providing the lowest possible search latency.

How is this relevant to cloud adoption?

First, Wardley maps make an excellent addition to help plan your approach to cloud migration. Second, Wardley maps shine when mapping your product strategy.

Going Deeper on Mapping Concepts

Genesis. This is the realm of testing hypotheses and experimenting with new product ideas. This includes the outcomes of hackathons, prototypes, and minimum viable products. Teams quickly create new concepts based on business hypotheses and test assumptions. These can be customer-facing user experience tests or core functional components in the back office.

This represents the unique, the very rare, the uncertain, the constantly changing, and the newly discovered. Our focus is on exploration. The low economic cost of the cloud, which enables experiments for hundreds of dollars versus the millions required to procure, rack, stack, and configure while making a Hail Mary bet, is why we have witnessed an explosion of digital innovation since AWS launched in 2006.

Custom Built. Applications that have passed muster during the initial hypotheses testing can be enhanced and tested further, and product ideas are honed and optimized. As you deconstruct or "strangle" your monolithic applications, you will place your microservices in this column until they mature into well-understood, rarely changing services. This column also includes your offerings and services built in-house using a more traditional approach. These are bespoke solutions, and hopefully, they are services that provide a unique value to your business and not things you have built simply because you can.

This column represents the uncommon and the things you are still learning about. It is individually made and tailored for a specific environment. It is bespoke. It frequently changes. It is an artisan skill. You wouldn't expect to see two of these that are the same. Its focus is on learning and craft.

Product. Place systems and services that are well-understood and evolving slowly through incremental improvement here. You may have stable systems that don't change much, which can be migrated to the cloud without modifying anything. These applications may be good candidates for the lift-and-shift pattern.

This represents the increasingly common manufactured through a repeatable process, the more defined, and the better understood. Change becomes slower here. While differentiation exists—particularly in the early stages—there is increased stability and sameness. You will often see many of the same products. Our focus is on refining and improving.

Utility. Can you replace systems in your estate with SaaS or PaaS solutions? Have you built standards-based services that are easily maintained and likely to stay the same? Then you enter the Utility column on the map. The simplicity of standard building blocks allows higher orders of complexity.

This represents production scale and volume operations, the highly standardized, defined, fixed, and undifferentiated. It fits a specific, known purpose and repetition, repetition, and more repetition. Focus on the ruthless removal of deviation, industrialization, and operational efficiency. With time you become habituated to the act; it is increasingly less visible, and you often forget it's even there.

Call to Action

Step 1. Pick a product or business outcome. Select a business outcome or revisit an existing one you want to offer your customers.

Step 2. Map its current state. Break out the intended or existing components.

Step 3. Understand user needs. Follow the steps working backward from the user to the back office.

Step 4. Bring the outside in. Validate your architectural assumptions based on what is now available as a service, focusing on removing undifferentiated heavy lifting by using elements on the right of a map in the Utility bracket.

Step 5. Build, buy, or use. In design reviews, ensure the CTO is constructively challenging when you should build, buy, or use a technology component.

Step 6. Execute. Execute with the understanding that every map is flawed and constantly changing due to the growth and availability of new services.

Final Thought

We see mapping gaining popularity around the world. This chapter provides just a small peek into the world of mapping. AWS customers often want to dive deeper on this topic. We highly recommend the book *Value the Flywheel Effect* by David Anderson.[29] David's book goes much deeper into both Wardley mapping and its uses with Serverless on AWS to allow you to focus on the maximum return you can get for your business.

We want to thank Simon Wardley for providing Wardley mapping under Creative Commons to the community and Adrian Cockroft for detailing it so effectively.

2.4 The CFO Matters

At the end of the day, finance leaders have to be proper storytellers. You have to be constantly on top of your data and tell the story behind the numbers.

—GERARDO ADAME

Each CFO plays a different role in the cloud adoption journey. This is entirely dependent on the nature of their business. A highly capital-intensive business has very different requirements, considerations, and sensitivities from a business in a services-based industry. Every cloud journey needs to be tailored clearly to individual needs. There is no one-size-fits-all approach; according to the *PwC 2023 Cloud Business Survey*, 80 percent of CFOs feel responsible for cloud investment decisions.[30] Nearly a quarter of CFOs feel they have either limited or no collaboration with the CIO compared to their other C-suite peers.

The roles of the CFO and CIO have been subtly changing. In many enterprises these roles have veered away from the strategic focus that you would expect from CXOs. As our colleague Mark Schwartz discusses in his book *War and Peace and IT*, enterprises must let their CIOs and CFOs refocus on strategy and empower them to move away from operational concerns, such as cutting costs, closing the books, and delivering IT services and projects on time, to driving competitive strategy and innovation.[31] The CFO and CIO can and should empower each other in accomplishing this transformation.

Fully aligning the CIO with the CFO can significantly accelerate your journey. While many CIOs have a base-level understanding of money and how it affects IT, they are usually not experts on the CFO's role or responsibilities. This reciprocated misunderstanding is at the heart of many stalled or delayed cloud journeys.

The CIO's relationship with other executive committee members will always be a fluid and nuanced element of any transformation. The CIO-CFO working relationship is one of the most crucial by far. Tenured CIOs must continually and efficiently adapt to high-frequency change and collaborate with their colleagues to deliver business value via technology. New CIOs have, at the very most, eighteen months to prove themselves capable of doing this while managing the inevitable stresses and blowups that occur. (Running from explosion to crisis can, unfortunately, be the norm—especially for new CIOs stepping into an existing enterprise.) They must achieve this while earning the trust and respect of their C-suite colleagues, something that cannot be given or bought, only earned. If a new CIO fails to do this, their time in the role may be shorter than planned.

The CFO's Point of View

We are not and have not been CFOs. However we have been privileged to engage with many on the CFO journey and have seen what those who have led cloud transformation from the finance side have achieved. So what do CFOs care about?

- ***Financial stability.*** Ensure the financial health and stability of the organization.

- ***Cost management.*** Focus heavily on cost efficiency to improve profitability.
- ***Cybersecurity and data privacy.*** Protect the company's data from cyber threats and ensure compliance with data privacy regulations.
- ***Digital transformation.*** Steward investments and ensure they deliver value.
- ***Capital allocation.*** Allocate capital in technology, acquisitions, or organic growth. Focus on prioritizations that maximize shareholder value.
- ***Regulatory compliance.*** Stay abreast of financial regulations and ensure compliance with reporting and disclosure requirements.
- ***Risk management.*** Identify, assess, and mitigate financial and operational risk.
- ***Environmental, Social, and Governance (ESG).*** Be increasingly involved in ESG reporting and initiatives.
- ***Finance transformation.*** Leverage technology as the backbone (data, machine learning, single version of truth, robotic process automation, etc.)
- ***Talent management.*** Attract and retain finance talent; develop leadership skills and succession planning.

Challenging CFO Truisms

Adopting and moving to the cloud can expose new stresses in the CFO's relationships and pain points unless they get ahead of the knowledge gap. These perceptions make or break a cloud journey. Even if they have a solid relationship with their CIO, the CFO may initially perceive moving to the cloud as a challenge to their truisms:

- ***Optimizing EBITDA.*** Earnings before interest, taxes, depreciation, and amortization (EBITDA) is a measure of a company's financial performance that excludes certain noncash expenses.

CFOs may struggle determining how to accurately calculate EBITDA accurately in the context of cloud computing because the allocation of costs between capital expenditures (CAPEX) and operating expenses (OPEX) can be complex.

- ***Maintaining control.*** How does the move from projects with perceived "known" costs and predictable depreciation timelines affect reporting and cash flow? The "Manifesto for Agile Software Development" was published in 2001,[32] but this issue still feels fresh for most CFOs.
- ***Managing risk.*** Absolutely no CFO wants to increase their financial risk. Is this change going to be hard? What if things go wrong?
- ***Leveraging available Research and Development tax credits.***
- ***Optimizing cost.*** Cloud computing provides a variable spend model compared to traditional IT infrastructure because costs are based on usage rather than upfront investments in hardware and software. However CFOs may need help with accurately forecasting and budgeting for cloud costs, especially if the business has fluctuating or hard-to-predict usage patterns.
- ***CAPEX vs. OPEX.*** CFOs may need help deciding between a CAPEX model (where costs are classified as capital expenditures) and an OPEX model (where costs are classified as operating expenses) when moving to the cloud. Cloud computing tends to be classified as an OPEX expense because the costs are based on usage rather than upfront investments. However, the classification can depend on the business's circumstances.
- ***Managing financial risk.*** CFOs may be concerned about the perceived increase in financial risk associated with relying on a third-party cloud provider for critical business functions.
- ***Consideration of reported ratios.*** CFOs may also be concerned about the impact of cloud computing on reported financial ratios, such as debt-to-equity ratios, return on assets, and efficiency ratios.

CFOs can fall into the sunk cost fallacy, the tendency to continue investing in a project or venture because of the resources already invested resources rather than the potential for future returns. CFOs may need help deciding whether to migrate to the cloud as upfront costs may be involved.

Cloud-Enabled Levers

Conversely, when the CIO-CFO relationship is effective, both executives understand cloud adoption enables transformational levers:

- ***Economies of scale.*** Leverage the investment to drive down costs.
- ***Operational risk reduction levers.*** Leverage the cloud's investment in security and operational resilience to reduce historic technical debt.
- ***Power of variable spend.*** Leverage the variable nature of spend to drive ongoing cost efficiencies.
- ***Cash redirection levers.*** CAPEX is cash-intensive; cloud adoption provides the CFO with flexibility to redirect cash investment to more critical priorities.
- ***Elastic capacity.*** Unplanned capital investment or overprovisioning of capital investments are intensively wasteful and disruptive; the cloud provides elastic pay-as-you-go levers that scale up and down.
- ***Transparency on "shared costs."*** The AWS account boundary provides a defined and evidenced operating zone on spend. Assigning accounts to teams or lines of business provides instant clarity and accountability.
- ***Investment decisions with usage data.*** Leveraging the cloud provides fuller cost insight into technology consumption to inform executive-level product decisions.
- ***Experimentation flexibility.*** Invest and experiment without a long-term commitment. Run small-scale tests with minimal costs.

- ***Tackling the sunk cost fallacy.*** Fully depreciated assets are not free. Continually rising maintenance costs, human resources required for upgrading, managing support risks, and general upkeep always need to be factored in.

Leverage and Inclusion

These levers lay the foundation of a well-managed culture that fosters strong FinOps practices inside an organization. (Our teammate Chris Hennesey, the former technology CFO of Capital One, provides awesome insight in his re:Invent 2023 session, "Making dollars and sense out of FinOps.")[33] Recognize the need for shared mental models and mechanisms to improve this symbiotic understanding of finance and IT. To do this, you need to leverage inclusion and education.

Inclusion. Foster and build the CFO relationship. In 2014 Thomas and his Experian Consumer Services colleague Michael Kilander, former SVP, developed a detailed business case for cloud adoption. They decided against a business case based solely on cost reduction, focusing instead on business agility and improving the customer experience. Business case in hand, Thomas and Michael went knocking on doors to build awareness (if not consensus) for what they were up to. This approach paid off, and they were able to address most, but certainly not all, concerns raised by various business leaders and stakeholders. We cannot overstate the importance of this critical step in the process. The original business case may need to be revised because this is an art and not a science (contrary to what some people may tell you). Empathy and collaboration are essential. The best results in our careers have been delivered when the objectives between C-suite members overlap and those individuals can agree and effectively collaborate on a goal and its delivery. Magic happens here.

Education. The CIO's expertise differs from that of the CFO. Teach; don't tell. Reciprocate. The CFO wants somebody on their team they can delegate to and work with on the change. AWS can help by offering the AWS Cloud for Finance Professionals course,[34] which shows how to:

- Define cloud business value.
- Estimate costs associated with current and future cloud workloads.
- Use tools to report, monitor, allocate, optimize, and plan AWS spend.
- Optimize cloud spending and usage through pricing models.

This is a critical and fundamental part of the journey for your finance colleagues. Get the CFO's assignee engaged, and you are well on your way. To really enable the change, why not embed the finance person straight into the cloud center of excellence (CCoE) from the start and ensure they become a part of the Cloud Business Office (CBO)? They can establish a mechanism to handle the monthly AWS Usage Report (the bill) as you scale and add more AWS accounts. This ensures correct engagement with the wider finance processes and controls are firmly embedded from the start and remain as you grow. This person can engage on the downstream business, producing compound benefits.

Leverage. Inviting thought leadership to address a problem is a great way to get buy-in. Virtually everything in the modern business world is powered by or touches technology. We don't know of any C-suite executive not looking for more levers to control costs and drive innovation. The possibilities opened for a win-win-win scenario are groundbreaking. One of the most compelling cases we've seen repeatedly is when the CFO, CIO, and COO align to improve the contact center's efficacy, efficiency, and empowerment. There is a reason that Amazon Connect is the second-fastest growing service at AWS. In our experience voice projects have always been the hardest IT experience; the legacy technology risk reduction, cost reduction and derisking, quality improvement of the actual customer voice, and technology possibilities of machine learning are profound. Everybody wins when executive objectives overlap and the way forward is delivered.

Advocate. Develop a shared vision to fully leverage cloud technologies' benefits. When presenting to your C-suite colleagues, you must be in lockstep with a strong, overlapping appreciation of each other's perspective. This work happens outside of the boardroom. Engage with the wider C-suite to unlock and address the unique challenges they face when understanding cost versus opportunity cost.

Call to Action

Step 1. Include your CFO and team on the journey.

Step 2. Educate them and your team and involve them from the start.

Step 3. Leverage the CFO and their team's expertise.

Step 4. Embed a dedicated finance resource into cloud adoption teams and mechanisms.

Step 5. Advocate with the CFO.

Step 6. Incorporate FinOps principles and practices inside your organization.

Final Thought

The business case is an essential part of the journey, so we recommend you employ the assistance of the AWS Cloud Economics team or an AWS Partner to help guide this process. Given the likelihood that running on the cloud becomes a part of operating procedures, training members of the CBO is a wise investment.

2.5 Measuring the Success of Your Journey

By failing to prepare, you are preparing to fail.

—BENJAMIN FRANKLIN (APOCRYPHAL)

Measure What Matters by John Doerr is the foundational modern book for businesses and governments to do precisely that—measure what matters. Maybe measuring what *should* matter is a better way to describe it. We like this book and recommend it with *Good Strategy/Bad Strategy* to (1) identify your strengths, (2) map your way, and (3) measure your progress. The last part is tricky. We can't just list metrics and say "There you go! Reach those and the transformation is done."

Sadly we find that (much like with principles) folks want to go straight to methods and measurements rather than take the more challenging route of linking them back to strategy before moving forward. People frequently seek vanity metrics, something they can focus on and drive everybody to achieve. It doesn't work.

As Goodhart's Law states: "Any observed statistical regularity will tend to collapse once pressure is placed upon it for control purposes." Borrowing metrics that don't correlate with your business strategy and goals is like adopting the emperor's new clothes fallacy. Goodhart wasn't the first to notice this problem. Campbell's Law likely has precedence: "The more any quantitative social indicator is used for social decision-making, the more subject it will be to corruption pressures and the more apt it will be to distort and corrupt the social processes it is intended to monitor."[35]

So humans play the system when you make a metric a target. Darn it!

Measuring against Primary Business Objectives

The cloud is not a strategy in itself; it's a potent tool for accomplishing business strategies. It's essential to connect the cloud initiative with the company's highest strategic objectives; doing so will provide the business case for the cloud initiative, the urgency to drive execution, the list of priorities to address, and the criteria for measuring success. Many enterprises we engage with are looking to grow—some by entering new geographical markets, some by broadening their customer base, some by introducing new products, and some by deepening relationships with existing customers. The cloud can help with all these things, but it's hard to do everything at once (i.e., make execution decisions about priorities). By choosing specific growth objectives, you can align your success measures with your business case and use them to guide your activities.

Maybe growth is not your primary objective; perhaps you have a manufacturing company that wants to use edge computing and machine learning for predictive maintenance, and you need to move to the cloud to do so. What success measures do you care about? Two things, probably: (1) whether you're successfully identifying problems with equipment and fixing them before the equipment fails and (2) whether you're accomplishing the business objectives behind that predictive maintenance (saving maintenance costs, not losing revenue). You can define a measure for each.

To put it another way: What's the business value of a hammer? It depends on what you build with it! Its value stems from whether you use it to build a house for sale, fix a piece of furniture with nails coming out, or store it in case you need it. (Keeping services on standby often has an unappreciated value in IT). It's the same with the cloud. Measure your results against what you care about, fulfilling your critical business objectives.

There's a potential trap when thinking in terms of return on investment (ROI). What's the ROI from a potential IT investment? Trick question—there's no ROI, just a projected ROI. Measuring success against that projection is often a test of the prediction's accuracy. What you care about is the actual benefit versus the costs. Measuring the true ROI has pitfalls because you often don't have a good baseline to measure against since the environment is changing quickly around you. Finally, the value of many investments is in risk reduction or creating options—both hard to measure in ROI terms. For those reasons, we suggest choosing operational measures that are more directly connected to your use of the technology. We used ROI in our past experience to (a) show off or (b) show how badly something had failed. Even then we struggle to recall more than four or five occasions where this was done in the hundreds of business cases we've been involved in.

Measuring Cost Reduction

There are three critical points to keep in mind with costs. First, when working in the cloud, costs are not a given—you have a multitude of levers available for actively managing costs. This differs from the company data center approach, where your hardware costs are fixed (step costs if you're growing), and cash goes out of pocket up front. Second, you can and should expect to gain lots of transparency in your costs and unit economics in the cloud. Third, your costs vary based on how much you use the cloud, depending on the course your business takes. If you grow your business, your costs will rise; if you develop new products for your customers, you'll pay the costs associated with those new products. You can't just consider IT costs in isolation; they're (hopefully) linked to new revenues or cost reductions in other parts of the business.

To continuously manage costs, develop a baseline for your costs and then work to reduce them against that baseline. You're probably already doing that with expenses like travel and telephone costs. It is hard to predict precisely how much your phone usage will be next year, but you can take this year as a baseline and work to reduce those costs. It's an empirical way to discover and control costs rather than relying on imprecise estimates.

You have to make trade-offs on the amount of effort you want to put into actively reducing costs. For example, you can have your software developers spend time optimizing their code to reduce its execution costs. There's a discipline called FinOps that provides a structure for doing so. But there's a trade-off with your developers' time—you'll pay an opportunity cost for the other valuable work they aren't doing.

Cost measurement is especially valuable. Using strategies in the cloud, such as resource tagging and separate AWS accounts for each business outcome, you can slice and dice your costs in many ways: by business unit, product line, resource type, transaction type—whatever is useful. This gives you unprecedented insight into your cost drivers and unit economics. You might even learn things from this analysis that cause you to rethink your business process or product mix.

Move toward treating technology costs as variable costs—they should vary with revenues, and the timing of your cash outflows should align with your revenues. Ideally—though this requires some sophistication—you can manage many of your technology costs as unit costs and work to increase your gross margins. Another helpful way to look at costs is in terms of leanness: are you achieving outcomes with minimal waste? Total costs become less interesting because they vary with the scale of your business, but unit cost measurements show how successful you are at streamlining your business and making it lean.

In many cases you can drive cost reductions in business operations that dwarf potential cost reductions in the IT budget. In the example above, predictive maintenance reduces factory operations costs; digital interactions with customers might reduce your call center costs; and robotic process automation can reduce the costs of your paper-handling processes. Just measuring IT costs misses those successes; an additional dollar of IT spending likely results in more than a dollar of cost reduction elsewhere in the business.

Measuring IT Delivery

Working in the cloud improves IT's ability to deliver for the rest of the business. While that sounds difficult to measure, the topic has been studied quite thoroughly, and there are some excellent ideas on how to do it. In the book *Accelerate*,[36] Dr. Nicole Forsgren and her coauthors show that a small set of IT metrics predicts business outcomes; these metrics are closely tied to certain IT practices. You want to measure:

- Release frequency: how often IT can deploy changes to IT systems.
- Change failure rate: how often those changes lead to problems.
- Cycle time for deploying changes: how long it takes to deliver IT capabilities once they're ready to go.
- Mean time to repair problems.

- Availability of systems.

This might seem too small a set of measures to encompass everything that IT does, but Forsgren shows that they indicate good IT practices such as automation, effective testing practices, and team accountability, which yield business results.

Rather than giving a poorly abridged version of *Accelerate*, we strongly recommend you get a copy and see if it helps you measure progress as you execute.

Measuring When Using Wardley Maps

In the previous chapter, we discussed leveraging Wardley maps to help you understand the landscape and where to focus your efforts. Maps can also be incredibly insightful for focusing on measuring the things that enable your strategy. Simon describes how to do this in detail in "A Quick and Easy Guide to Measurement."[37]

Measuring Business Agility and Leanness

Let's define agility as the ability to respond to changes in the business environment quickly, inexpensively, and at low risk. It's a capability, a potential, to use when needed (though that's probably often in the fluid business environment). Like risk, agility can be difficult to measure because it's about the potential for capturing opportunities and avoiding losses. So it often needs to be analyzed like a financial option. And you have a limited sample size to measure—how often do you bring a new product to market, and how quickly have you done it in the past? Anecdotal evidence of agility might be the best you can do.

But this is less of a problem than it might seem. You can still guide the transformation journey to ensure you gain speed and agility—for example, by using the *Accelerate* metrics discussed above. You can also draw a value stream map of your product or feature delivery process to find measurable ways to reduce waste (often with a sustainability benefit). Your typical time between sensing a change in the environment and responding to it is your lead time; the value stream includes things like governance processes, resource provisioning, team assembly, and technical delivery. The cloud is a powerful tool for removing waste in many parts of this process, but you'll have to address governance and funding to make the most of it.

Measuring Risk Reduction

The cloud helps reduce many types of business risks. Focus on (1) security risk, (2) resilience risk, and (3) compliance risk. The best approach to measurement is identifying the sources of risk in each category and measurably reducing them.

Compliance risk can be managed through automated policy enforcement, continuous auditing, and transparent reporting; you can best measure it by counting the number of fully automated controls and the number continuously verified. To address resilience risk, define potential disaster scenarios, simulate them if possible (or do a tabletop exercise), and verify that you can respond to each scenario successfully. You can also set up a maturity model for your nimbleness in responding to completely unexpected (untested) scenarios and measure your capabilities against it. Or you can itemize your main vulnerabilities—let's say legacy systems that weren't created with resilient architectures or technologies—and measure your progress in modernizing them. The approach is similar for security—itemize vulnerabilities and work to reduce them. You can also identify general solution areas and assess yourself against them—the quality of your identity validation, authentication and authorization, logging and log analysis, and so on.

How Does AWS Measure Things?

The first thing to know about AWS is that everything changes frequently, and how we do business is undoubtedly one of those points. While the AWS mission has been immutable during our tenure, the principles and mechanisms have matured. All three—mission, principles, and mechanisms—form the critical aspects of execution. That said, it's unlikely that the two-pizza team ownership model typically led by a general manager will change soon (and this is the CEO's call, not ours!). These teams own their execution and, crucially, their data or metadata, depending on the service they offer. Each team typically reports their key measurements, lowlights, highlights, and "dogs not barking" (i.e., what isn't getting the attention it should!) within a two-by-two matrix. This is an inspection mechanism for the team to provide commentary to its Director/VP/SVP on what is and isn't working. Being vocally self-critical with these reporting mechanisms is AWS's norm, not the exception. Any overly glowing team report gets senior leadership asking questions; as Jeff Bezos says, "No one's body odor smells better than anyone else's." This is cultural, led from the top, and crucial to AWS's truth-seeking culture. We have found that the most insightful conversations come from leadership engagements where being vocally self-critical is the norm.

How we set goals at AWS is an entirely other mechanism and system that we have developed internally to give any leader (i.e., everyone) a view of their rolled-up goals; these are tracked and held accountable to individual leaders. Only occasionally are goals shared between executives.

Call to Action

Step 1. Understand your business strategy and have a map.

Step 2. Select a few key measurements.

Step 3. Keep it simple.

Step 4. Automate the heck out of the reporting.

Step 4. Communicate.

Step 5. Revisit continually.

Final Thought

Moving to the cloud has many benefits, including better security and availability. But that probably isn't the reason you're moving to the cloud. Whatever your reason is—gaining access to machine learning, better analytics, edge computing, etc.—it probably requires you to actively build or modernize. And that means that you need to drive behavior and measure and celebrate results. If you want to reduce costs, you must work to reduce costs. If you add new services for customers, you've got to add new services for customers. Getting the correct data to guide these activities should be a key goal in measuring results. So for a CFO who wants to know how to measure the value they're getting from the cloud, we suggest formulating business objectives—the "why." Then work with the CIO to establish the plan to get those benefits. Agree on how to measure success, then execute that plan. (The plan does not have to be detailed or deterministic.) When we meet with AWS customers to discuss the cloud's value and how to measure it, it's far better to meet with the CFO and CIO together. Finding ways to measure results is just an aspect of gaining clarity on goals and formulating approaches to accomplish them.

PART III

CULTURE AND ORGANIZATION

3.1 Culture

Culture is simply a shared way of doing something with passion.

—BRAIN CHESKY

Peter Drucker is famously quoted as saying that "culture eats strategy for breakfast," and he's right. Most leaders quickly realize that the cloud's technical implementation is not the most challenging part of the journey. Culture and organization are.

Geert Hofstede, Professor Emeritus of Organizational Anthropology and International Management at Maastricht University in the Netherlands, is well-known for pioneering research on cross-cultural groups and organizations. He defines culture as the "software of the mind."[38] Culture encodes how we interact with one another. It has written and unwritten rules and norms that have evolved—whether in response to some problem or calamity or based on what has worked in the past. While some cultural norms are explicit—for example, mission statements and codes of ethics—others are hidden. Regardless of how it manifests, culture is wholly intertwined with how things are done in every organization.

Culture is compelling. Anytime someone tries to fiddle with culture, corporate "antibodies" emerge to defend the corporate body from foreign influences. These defensive reactions can manifest in various ways—from public opposition to political shenanigans to outright sabotage. Some may adopt a passive-aggressive hope that the new endeavor fails and goes away. The only one of these responses we consider healthy is public opposition. You can have a dialogue and exchange with outspoken critics to sort out the issues. Critics probably have important concerns that should be heard and addressed, and incorporating this feedback into the process invariably strengthens the outcome. Be worried about the apathetic employee.

Successful leaders cultivate the culture they want for their organization, which requires employees to change and adapt. Humans are naturally biased toward maintaining the status quo, what is perceived as normal, traditional, and ordered. People naturally shy away from what they think of as new-fangled ideas, which they often equate with uncertainty or chaos. They think staying with the familiar is better—even if it is less efficient or more expensive. Better the devil you know.

Fear, Uncertainty, and Doubt (FUD) are personal. Whenever there is a change in the wind, people naturally wonder how it will affect them personally. People may worry about the long-term impact of cloud adoption on their careers, whether automation will eliminate their jobs, or if they are in danger of becoming irrelevant or obsolete in this new world. This all contributes to doubt—uncertainty about whether the transformation will succeed, whether it is the right thing to do, or whether it would be better to leave things be.

As we've seen, FUD is one of the primary sources of resistance to change. One way to deal with FUD is to understand the interests and motivations of key players in the organization. You need to understand the obvious stakeholders and the nonobvious influencers. Stakeholders include all members of the C-suite, the board of directors, and business and IT leaders. The nonobvious influencers could be respected long-tenured engineers, such as senior network engineers, architects, senior developers, and many others. You can identify who they are simply by asking members of IT who the go-to people are in their respective disciplines. Sometimes influencers are well-known because they are not afraid to ask hard questions in public, but other times they are silent and influence IT through the expert power they wield in the organization. Brent, the indispensable IT expert in the previously mentioned novel *The Phoenix Project*, famously describes this dynamic. Brent is a human bottleneck, essential to all significant IT efforts. While this gives Brent strong job security, it harms the organization. Brent is not malicious in any way, but his role and influence put the success of any transformation at risk.

To turn around a culture of fear, focus on success. You must think about how cloud adoption enables success for each stakeholder. Can you help reduce costs for the CFO? Can you help drive desired cultural norms, such as hiring for diversity? Can you prioritize components or systems in the cloud journey to automate onerous tasks for the compliance team? If you think about these questions, you will find many opportunities to align the transformation's goals with the key stakeholders' ambitions. Find simple solutions that have a potentially high impact on the stakeholder to limit the impact on the overall roadmap. This needs to be more than an IT-only initiative.

In the case of someone like the fictional Brent, you need to train others to do and know what Brent knows so that the resource constraint is removed and Brent's veto power is limited. To sway the opinions of critical influencers who command the respect of IT employees, you need to spend time understanding their concerns. This is time well spent because the years of experience they bring to any problem lets you anticipate challenges. Dispel misconceptions by educating and clarifying each concern they raise, or you will have to mitigate concerns that pose potential problems. Mitigation can be as simple as clearly articulating a plan, which you might assign them to create directly so they have skin in the game.

Management is not about enforcing control in a hierarchy of functional responsibilities. It is about gaining the power that a team-oriented approach offers by amplifying the team's ideas, creating clarity around goals, removing impediments, and devising and allocating resources to support the team's activities. You need to engage the middle manager's ingenuity in accomplishing new goals where impact can be tied to business success and which, collectively with other goals, supports new ways of working. An important task for leaders today is to find ways to creatively redefine their middle managers' goals and incentives, aligning them with transformation.

Cloud transformation is primarily a leadership effort based on influence and persuasion rather than command and control or top-down authority. The cloud, DevOps, and other best practices for IT delivery can make heroines and heroes of everyone. They add so much value to the enterprise that there are more than enough superpowers to go around. The goal of transformation is to *empower* everyone across the organization—middle managers included—and make them successful. As Mark Schwartz succinctly states, "The cloud, DevOps, and today's other best practices for IT delivery can make heroes of everyone."[39]

The principles you can hold everyone, including yourself, accountable to are a significant part of the enabling mechanism. The ability to ask why somebody did something contrary to the principles that the leadership team has declared is the difference between being in control of a conversation when things go wrong and not.

Speaking of principles—they need to be well-defined. Here are some examples using the AWS pattern:

We believe that:

- ***All of your assumed constraints are debatable.*** We strive to debate our perceived constraints consciously and subconsciously and not accept them at face value.
- ***We should keep the customer, employees, and company safe.*** However, doing nothing carries a much greater risk than doing something.
- ***We should not fight gravity; the apple always falls.*** Moving to the cloud is essential for our enterprise to get the cost, security, elasticity, availability, and flexibility benefits our business needs.
- ***Using data and customer anecdotes drives better decisions.*** Whenever possible, we use data, rather than opinions and conjecture, to drive measurable results.
- ***Setting a few bold goals is an enabler, not a target.*** Hands down, the most successful transformations come from bold leadership combined with best practice experience. GE's and Enel's experiences are fantastic case studies in their own right—all have audacious goals combined with superb tactical experience-led execution.

Call to Action

Step 1. Define your leadership principles.

Step 2. Dispel FUD.

Step 3. Create quick wins.

Step 4. Find complementary stakeholder objectives.

Step 5. Deliver objectives.

3.2 Teams

If you can't feed a team with two pizzas, it's too large.

—JEFF BEZOS

Much of Thomas's approach to cloud adoption stems from his experience in the US Army. The US military is as hierarchical as an organization can be, yet small units are afforded a great deal of autonomy while they execute their missions. The US military organization is modeled on the organization deployed initially to great effect by the ancient Roman military. The smallest unit is a squad, usually comprised of eight to twelve members; four to six squads form a platoon, and three to six platoons form a company. Companies are then aggregated into battalions, which make up regiments, which roll up to divisions, on to corps, and finally armies. While there are many reasons why this structure has proven effective over the past two thousand years, two aspects are pertinent to our discussion: command and control and local autonomy.

Squads are small because one squad leader can effectively lead a small unit of fewer than fifteen people. Trust and cohesion at the squad level are crucial and are based on shared experience (sometimes hardship) and intensive training as a unit. It is relatively easy for a small unit to pull together and focus on achieving a particular mission or outcome. Each team forms solid internal bonds, and team members identify with their squad. Each subsequent level of command has a small number of direct reports (similarly many business publications suggest an optimal span of control comprises seven direct reports). Teams develop common skills, such as first aid, marksmanship, or land navigation, diving deep into their team and individual specialties. This ensures the team can operate autonomously in pursuing their mission while other units provide support when needed.

While the popular concept of military leadership is that leaders simply exercise command and control over their people, the reality is much more nuanced. Effective leaders earn the trust and respect of the men and women they lead. While certain decisions are not up for debate, the whole team debates and discusses many other decisions. The best leaders encourage and seek this kind of open, back-and-forth discussion to benefit from the experience and knowledge of all team members. Regardless, the leader makes the final decision and is responsible for outcomes.

Team leaders and members receive orders from their command structure. When the command structure defines the mission and objectives, the commander will specify what is known as the "commander's intent," which is designed to enable disciplined initiative to empower agile and adaptive leaders.[40] A retired general wrote, "Because tight centralized control of operations isn't possible or desirable...leaders must train their juniors to do the right things and then trust them to act independently."[41] This is a critical component as team leaders decide how to accomplish a particular objective. The commander's intent is not a free-for-all; the "concept of operations" describes principal tasks, how the principal tasks complement one another, and responsible units or teams.

The commander's intent is deliberately sparse on execution details. This provides the team with the autonomy to react to local conditions and the tactical situation without constantly asking for guidance and detailed orders on how to proceed. When applied to business, the commander's intent is informed by the business vision, strategic roadmap, and epics for the next quarter or two. At the same time, user stories correspond to the concept of operations for the sprint.

The similarity ends here since business leaders and managers don't have the same command authority as their military counterparts. There are typically no life-and-death situations, no potentially catastrophic emergencies, and no requirement to manage the health and welfare of each "soldier."

So what other benefits do small teams afford? First, they allow personal and human interactions to take center stage. Team members form strong bonds inside the team, which allows a team identity to form and team spirit to emerge. This is invaluable when weathering difficult times or traversing the trough of disillusionment (a.k.a. the "valley of despair") when a problem seems most intractable. Teams must have the mental toughness to persevere to experience a breakthrough and arrive at the solution. Team members must build trust, which can be strengthened by encouraging team-building exercises and fun team activities.

Consider this description of the book *Turn the Ship Around!,* written by retired US Navy Captain David Marquet:

> "Leadership should mean giving control rather than taking control and creating leaders rather than forging followers." David Marquet, an experienced Navy officer, was used to giving orders. As newly appointed captain of the USS Santa Fe, a nuclear-powered submarine, he was responsible for more than a hundred sailors, deep in the sea. In this high-stress environment, where there is no margin for error, it was crucial his sailors did their job and did it well. But the ship was dogged by poor morale, poor performance, and the worst retention in the fleet. Marquet acted like any other captain until, one day, he unknowingly gave an impossible order, and his crew tried to follow it anyway. When he asked why the order wasn't challenged, the answer was "Because you told me to." Marquet realized he was leading in a culture of followers, and they were all in danger unless they fundamentally changed the way they did things. That's when Marquet took matters into his own hands and pushed for leadership at every level. *Turn the Ship Around!* is the true story of how the Santa Fe skyrocketed from worst to first in the fleet by challenging the US Navy's traditional leader-follower approach.[42]

Second, small teams facilitate clear and consistent communication. This is simply a consequence of Metcalfe's law, which states that the effect of a (telecommunications) network is proportional to the square of the number of connected users of the system. So the more users you add, the more you have to communicate.[43] Small teams can gather around a whiteboard and debate a particular technical problem by thinking aloud and drawing out ideas on the board. Training within small teams can be accomplished peer to peer or by bringing in a coach for hands-on experiences. Individuals can also easily propagate learning through the entire team.

Third, small teams identify with their work and outcomes, facilitating a huge sense of ownership. This ownership can be further cultivated to pursue something former Navy SEAL commander Jocko Willink calls "extreme ownership."[44] Team members come to believe that they are entirely responsible for the success or failure of their mission. This means teams candidly discuss impediments, seek innovative solutions when encountering obstacles, and accept personal responsibility rather than look for excuses or blame others. This level of ownership must be carefully cultivated and is difficult to achieve. However, teams that exhibit this level of ownership are extremely effective and impactful and can dramatically increase productivity and innovation within an organization.

Other nonmilitary models are worth examining, such as AWS's two-pizza teams or Henrik Kniberg's work with Spotify's tribes and guilds.[45] How you structure your teams ultimately depends on your organization's needs, desired business outcomes, and the culture you already have. We will cover this more in the section on target operating models in Chapter 4.3 Your Evolving Target Operating Model.

Call to Action

Step 1. Define your target team size.

Step 2. Evaluate moving from command and control to empowered teams.

Step 3. Understand and address the impact on middle management.

Final Thought

The aspiration in technology has long been to enable teams to deliver with autonomy and ownership. It has been hamstrung by the fact that many Agile teams still depend on siloed teams that only specialize in their technology or discipline and always end up on another team's critical path. The cloud is the inflection point. It allows small teams to finally take ownership end to end and operate with commander's intent—a.k.a guardrails—to deliver an outcome. Don't forget to embed a cloud engineer into your delivery teams if you need to—interteam human dependencies are defects!

3.3 Principles for Your Cloud Journey

Obey the principles without being bound by them.

—BRUCE LEE

Tenet: (noun) a principle or belief, especially one of the main principles of a religion or philosophy. These tenets are held by the group. To be a member in good standing, you are expected to hold to its particular teaching.

We have mentioned principles and tenets in previous chapters. Let's dive deeper and provide some concrete examples; it's nice to think everyone starts a transformation journey at the same time and place. It's easy to assume everyone understands the *why* and *how* behind the journey. Even leadership teams seemingly aligned on problem scope (and we have sat on many) often never have the actual conversation to align on the why and the how.

As a leadership team, how can you ensure your team—and the teams working for you—stay aligned and make most decisions autonomously that still align with your principles?

One of the mechanisms at AWS that deals head-on with potential misalignment and ambiguity is the effective use of tenets. Tenets exist at Amazon on a global holistic level and within individual teams. Each team defines its own tenets. Any team member can appropriately challenge the tenets, and if any member thinks they know a better one, then they own making a recommendation for change.

Taking just a small amount of time (yes, we know you are running from crisis to fire!) to define the tenets for your cloud adoption and consciously allowing them to be challenged and amended as you know more saves you incalculable time as you go forward. We have personally experienced and seen teams that have spent days, weeks, months, and yes, even years building software and infrastructure that seems essential to them, only to find no one uses it. One of the most common examples in our industry is the term *data lakes* (we discuss lessons learned on this later). We've lost count of how many enterprises we've worked with where a siloed team constructs a thing of beauty around Hadoop and fast backend storage, only for no one to place their data in it or use it for answers. What a waste. A simple tenet constructed around data can holistically prevent this. Even something as simple as "Each team owns their data and makes it securely accessible on an as-needed basis by everyone via an API" can help remove a massive waste of time and energy.

Unfortunately it's not unusual to work with technology leadership teams that have spent the best part of two years working incredibly hard to build a new, automated, fully featured development model for their engineers. Their CI/CD pipelines are deemed perfect; they tried to force a particular technology choice, and they had all the controls they thought they needed in place. There was just one problem. No one was using it, and they had no production workloads running.

In times like this, we find ourselves acting as cloud shrinks; it's our job to ask the challenging questions most folks in their respective companies would be too polite to ask. "What are your group tenets to building securely, operating, and migrating to the cloud?" They often don't have a single one, not even a business case they could point to. This story is, sadly, not unique. In our previous positions, we found ourselves looking at the latest technology offering—thinking it was the best thing since sliced bread—only to get back to the office, discuss it with our engineers and developers, and then take the time to sincerely listen to critiques from our experts. We could fortunately pivot and drop the whole thing, with nothing lost but a few hours. But the thought of wasting two years on such initiatives in today's economy sends shivers down our spines.

A better approach is one of seductive adoption. What you offer is so good, easy, and compliant; why wouldn't you use it?

So what is an excellent example of a tenet? The most powerful ones we use are the Amazon Leadership Principles (LPs). These tenets drive every single Amazonian to use their judgment with a set of consistent principles. Our team is over 1.5 million strong at the time of this writing, and we can have a conversation with any one of them about "diving deep" into a customer problem or not turning up for an internal meeting because the first LP (Customer Obsession) requires our undivided attention.

Amazon Leadership Principles

Customer Obsession. Leaders start with the customer and work backwards. They work vigorously to earn and keep customer trust. Although leaders pay attention to competitors, they obsess over customers.

Ownership. Leaders are owners. They think in the long term and don't sacrifice long-term value for short-term results. They act on behalf of the entire company, beyond just their own team. They never say "that's not my job."

Invent and Simplify. Leaders expect and require innovation and invention from their teams and always find ways to simplify. They are externally aware, look for new ideas from everywhere, and are not limited by "not invented here." As we do new things, we accept that we may be misunderstood for long periods of time.

Are Right, A Lot. Leaders are right a lot. They have strong judgment and good instincts. They seek diverse perspectives and work to disconfirm their beliefs.

Learn and Be Curious. Leaders are never done learning and always seek to improve themselves. They are curious about new possibilities and act to explore them.

Hire and Develop the Best. Leaders raise the performance bar with every hire and promotion. They recognize exceptional talent, and willingly move them throughout the organization. Leaders develop leaders and take seriously their role in coaching others. We work on behalf of our people to invent mechanisms for development like Career Choice.

Insist on the Highest Standards. Leaders have relentlessly high standards—many people may think these standards are unreasonably high. Leaders are continually raising the bar and drive their teams to deliver high-quality products, services, and processes. Leaders ensure that defects do not get sent down the line and that problems are fixed so they stay fixed.

Think Big. Thinking small is a self-fulfilling prophecy. Leaders create and communicate a bold direction that inspires results. They think differently and look around corners for ways to serve customers.

Bias for Action. Speed matters in business. Many decisions and actions are reversible and do not need extensive study. We value calculated risk taking.

Frugality. Accomplish more with less. Constraints breed resourcefulness, self-sufficiency, and invention. There are no extra points for growing headcount, budget size, or fixed expense.

Earn Trust. Leaders listen attentively, speak candidly, and treat others respectfully. They are vocally self-critical, even when doing so is awkward or embarrassing. Leaders do not believe their or their team's body odor smells of perfume. They benchmark themselves and their teams against the best.

Dive Deep. Leaders operate at all levels, stay connected to the details, audit frequently, and are skeptical when metrics and anecdote differ. No task is beneath them.

Have Backbone; Disagree and Commit. Leaders are obligated to respectfully challenge decisions when they disagree, even when doing so is uncomfortable or exhausting. Leaders have conviction and are tenacious. They do not compromise for the sake of social cohesion. Once a decision is determined, they commit wholly.

Deliver Results. Leaders focus on the key inputs for their business and deliver them with the right quality and in a timely fashion. Despite setbacks, they rise to the occasion and never settle.

Strive to be Earth's Best Employer. Leaders work every day to create a safer, more productive, higher performing, more diverse, and more just work environment. They lead with empathy, have fun at work, and make it easy for others to have fun. Leaders ask themselves: Are my fellow employees growing? Are they empowered? Are they ready for what's next? Leaders have a vision for and commitment to their employees' personal success, whether that be at Amazon or elsewhere.

Success and Scale Bring Broad Responsibility. We started in a garage, but we're not there anymore. We are big, we impact the world, and we are far from perfect. We must be humble and thoughtful about even the secondary effects of our actions. Our local communities, planet, and future generations need us to be better every day. We must begin each day with a determination to make better, do better, and be better for our customers, our employees, our partners, and the world at large. And we must end every day knowing we can do even more tomorrow. Leaders create more than they consume and always leave things better than how they found them.

These tenets are designed to be contentious and provoke conversation. Every day every Amazonian reflects on and balances them. Sometimes we have to Dive Deep before showing Bias for Action, and sometimes we need to make things happen fast. Using the tenets requires judgment, and we recruit vigorously for that judgment.

So what makes a good cloud tenet for your enterprise? We have encountered quite a few in our travels and journeys. This list is by no means definitive—our goal is to present the best we have seen. Of course "the best" is subjective, but all good tenets begin with "We believe that."

Aside from the LPs, what have we used as principles ourselves? What have we seen AWS customers use? They can be grouped in a few buckets. You don't need to copy these principles; they're simply pointers on what might work well for your business.

Agility Examples

Small, autonomous, multiskilled teams deliver business outcomes faster. We organize ourselves into teams no larger than twelve. Wherever possible, the teams will be self-contained and can essentially own their work schedule and deconstruction to deliver it.

If you build it, you run it. As the small new teams create features, they will own their support 24-7-365 (DevOps in its simplest form).

We are often asked about segregation of duty. You ultimately want all code deployments and operations to be highly automated, using code pipelines for everything. If you need to retain two-person control for specific tasks (e.g., administrator access to a production datastore, pushing code, changing the pipeline), consider different employees within one team or two-person automated approval roles for pipeline deployment. Automation with mandatory, nonbypassable logging is key. In the book *DevSecOps,* Glen Wilson writes:

> "The short answer is that in DevOps the developer is responsible for writing code, and operations is responsible for writing the automated process that pushes this code through the pipeline all the way to production. As long as this practice is followed and evidenced, it will fulfill the needs of compliance. The additional involvement of security engineers who build the automated security tests as part of the CI/CD pipeline lends further weight to this end-to-end process supporting segregation of duties."[46]

The team we have is the team we need. We always work first to reskill, retool, and promote our workforce with the best knowledge so they can execute our cloud vision before trying to hire externally.

Teams get to choose. The team decides with their product/business outcome manager how to build and what tools to use as long as they meet the company's security and business objectives.

One size doesn't fit all. Our business is large and diverse. Use the right tool for the job. We don't assume one size fits all for tools or products, but we do have strong opinions on how to solve common problems. We automate and codify our opinions into simple, integrated experiences. We remove and deliberately avoid undifferentiated heavy lifting in engineering.

Leaders should get out of the way. We decouple and decentralize development by allowing service teams to own their adoption. We prefer to build guardrails, not gates. We automatically audit for compliance. Leaders should help folks remove blockers.

We should publish our API. Ensure our product and data are accessible securely via an internal (and, if appropriate, external) RESTful API.

Cost-Conscious Examples

We should be cloud-first. All new development will be cloud-native to remove as much undifferentiated heavy lifting as soon as possible.

We should be cloud-native. Wherever possible, we leverage AWS features rather than build our own solutions. We build the thinnest possible control plane over AWS to leverage efficiencies of scale. We acknowledge that "perfect" is the enemy of "good enough." While we are biased toward using AWS services, we will innovate with our own temporary solutions when blocked.

We should run less software. If a component has become a utility, we shouldn't spend precious development time maintaining it. Instead we should consume it as a service.

(This can be a hard shift for technology professionals. They want to build their own thing. But containers are now run and operated as a service; do you really need that bespoke "widget"? That means you need to roll your own stack. If your engineers are no longer building data centers, why are they building container platforms? This will only lengthen TTV and create technology debt for you to manage perpetually.)

Focusing on the business outcome wins. We focus on building and supporting the company's data and business logic, not systems we don't need.

Using a primary public cloud provider enables speed and reduces complexity. Focus and skill curves matter. We will focus on a chosen cloud provider to enable speed—avoiding the distractions that come with too many services.

The cloud and shipping of a minimum loveable product enable speed. We investigate the appropriate security, availability, and efficiency objectives to get the first production workload to the cloud. We expand our research to other tools as customer features demand.

Setting a date to exit the on-premises data centers matters. We will migrate or find suitable homes for all our systems so we can close our data centers by a specified date.

We can save as we earn. The team and business outcome/product manager are accountable for their cloud spend. If a means to an end justifies using something that delivers material fiscal benefit to the organization, they can reinvest it.

Frugality matters. Being prudent and owning your cloud spend is important—teams should continually strive to lower costs. Money spent on wasted resources could be better spent on customer features.

Teams are accountable for the costs they incur. The AWS account boundary is the ultimate boundary for cost.

Elasticity Examples

Everything fails all the time; design for it. Design and test for failure at levels appropriate for the customer problem being solved. Use reliability engineering principles as we go.

Production always runs in multiple AZs. Production services and their data are always run in more than one AZ.

Auto scaling rules. We will leverage auto scaling as appropriate to mitigate potential bottlenecks occurring in production.

Innovation Principles

Everyone is a security engineer. Everyone focuses on necessary security every day.

Pair programming works. For training, development of production code, and support, two developers frequently work side by side on a single machine. The sum is greater than the parts.

We should be tooled correctly for continual learning. We ensure developers have the tools they need for the job. We put mechanisms in place to encourage and reward continual technical self-development.

Certification helps significantly. We encourage, recognize, and reward engineers and developers who attain AWS Certification.

Getting to 10 percent of certified engineers matters. Getting 10 percent of all engineers and developers certified is our goal. (Read Chapter 4.1 Becoming Cloud-Fluent at Scale to learn why.)

We should recruit for alignment with our tenets. Ensure the folks we want to hire have demonstrable experience that is aligned with our tenets.

We should recognize what motivates engineers and developers. Motivation comes from autonomy, mastery, and purpose. Allowing people to run with their ideas, master them, and impact them can nurture this.

Bad ideas should fail fast; production should not. We encourage people to test ideas and fail quickly, so production doesn't.

Going Global Examples

We should trust but verify. We intrinsically trust our leaders, engineers, and developers to make the right decisions to protect our data and systems. But we also have mechanisms in place to verify that trust (we address this in Chapter 3.5 The Cloud Center of Excellence).

Source code security matters. All code is securely held in an enterprise repository, and access is monitored.

Policies matter. While teams can choose their tooling, the tools and solutions must comply with security and availability objectives.

We should work to reduce credential operating zone. We appropriately reduce access to the minimum.

We should assume the enemy knows our code. Dance like no one is watching; encrypt like everyone is.

We should radically restrict and monitor human access to data. Drive people to use tools to access data rather than by hand.

Immutability rules. The authoritative data source and logs will be immutable.

This list is by no means exhaustive. These are just a small selection of tenets you can copy, paste, and adapt as you see fit for your business and teams. Hopefully you can see a long thread of Agile and innovation at the edge (i.e., from the teams themselves). Trust that your teams will be accountable and responsible for the how and why while verifying their compliance.

At their very heart, principles and tenets reflect an organization's culture and most deeply held values.

Call to Action

Step 1. Agree on your principles. Be sure that your principles and tenets reflect your organizational culture and values. If they are out of alignment, employees will pursue less-than-optimal activities and inefficiencies will emerge.

Step 2. Challenge and update. Don't just set and forget your principles and tenets. Publish them clearly and embed them into your design reviews at every stage. Continually revisit them to ensure they still reflect your organization's culture and values.

Step 3. Publish and use them continually. As Amazonians, we have seen the power of well-crafted principles and tenets, and we live them every day of the week. Make them a vital part of your organization too.

3.4 Leveraging the Leadership Team

Tell me and I forget. Teach me and I remember. Involve me and I learn.

—ANONYMOUS

Enterprises on this journey can stall. We experienced it on our journeys, and we've seen it on the journeys of the AWS customers we work with. It is vital to have an aligned leadership team that feels ownership in the journey and is empowered to exercise its ability to question and get answers to those questions. When this alignment has not occurred, it very often materializes as a "frozen middle," where chief executives, engineers, and developers can clearly see the benefits of cloud adoption and actively want to move that way, but managers, directors, and junior executives are concerned about the impact on their roles. So this latter group consciously and unconsciously tries to block or control such a move.

Nearly every enterprise cloud journey will suffer from this frozen middle at some point, which can be fatal to transformations. At times we both felt stuck in parts of our own journeys. It's frustrating and akin to walking through a room filled with molasses (*Treacle to us in the UK,*

Thomas—Jonathan) while everyone shouts from the sides for you to go faster.

So what mechanism works to remove these stalls? We often see customers moving at pace when they have an aligned cloud leadership team (CLT) in place.

What Does a CLT Do?

The CLT ensures effective governance for the organization to adopt and accelerate public cloud use across the business. It does this through the holistic representation of critical stakeholders from across the business who form a quorum and commit to being broadly educated on key cloud differentiators across security, reliability, availability, cost, sustainability, and TTM. The quorum establishes and agrees to bold objectives and principles to meet and fulfill the business case. It acts positively to encourage the workforce to adopt the cloud at scale and address and remediate any risks or blockers that arise in its course.

The CLT ultimately exists to ensure the alignment and strategic, tactical execution of cloud goals with business goals across people, processes, and technology in a well-governed and inclusive way.

Getting the Right Leadership Team Together

Cloud Transformation Leader. The most effective individual has the implicit authority to accept or mitigate perceived risks in line with the board's risk appetite and set appropriate controls. The position works best when the CIO or CTO—or at the very least, a direct report of these two roles—assumes it. The Cloud Transformation Leader has an expansive role in leading the CLT and taking everyone on the journey across people, processes, and technology in congruence with the board's risk appetite. This is a senior executive role.

Chief Information Security Officer (CISO). Having either the CISO in this position—or an empowered direct report—is crucial. This person has multiple roles within the group: (1) to educate themselves in the AWS Shared Responsibility Model, clearly understanding which parts AWS handles and which parts customers are responsible for; (2) to educate others in the new security paradigm that now exists; (3) to ensure potential blockers are scrutinized appropriately; (4) to ensure the security objectives for the organization's move to the cloud are clear and appropriate. We cover security in depth in Chapter 7.1 Security Is Always Job Zero.

Legal and Procurement. In the old business world, supplier contracts were heavy with CAPEX decisions and guesstimates of required capacity. The contracts, which took months or even years to negotiate, were often packed with numerous SLAs that proved to be mere words on paper when an actual outage occurred.

By default, supplier contracts in hyperscale public cloud are different, with no committed spend, pay-as-you-go consumption, a high security standard, and the natural requirement to protect every customer from every other customer. Legal and Procurement must be involved from the start and have a chance to understand these differences.

Risk and Audit Representation. Ensuring the Risk and Internal Audit teams (if appropriate for your organization) are present within the CLT is important. As you look to adopt the profound benefits to your business that the public cloud brings, these functions help ensure that frontline leaders are raising, accepting, or mitigating risks across these areas.

Head of Infrastructure and Operations. The head of infrastructure and operations typically commands 51 percent of the vote for any decision that comes to the CLT regarding the cloud. This makes some sense from their perspective. The CLT, likely called at 3:00 a.m. when things fail, must maintain critical operations 24-7-365, patching, availability, DR, and all the infrastructure in between—so it always has a powerful voice in the CLT quorum. And thoughts like "Wait a minute, I build infrastructure—what do I do when we move to the cloud?" can be an elephant in the room.

In our experience the infrastructure engineers who previously built, ran, and continually upgraded data center-based infrastructure have a crucial role in cloud migration and growing the business. Their ability to understand infrastructure as code (IaC) through their experience with command line subsystems of legacy data centers (Linux, Windows, network, storage, and databases) is a profound advantage. This is especially true when using those same command line interface skills to configure scripted API calls as AWS CloudFormation scripts. These scripts build not just servers or networks but entire Regions of servers, data services, and everything in between as CI/CD code. We cover CI/CD more in Chapter 4.3 Your Target Operating Model—DevOps.

The motivation boost as infrastructure engineers become skilled AWS experts, ready and able to perform scripted wizardry across any of the AWS Building Blocks (covered more in Chapter 4.1 Becoming Cloud-Fluent at Scale) ensures they always have an important place within Agile teams. Helping engineers through this profound change curve is the job of leaders.

Head of Delivery and Line of Business Representation. The most rapid transformation drivers occur when business leaders demand to leverage new AWS Cloud tools to transform their lines of business, enabling them to deliver different and better customer results.

It's potent stuff when business leaders can clearly articulate a vision of value, leverage the new building blocks of the digital age, and rapidly engage with teams to deliver this change. Using data to make better automated customer decisions in areas like credit risk, decisioning, fraud reduction, cross-sales opportunities as a financial services company for example, is extraordinarily impactful.

Having business leaders' representation for the first workloads is like jumpstarting your journey to the AWS Cloud. It provides a problem catalyst, funding, and goal. Everything else follows.

Human Resources. As you reskill your current and future employees at all levels for the public cloud, HR needs to act as trusted advisers to ensure you engage effectively and appropriately with your workforce. This is especially the case as you look to continually adapt and transform your workforce and job roles.

CCoE Leader. In the next chapter, we delve deeper into the prerequisites of the CCoE Leader and their crucial role as both leader of the CCoE and trusted adviser to the CLT.

The Head of Architecture. Over the last few decades, the role of enterprise architecture has been vaunted and derided in equal parts. In waterfall project management, its role as a key early stage and ongoing governance function often makes or breaks a business case in equal measure.

We respectfully argue that technology architecture has never been more important (see Chapter 5.6 Using the AWS Well-Architected Framework). But the Head of Architecture role has changed significantly with the shift to Agile and teams that build and support using an API-based, pay-as-you-go cloud model. Today's enterprise architects can no longer sit in their ivory towers and act as the authoritarian old guard. The role has changed. The current expectation is that architects can code as well as any developer. They are expected to operate as senior principal developers/engineers with significant multidisciplinary experience, technically leading and mentoring engineers and developers in their teams to ensure consideration of all interrelational components required by modern architectures. Within their teams, architects refine all the architecture assets for their fit-for-purpose and adapt them in line with the product managers to effectively manage technical debt. Their role in the CLT is crucial to ensure a controlled move to the cloud.

Call to Action

Step 1. Set a north star. (We cover this in Chapter 2.2 Your Business Strategy and Principles Matter.)

Step 2. Ensure goals align with business objectives. (We cover this in Chapter 2.5 Measuring the Success of Your Journey.)

Step 3. Catalog, prioritize, and answer all questions—eventually. Everyone will have questions—you can count on it. Most senior executives are consciously curious, which materializes in the form of questions. Do not simply give these questions lip service; capture every single one. Each question is important to the person who asked it, and if left unanswered will act like an anchor dragging down your transformation. *Eventually* is the key term. If the CLT tries to answer every question before doing anything, it will never achieve anything. Don't let this stop you from getting started! It's natural for an organization to prevent customer data from existing in the cloud until the CISO and their teams understand the AWS Shared Responsibility Model. But that doesn't preclude a team from working toward a first workload. Focus on providing just-in-time answers and eventually answering everything later rather than answering everything before starting. An executive briefing session held locally, or ideally at AWS in Seattle, can answer whole swaths of questions, be highly educational, and enable the rapid building of executive relationships.

Step 4. Agree on your principles. (We cover this in Chapter 3.3 Principles for Your Cloud Journey.)

Step 5. Remove roadblocks. Rapid removal of roadblocks builds and maintains momentum and neutralizes ambiguity around committing to the transformation.

Step 6. Agree on the first production workload. Pick something important. It needs to matter to your business peers, demonstrate value, and define a new way. A simple microservice for your production website can work well and is still important to your business. We don't encourage proof of concepts—nobody cares about science projects.

Step 7. Establish a CCoE. (We cover this in Chapter 3.5 Creating the Cloud Center of Excellence.)

Step 8. Assist in the contracting process as required. Pay-as-you-go public cloud contracts are different from capital expenditure-intensive, fixed-term contracts. Leaders should be informed and supportive of these differences. The leadership team may also want to ensure appropriate commercials are in place, including entering a private pricing agreement.

Step 9. Ensure funding is available, specifically for assigning dedicated resources and cultivating priorities. This becomes especially important for establishing the business case and migration decision points.

Step 10. Agree, execute, and monitor migration of applications and data. Ensuring congruence, priority, and awareness of *what* and *when* in migration is a key role of the CLT. Migration is discussed in detail in Chapter 5.4 Completing a Large-Scale Migration and Modernization.

Step 11. Communicate broadly and consistently. The information vacuum will be filled with FUD if you don't communicate.

Step 12. Establish a broad reskilling program. (We cover this in chapter Chapter 4.1 Becoming Cloud-Fluent at Scale.)

Step 13. Establish a regular review cadence. Meeting daily or weekly to check progress and ensure perceived risks are appropriately decisioned is crucial to maintain momentum.

3.5 The Cloud Center of Excellence

Give me a lever long enough and a fulcrum on which to place it, and I shall move the world.

—ARCHIMEDES

One of the key principles of AWS is to level the playing field for every customer by ensuring they have access to the world-class technology previously available to only the largest and wealthiest businesses.

Anybody can start using the AWS Cloud with just a few simple clicks and a credit card. Self-service has enabled hundreds of thousands of customers to make the journey to the cloud quickly and autonomously. But what is the right way for an enterprise to start?

Enterprises can start with just a company credit card. But if you want to learn from those who have gone before you and develop a holistic AWS Cloud experience that can scale across your business and give you maximum benefits from the cloud, then you should seriously consider establishing a CCoE.

What Does the CCoE Do?

A CCoE team coalesces all applicable technical and business product expertise into one team to bring the first production cloud-native workload or migrated workload to the cloud. It establishes the technical objectives, reusable architecture patterns, and associated code for the organization's use of the cloud across the paradigms of security, availability, durability, performance, scalability, services, cost, sustainability choices, the ecosystem, and TTV differentiation. Its members commit to becoming intensely curious about the AWS Cloud and aspire to become cloud experts.

We started our journeys by bringing together the right engineers and developers with the right leaders and goals. Of the many steps you take in your journey to the cloud, creating the CCoE team is one of the most important. This team has a tremendous, disproportionally positive impact on the momentum and outcome of your cloud journey. The team that executes your first cloud workloads and sets the first design patterns will set the bar for everyone who follows (and they should keep raising it). This team's efforts, actions, standards, and engagement with other teams are crucial.

The nature of the relationships between the people you assign to the CCoE directly impacts its ultimate success—or failure.

The purpose of the CCoE is to be a beachhead, a leading light, and a fulcrum of technical change for your cloud transformation. As you scale your talent transformation, success will change this team's requirements and nature.

The team should rightsize over time as you automate more of your processes and, if you choose, transfer much of the responsibility—build and run—to the business outcome teams (which we argue you should).

A CCoE team should work hard to make its function unnecessary as the cloud becomes the way you deliver IT. We discuss this more in Chapter 4.3 Your Evolving Target Operating Model—DevOps. Eventually you'll have a cloud operations team that ensures the critical mechanisms that need to be in place are running smoothly, such as account vending, IP addressing, controls, IaC, and networking.

Where can this go wrong? We have sadly seen customers on the second or third incarnation of creating a CCoE due to some common pitfalls that come from well-considered mental models.

This team needs a mental model that will be an ephemeral construct, not an immutable one. The CCoE should be staffed with dedicated individuals on a temporary team. *Dedicated* means just that—not a side project or shared resource. It's best to set the expectation that this team is a means to an end, not an end in itself. The mindset that all cloud decisions will route through this team forever leads to failure into the second trap, the bottleneck.

Bottlenecks occur as the amount of cloud patterns or manual cloud creation work that the CCoE needs to do exceeds its demand. We have seen this happen repeatedly around the world. There is a desire to "do things right" and "build things in the right way"—a natural reaction from anyone who has had to maintain clunky systems. Early iterations of the CCoE often try building every pipeline and permutation a developer could ever need, which usually fails. The fact is there are infinite ways to solve a problem using the cloud. If you want teams to use TTV as a key metric, you have to remove dependencies and empower application teams to service cloud IaC themselves. That doesn't mean you can't set the right controls and baseline from the start; we encourage everyone to use AWS Control Tower (more on this a little later). Establish a principle that the CCoE's primary goals are to avoid becoming a bottleneck, correct the basics (including security), and empower other teams to use self-service. If this means all future teams that want to build and support need their own cloud engineer or skills, that's fine.

In conjunction with the first two potential issues, the team can fall into the trap of wanting to boil the ocean and create the perfect platform. It may take the approach of "I will create the perfect gold-plated platform," and unfortunately spend years getting there. The principle of the minimum loveable product is a good one to adapt.

Another failing is when the team attempts to extend the existing architecture or tooling to the cloud. Now there can be entirely sensible reasons for doing this. We know companies that have extended that IP address space at layer three straight into AWS and started migrating applications immediately because there was a business reason to do so. But taking a moment to think of the medium- to long-term effects pays time dividends in the future. As long as the team understands the words of Dr. Werner Vogels ("Thou shall not use old IT concepts for new applications") and recognizes that the tooling, design patterns, and needed are likely different, being deliberate about tooling choices and the reasons behind them is very important. Your AWS Solutions Architect is your very best friend here.

In a very large enterprise with multiple divisions or lines of business, a central team can find itself in competition with federated CCoEs. This challenge requires leadership at the group level to define principles and ensure congruence.

Centralized vs. Federated Model

It is common in very large enterprises for divisional CIOs to report to divisional CEOs, who have their own delivery mandates, goals, and budgets. This can create contention with what the central IT team should be doing. We are often asked to provide advice in this regard, and here is what we recommend.

Global responsibilities should include:

- Enablement of federated CCoE teams
- Private pricing agreements
- Global networking and IP address allocation
- AWS management account responsibility
- Security standards
- Compliance standards
- "Traffic light" of service usage

Federated responsibilities should include:

- Enabling line of business application teams
- Availability choices
- Region choices
- AMI creation as appropriate
- Creation of service usage standards as needed
- Ability to customize DevSecOps pipelines
- Ensuring all IaC
- Ensuring AMI rehydration (typically the OS image) is rotated with a consistent date to ensure the latest and greatest is used
- Local IP address allocation
- AWS Control Tower vending as needed

What Makes the Right Team

It's worth restating that side-of-the-desk or matrixed resourcing does not work well—at all. You need a dedicated, hand-picked team with complementary skills that allow them to overcome technical hurdles without seeking much, if any, external technical assistance from other teams.

Consciously acknowledge that you are blending multiple skills together. While many organizations aspire to "do" DevOps, so many we work with forget the "Ops" bit of the equation. Our goal is to bring together diverse skill sets that can overcome any and all potential technical roadblocks.

Creating a diverse team helps increase performance. Researchers Brian Uzzi and Jarett Spiro studied the relationships between collaborators (composers, directors, lyricists, and producers) from nearly 500 musicals produced on Broadway between 1945 and 1989. Using a ratio for density of past working relationships (*Q*), the researchers found that musicals with low *Q* among collaborators were unlikely to become commercial or critical successes. Uzzi and Spiro also discovered that so-called "A-teams"—teams with very strong connectivity or a track record of working together (high *Q*) on other musicals—were not a good indicator of success either. Broadway teams with a good mix of new and existing relationships (midrange *Q*) were three times more likely to achieve box office success.[47] The most successful musicals were by teams comprising a good balance of people who had worked together in the past and knew how to pull off a top production, as well as new blood that brought in a steady supply of new ideas.

From our painful personal experience, the virtual team construct is initially crucial due to the diversity of complementary skills in your CCoE team. Attempting to change reporting lines (which is always emotional) slows things down, potentially terminally. You can revisit this important organizational topic in Chapter 4.2 Your Interim Operating Model.

Effective teams have a broad, deep set of technology skills. For this initial team, permanent employees may prefer outsourcing or contracting resources. It's okay that the foundational team almost certainly won't have the necessary AWS Cloud from the outset. We will get to this later.

Below is the ideal list of CCoE team members. The number of people who comprise this team is not important. It's entirely possible for a single builder to do all these tasks, and thousands of startups get going this way!

Many organizations don't have these individuals in discrete roles but have great engineers and developers doing one or many tasks. That is perfectly fine. We also recognize that assigning some of your most effective employees to this team can be a huge challenge. These individuals are likely already assigned to critical work elsewhere, and budget constraints may make it difficult to replace them with contractors. The CLT's involvement is crucial to ensure resources and trade-offs can be made as needed.

CCoE leader. The individual leading this team has a profound responsibility. This person's performance can (and often will) make or break journeys. When we designated CCoE leaders for our own teams, we chose individuals who overindexed on empathetic people skills and had a firm collaborative bias for action. While strong technology appreciation is required, emotional intelligence is more important here. Consider this description of emotional intelligence from the great book *The EQ Edge* by Steven J. Stein, PhD and Howard E. Book, MD:

> "It's a set of skills that enables us to make our way in a complex world—the personal, social, and survival aspects of overall intelligence, and the elusive common sense and sensitivity that are essential to effective daily functioning. Emotional intelligence also encompasses our ability to read the political and social environment, and landscape them; to intuitively grasp what others want and need, what strengths and weaknesses are; to remain unruffled by

> stress; and to be engaging and the kind of person others want to be around."[48]

This role is best suited for an individual with an appropriate level of seniority, which should be explicitly stated and implicitly understood within the organization.

Security engineer. Security is job zero for us all. Everyone—especially the CISO—wants to ensure that the right security decisions are made. Having a hands-on, code-centric security engineer or developer with a constructive attitude toward outcomes and a reporting line to the CISO is crucial. This individual is responsible for ensuring the first cloud components you choose align with your security objectives.

Carl "CJ" Moses, VP of security engineering at AWS, puts it well: "The security group should not be the group of "no." If your security team is the group of "no," you have got the wrong security team... Security should be an enabler, and we should be part of the process all the way through."[49]

Network/firewall engineer. Ensure you can securely design and connect your existing enterprise network to the AWS Cloud with AWS VPN or AWS Direct Connect while ensuring harmonious IP address ranges, adequate bandwidth and latency calculations, Domain Name System (DNS) server integration, and network routing. Having a network engineer on board who can do this while working with the rest of the team on a shared outcome is critical.

Add someone with firewall expertise to the team to ensure you can appropriately set firewall ports as required from your on-premises infrastructure to the AWS Cloud and enable correct routing of any network segmentation you have in place.

Automation engineer. All AWS engineers and developers learn the importance of using CloudFormation or the AWS Cloud Development Kit (AWS CDK) to ensure repeatable and well-managed IaC as a foundation for DevOps. If you build on Amazon EC2, you need an expert-level engineer familiar with AWS CloudFormation who can assist in automating key elements for secure, scalable Amazon EC2 operation across the various OS your enterprise requires. Having someone who can do this from the start will save you a lot of time and rework later. This person will likely maintain the AMIs,[50] which is an ongoing process as long you use Amazon EC2s rather than AWS

Serverless. The automation engineer should specialize in Ansible, Chef Automate, or Puppet Enterprise to assist your application automation efforts and create the right guidelines to ensure consistent IaC. The goal is to automate everything possible. Everyone needs to learn intrinsic IaC automation delivered through code pipelines.

Operating system engineer. Whether you prefer Windows or Linux, having an experienced engineer who can understand the breadth of critical OS interdependencies in a corporate OS landscape is crucial. This position is similar to that of the automation engineer. Engineers familiar with Unix/Linux and its fundamental elements typically have a shorter learning curve with AWS Command Line Interface (AWS CLI) or AWS CDK.

Software development engineer (SDE). You need experienced developers to create business logic in whatever language your teams prefer. They create the business logic required for your first production instance. Putting them on the team is crucial and lays a constructive path toward Build IT/Run IT if the CLT chooses that principle.

Software quality engineer (SQE). As you move toward CI/CD and DevOps practices, testing what you do does not go away; it becomes a core part of the cycle. If you want to move to small DevOps teams, get your testers to move toward developing test cases before moving to cutting code. In recent years we have seen a swing from test-driven development (TDD) to Observability-Driven Development (ODD). According to Splunk, ODD has been associated with a 2.1 times higher likelihood of issue detection and a 69 percent improvement in the mean time to resolution.[51] TDD focuses on detecting and fixing bugs before they can harm the system or its users, while ODD focuses on monitoring the software system's behavior in real time to identify potential problems and understand its behavior in different scenarios. Whatever method is right for you, testing is a crucial step in CI/CD. TDD and ODD development are software development processes that rely on repeating a very short development cycle. Previously defined "requirements" in a waterfall process are turned into specific minimum test cases as part of an Agile sprint. The developed software must pass tests defined in the sprint. SQEs help the team break down their story steps into the necessary test cases and take input from all team members with an emphasis on security.

Operations engineer. How infrastructure and applications are monitored, where logs go, and how the existing Information Technology Infrastructure Library (ITIL) processes integrate are important. Although mature DevOps can automate many ITIL functions, you might not be there yet. Having a team member who knows how to get the important application/database/infrastructure telemetry data and access a performance baseline eases the integration of existing systems and processes appropriate to use in the cloud.

Data engineers. Having engineers who know where your data is, how to access it, how to move it appropriately, and how to establish the first cloud data stores can accelerate your journey. This team member might be a system database administrator normally responsible for the underlying database engine, performance, operations, backups, and upgrades. Or they might be an application database administrator normally responsible for writing and debugging complex SQL and understanding the best ways to incorporate database requests into application programs and performance tuning. You might also enlist a data scientist in this role to create machine learning-based tools or processes within the company, such as recommendation engines or automated lead-scoring systems and statistical analysis. Regardless of who you assign, one of these people can help reduce cycle time for the team. Databases and analytics are covered in far more detail in Chapter 6.1 Data and Data Mesh.

AWS Solutions Architect and Partner Resource. Engaging both your AWS Solutions Architect and approved AWS Partner or AWS Professional Services resource can accelerate learnings and help guide you. This allows you to grow your knowledge, which is a real catalyst for development time.

Creating Your Landing Zone

Landing zones in the AWS Cloud need their own subtopic in this chapter. We cannot overstate how much work has gone into reinventing the landing zone wheel oh so many times. AWS offers over two hundred services and infinite ways to configure your accounts, controls, and networking. The choice of whether to use CloudFormation, Terraform by HashiCorp, or Pulumi is intensely debated. Making the right decision is crucial for setting your cloud journey on the right path.

What is a landing zone? A landing zone is a well-architected, multi-account AWS environment that is a starting point from which you can deploy workloads and applications. It provides a baseline to get started with multi-account architecture, identity and access management, governance, data security, network design, and logging.

Your AWS Solutions Architect, AWS Partner, or AWS Professional Services team can help you with the latest and greatest information to allow you to make an informed decision. They will almost certainly recommend using AWS Control Tower, which ensures that AWS takes all the heavy lifting of maintaining this for you in perpetuity. You can bespoke it if you want—it is your part of the Shared Responsibility Model. But any bespoke choices you make become technical debt you have to manage forever.

AWS Control Tower offers a straightforward way to set up and govern an AWS multi-account environment following prescriptive best practices. It orchestrates the capabilities of several other AWS services, including AWS Organizations, AWS Service Catalog, and AWS IAM Identity Center (successor to AWS Single Sign-On), to build a landing zone in less than an hour!

Prior to using Control Tower, many AWS customers handcrafted code to build their own landing zones (we did it, too, when we led our digital transformations), and it took them a very long time.

When you use Control Tower, resources are set up and managed on your behalf. It extends the capabilities of AWS Organizations and helps keep your organizations and accounts from drift (i.e., diverging from best practices) and the applications it controls. For example, you can use controls to ensure security logs and necessary cross-account access permissions are created and not altered.

If you host more than a handful of accounts (any Enterprise will be), Control Tower provides an orchestration layer that facilitates AWS account deployment and account governance. You can adopt it as your primary way of provisioning accounts and infrastructure. Users in your federated teams can provision new AWS accounts quickly through configurable account templates. Meanwhile your central cloud operations team (which should be formed when the CCoE disbands) can monitor that all accounts are aligned with established, company-wide compliance policies.

What if You Want to Use Terraform by HashiCorp?

Since November 2021 Control Tower has worked with Terraform through the availability of AWS Control Tower Account Factory for Terraform (AFT),[52] a new Terraform module maintained by the Control Tower team that allows you to provision and customize AWS accounts through Terraform using a deployment pipeline. The source code for the development pipeline can be stored in AWS CodeCommit, GitHub, GitHub Enterprise, or Bitbucket. With AFT you can automate the creation of fully functional accounts with access to all the resources they need to be productive.

Controls within Control Tower

For those companies that must comply with multiple compliance frameworks and assertions, there is one final compelling reason to use Control Tower. Highly regulated entities typically leverage controls to ensure adherence to a compliance framework. A control is a high-level rule that provides ongoing governance for your overall AWS environment. It's expressed in plain language. Control Tower implements preventive, detective, and proactive controls that help you govern your resources and monitor compliance across groups of AWS accounts.

After the CCoE

When the CCoE team becomes a bottleneck, it is time for change. This team eventually needs to become a cloud operations team with the key tenet: "We should be enabling other teams to use the cloud autonomously" (which means focusing on a few things really well). This includes ensuring Control Towers use, maintaining networking and security, configuring controls, adhering to AMI standards, and preventing IaC from drifting, among other things.

The CCoE is there to escalate blockers that need removing to the CLT. Ensuring a regular cadence of daily standups and the appropriate escalation of blockers to the CLT, especially in the first workloads, is crucial. The CCoE leader—and ideally another member of the CLT who is empowered to remove blockers that arise for this team—should be in attendance.

Call to Action

Step 1. Help establish security objectives. Refer to Chapter 7.1 Security Is Always Job Zero.

Step 2. Oversee the creation of landing zones using Control Tower.

Step 3. Ensure consistent code repository. You'll already have existing code repositories in one form or another. But over the last few years, the de facto standard has become Git, a code version control system for tracking changes and coordinating work on files among multiple people. A consistent mechanism for code sharing is crucial, especially as everything becomes IaC.

Step 4. Establish initial availability objectives. Refer to Chapter 5.3 Resilience and Reliability.

Step 5. Establish a training and reskilling program. Refer to Chapter 4.1 Becoming Cloud-Fluent at Scale.

Step 6. Ensure resilient and secure network connections. Review and select the right connectivity patterns so you can route and secure networks from your existing on-premises environment to the AWS Cloud in a scalable and efficient way.

Step 7. Conduct quick-win analysis with business partners. You always aim to create strategic change, but quick tactical wins generate "small victories" that can materially demonstrate success.

Step 8. Complete the first production workload. If you don't have anything live in AWS, you should aim to go live in twelve weeks or less! This is your goal. Use the mechanisms in this book to accelerate your journey. Choose something that gets you live and generates positive news internally. Speed in business matters.

Step 9. Establish an initial billing/payment process review. Getting your first AWS bill is like throwing sunshine in a dark corner. It is your pinnacle point of truth in what and when it was used. Ensuring the right mechanisms are in place so that teams or product owners are accountable for their spend and budget can help make the right decisions. Engaging the correct Financial Analyst from the CFO's team is important.

Step 10. Establish appropriate identity access management.

Step 11. Establish initial run books. Setting patterns for effective support 24-7 as you approach production and establish monitoring canaries is needed with today's systems. You've built IaC via CI/CD pipelines, but does the team understand how to gain bastion host access if necessary?[53] Do appropriate on-call individuals have the right access? Do you have an on-call rota? The AWS Well-Architectured Framework is an excellent resource.[54]

Step 12. Initiate effective communication of technical patterns and feedback. If the CCoE team operates in a vacuum, expect the rest of the organization to be clouded with FUD. Establishing an internal wiki site and communicate what the team is doing weekly. Being humble in its engagement with other teams and ideas is important, especially as you approach production and scale the teams.

3.6 The Cloud Business Office

A year from now you may wish you had started today.

—ANONYMOUS

The leadership team can't get and the keep show on the road with only good intentions. There needs to be a mechanism in place.

The enterprises we've worked with typically have a project management office (PMO), an office of the CIO, a chief of staff, or elements of all three.

What mechanism can join the strategic oversight of the CLT, understand the tactical build that the CCoE is doing (which needs to scale), handle the other significant moving parts, track all the action items, relationships, and interdependencies, and be there to scale and communicate what's new? For that you need a CBO.

What Does a CBO Do?

The CBO guides and informs cloud adoption. It acts on behalf of the CLT, ensuring their intent is well managed. It identifies blockers and tracks progress, architecture alignment, vendor relationships, delivery methodology, migration tracking, reskilling, communication, budget, governance, risk management, and compliance.

Because of the significant governance, risk management, and compliance focus in highly regulated businesses (e.g., financial services institutions, healthcare, and government), we have also seen the CBO called a cloud governance office. There is no hard or fast rule here. Name this function as you see appropriate. It needs a single-threaded leader (SLT), somebody whose sole role is to make this journey successful. They likely don't have direct managerial accountability of the folks assigned to the team, but they wake up each day focusing on this role only.

The CBO exists to ensure alignment between the thousand-and-one elements that need to be coordinated as you execute any well-managed change program. If you don't have a team to help address not only the technology but also the change management, complementary processes, and mechanisms that the rest of the organization leverages, you run a significant risk of the "great stall" caused by being stuck in the frozen middle.

Getting the Right Team Together

Architecture alignment. Although the enterprise architect role is experiencing seismic change, it's still important to provide reference architecture alignment, work decomposition, and engineering support. The CBO is the place to corral this effort and change.

Product management and delivery management. Most organizations have an obsession with a backlog of projects and what can and can't be funded, so this topic is always charged. The PMO is the lynchpin. Managing the change is paramount if you move from project management to a product- or Agile-based delivery method. Ensuring demand management, decomposition, and prioritization of functional work is essential. A product roadmap strawman or epic should be available for account executives to groom. Agile execution support and overall status reporting are also important components of this process.

Financial management and cost optimization. Budget management has always been a focused effort in technology. The ability to clarify infrastructure costs when using the cloud is a revelation.

AWS's breadth of services and pricing options offer the flexibility to effectively manage your costs and keep the performance and capacity your business requires. You can easily rightsize your services and use powerful cost management tools to monitor your costs so you can always be on top of how much you're spending.

Establishing principles and mechanisms for your organization as you scale your AWS usage helps with speed and execution, keeping the CFO on your side.

Onboarding. New employees need to get up to speed with the right knowledge and appropriate access. Existing employees need to know how they can access the new platform. Make sure whoever oversees onboarding has an effective content creator assigned to work hand in hand with the communications output. Clearly and continually communicate that as you build more capabilities in this space and it grows, it will change.

Training and reskilling. See Chapter 4.1 Becoming Cloud-Fluent at Scale.

Organizational change management. Organizational change management and strategy execution are the CLT's responsibilities. The office of the CIO typically handles the change delivery at a macrolevel and appreciates the complex interdependencies that make up the modern enterprise landscape. As your organization moves to small teams, the CBO should focus on what differentiates the business and present the pros, cons, and risks of different possibilities to the CLT.

Clearly communicate what is happening, why it is happening, and when it is happening in a timely manner. Ensure both push-type information (e.g., emails) and pull-type information (e.g., websites) are available and digestible.

Call to Action

Step 1. Identify the leader for the CBO. Balancing EQ and IQ is important in this role. This team member needs to recognize that the CLT has the final say on execution and work hand in glove with the CCoE leader to establish and scale the *how.*

Step 2. Note that the CBO's tactical responsibilities include helping the CLT by tracking actions, identifying blockers, ensuring the cadence of standups, and tracking everything else mentioned throughout the CLT, CCoE, and CBO chapters (and indeed this entire book). The scope is very, very broad. Ultimately the CBO supports the CLT and keeps the wheels from falling off.

Step 3. Build and reskill the team. Building the right team with complementary skills as you adopt the cloud and engage with adjacent teams across the enterprise leads to this team's success.

Step 4. Establish an OODA loop or its equivalence. The OODA loop (observe, orient, decide act) is a decision-making model developed by military strategist and US Air Force Colonel John Boyd. Boyd applied the concept to the combat operations process during military campaigns, often at the operational level. Businesses now apply it to understand commercial operations and learning processes. The approach explains how agility can overcome raw power in dealing with human opponents and is especially applicable to cyber security and cyber warfare.[55] Observing what is going on and adjusting accordingly is very good advice for the CBO leader. Things will change, and curve balls will come. You need to handle them.

Step 5. Communicate. Establish and maintain both push comms and pull comms. If you don't fill the communication vacuum, folks will fill it for you. So communicate!

PART IV

PEOPLE AND PROCESS

4.1 Becoming Cloud-Fluent at Scale

A leader takes people where they want to go, a great leader takes people where they don't necessarily want to go but ought to be.

—FORMER FIRST LADY ROSALYNN CARTER

We all know the importance of learning—it's how we keep up and stay ahead of the change swirling around us. Becoming cloud-fluent is primarily about education and learning. Our own (sometimes painful) experience as leaders has taught us that it's easy to oversimplify gaining cloud fluency as "teams just need a little classroom training." This is not the case at all. As our journeys can attest, training is useful but only the tip of the iceberg.

There are many factors at play here. Your business may be a complex mixture of divisions, outsourcing, siloed resources, some Agile practices, some waterfall practices, some DevOps, operations teams, and third-party vendors with their own project delivery processes. Leading people to upskill so you can remove thankless tasks and empower them to innovate can be daunting.

Motivating people to learn, ideally through self-motivation, is challenging enough. Getting people to unlearn ways and methods they may have used with some success for decades is even more challenging—especially when those methods yield traditional results. In his book *Unlearn*, Barry O'Reilly explains, "We must unlearn what brought us success in the past to find continued success in the future."[56]

You can lead a horse to water, but you can't make it drink. You can't force reskilling; people need to be motivated. Some people tenaciously cling to their previous way of working and remain attached to incumbent technology skill sets.

As a leader, consider how your strategy will be impacted by three human drives closely tied to professional identity: autonomy, mastery, and purpose. These drives motivate people to perform a role, receive an income, pay their mortgage, and live their lives. As long as the cloud remains a mystery, people will fear it. Humans naturally fear the unknown.

Fear is a fickle thing. We won't wax poetic, but we know from personal experience that fear can lead to all sorts of irrational decisions—nearly all of which will delay your transformation. And delays in business can be costly or even fatal.

Okay, let's reset for a second. At this point in the journey, it's important to remind you that this emotion—fear of the unknown—will occur. It's natural. You can't avoid it, but you can lean into it by sparking motivation, interest, and courageous honesty from all leaders so that you can learn together.

Getting this right is so very important. If you succeed in reskilling, your people will understand how to solve challenges, and everything else will largely solve itself. We see this with AWS customers all over the world. Successful reskilling needs motivation (especially for engineers and developers), a mechanism like the twelve-step process detailed later in this chapter, and funding of time and money to allow your business to become cloud-fluent at scale.

Tackling Motivation

Motivation is incredibly nuanced. As individual contributors, managers, and leaders, we've learned that what motivates one person may not motivate another. You need multiple motivational levers in place to support different people.

In his book *Drive*, Daniel Pink argues that human motivation is largely intrinsic and can be divided into three categories: autonomy, mastery, and purpose. He argues against old models of motivation driven by rewards and fear of punishment, dominated by extrinsic factors such as money.[57]

Autonomy. Our desire to be self-directed. It increases engagement over compliance.

Mastery. The urge to get better skills and be known as an expert.

Purpose. The desire to do something important and with meaning. Businesses that focus on profits without valuing purpose end up with poor customer service and unhappy employees.

Having gone through tremendous reskilling journeys ourselves and working with AWS customers around the globe, we agree that Daniel Pink has nailed a significant part of the motivation formula—especially for builders. And today's builders are not only engineers or developers but also product managers, entrepreneurs, and leaders from all walks of life. The ability to act autonomously, leverage mastery, and execute purposefully—without having to build massive, capital expenditure-intensive data centers—has enabled thousands of startups to challenge the status quo like never before. Pinterest, Lyft, Monzo, Peloton—the list goes on and on.

Everything you do as a leader should focus on the short-term fear that reskilling for the cloud will cause for your engineers. They will have to slow down to learn before they can go fast—faster than they ever thought possible. In the 2018 *Accelerate State of DevOps* report, the authors write, "How you implement cloud infrastructure matters. The cloud improves software delivery performance, and teams that leverage all of cloud computing's essential characteristics are twenty-three times more likely to be high performers."[58]

With the launch of Amazon Q Developer, organizations can accelerate reskilling even further. AWS ran a productivity challenge, and participants who used Amazon Q Developer completed tasks 57 percent faster and were 27 percent more likely to complete them successfully than those who didn't.

There is a complication. When it comes to reskilling—particularly with engineers, developers, managers, etc.—autonomy, mastery, and purpose are not the only elements to contend with. People need to unlearn what they've previously done before learning something new. A Linux engineer who has racked, stacked, cabled, installed, configured, and maintained servers from the hardware up probably has a high level of autonomy, mastery, and purpose with the status quo. Introducing this engineer to cloud-first and cloud-native principles creates a fear of the unknown.

According to Barry O'Reilly, the cycle of unlearning is a three-step process: (1) Unlearn—what do you want to unlearn and why? (2) Relearn—as you unlearn limiting but ingrained methods, behaviors, and thinking, you can take in new data, information, and perspectives (3) Breakthrough—as you break free of existing models and methods, you can achieve extraordinary results. Then use what you learn from your breakthroughs to tackle bigger and more audacious challenges, starting the cycle of unlearning all over again.

As Stephen Orban writes, you already have the people you need to succeed with the cloud.[59] We often see organizations think they need to recruit new builders for the cloud. While it's always important to onboard new folks aligned with your culture and expertise requirements, having a scalable reskilling mechanism that addresses individual motivations for each learning style is especially important. See this chapter's Call to Action for twelve steps that work.

Call to Action

Step 1. Acceptance through the art of doing. Your engineers need to realize they can learn AWS Cloud skills and become experts (mastery) operating (autonomy) in a far more valuable way (purpose) when building customer products. This is far more exciting than building and endlessly refreshing hardware. Technology leaders within your organization need to accept this and realize that your existing approach has diminishing returns and needs to change. Discuss this in town hall meetings, team meetings, and water cooler one-on-ones. Engage in humble yet confident communication that you will all learn together.

Step 2. Training. Working in a classroom environment with an instructor creates a safe space for many people and is important to their learning. AWS facilitates training via AWS Training Partners. AWS Cloud Practitioner, AWS Technical Essentials, and AWS Associate Architect are all excellent starting courses, depending on your team's knowledge level. The classroom courses offer an eye-opening and delightful peek into the art of the possible and can radically change your perspective on where you've wasted time with previous practices. The AWS website has hundreds of videos that provide online training for a range of technical topics, from novice to advanced. We recommend offering training immediately prior to a team coming together to use AWS. Resist compelling people to attend training without offering them time and motivation to apply and reinforce what they learn. A whole list of classroom training courses is available.[60] AWS Skill Builder is also available online with a subscription, allowing learners to pursue a bespoke training path, with options available for solutions architects, developers, DevOps engineers, cloud operators, and decision-makers.[61]

Step 3. Hands-on time. There is no compression algorithm for experience, so safe hands-on time is required. Consider offering your engineers an AWS sandbox account—a place that never hosts production; has a set billing alert, and ideally allows engineers and developers to configure everything, including an account's IAM, VPC, and associated IP address space. At re:Invent 2017 Thomson Reuters announced they were giving their engineers and developers a safe sandbox account in which to learn.[62] The cloud gives you a million ways to accomplish the possible; it can be overwhelming. Your engineers can become both very excited and slightly disillusioned by the possibilities. Recognize the normal change curves everyone goes through; some are short, and some are long—it's personal. Continual encouragement is the key!

Step 4. Create your own two-pizza cloud team. The first engineering team you put together should comprise a holistic skill set—network, database, Linux server, application, automation, storage, and security. Provide whatever resources it needs to be autonomous.

Step 5. Add expert-level engineers with the right attitude about sharing learnings and best practices. We both found that embedding engineers from AWS Partners into the CCoE team was a significant and material accelerator for our teams' journeys. Enabling engineers to pair program and go from a bash shell on their laptop to configuring AWS CLI, working with a code repository, and actually building and executing CloudFormation code is a proven way to accelerate learning. It has a transformative effect. Humans learn from other humans by watching, asking questions, and repeating. Engineers prefer learning from fellow engineers. Working in small teams, they get to ask questions and try things they wouldn't be able to in a time-bound classroom course. The jumpstart via pair programming often takes no longer than a day and can be repeated to enable learning more advanced configurations. Pairing a new engineer with an expert when they join the team scales effectively, radically reducing the lead time for an engineer to be effective and understand how your CI/CD pipeline operates.

Step 6. Make it real. The Agile two-pizza team should build something real and in production. Your foundational AMI can host a small app and associated network setup. The objective is to find something important that solves an existing business challenge. Get it done in weeks, not months. Track progress. Show an interest. Set a demo deadline. Be there to see progress as well as the results. A word of advice: don't let the team boil the ocean here. Only work with the AWS building blocks you need; you'll have plenty of time to expand as needed. The advantage of experimentation is key; AWS makes discarding and starting over as many times as needed to learn feel natural.

Step 7. Scale learning with cellular mitosis. Once the first team achieves AWS proficiency and delivers a product, oversee the team's cellular mitosis. Gently and consciously split this first team in two, introducing no more than one new engineer per person. This is difficult and should be handled with care. Be honest with team members and positively acknowledge their collective achievement. Ask for their help passing on learnings and best practices to their new teammates.

Keep splitting and reforming teams in this mitosis-driven approach until all engineers rotate. The precise composition of skill types should be appropriate to the task at hand. The initial CCoE team may no longer exist; this is not bad—it was always an ephemeral construction. Every team needs to be experts on the cloud.

Step 8. Certification. After training, peer programming, and hands-on time, your team can work toward AWS Certification. Ensure everyone can prepare themselves by providing resources to self-service their learning. The AWS

Marketplace offers enterprise licenses from A Cloud Guru that allow anyone with your company's email to access excellent preparatory training material for exams. Engineers can pass the certification in their own time at their own pace. We suggest starting with the Associate Certification and building up to Professional.

Certifications are broad and deep, allowing real mastery to develop.

There are many benefits to AWS Certification. Some enterprises cleverly use certification as a license to achieve account access levels. We've also seen it built into graduate induction courses, which is awesome.

Step 9. Scale certification and associated leadership. According to research and confirmed by our experience, you need a critical mass of just 10 percent of employees advocating a platform before the network effect takes hold.[63] Scaling learning and certification to 10 percent of your engineers is a major milestone in your journey. You'll get a compelling halo effect that influences your company's perception externally and internally. Outside engineers who want to work with only cloud-native companies will seriously consider working for you. Your transformation's pace increases exponentially as you attract or convert more cloud-fluent talent. Internal engineers don't want to be left behind, further increasing the pace of reskilling. Some may want to coast to retirement rather than relearn, which can be fine; these folks can then manage the sunset period of remaining legacy systems.

Step 10. Recognize and reward expertise loudly and proudly. Your goal as an IT executive is to shout from the rooftops the name of every person who passes each certification exam. Reward and recognize technical progress in any way you can—meals, vouchers, drinks, special team chairs, novelty awards, you name it. Many large enterprises establish a global roster of each person and their AWS certifications. Certification is a tangible and visceral achievement. Nearly every engineer we've ever met craves peer respect, and certification—combined with what you build—contributes to community kudos. This goes a massively long way in addressing the mastery part of motivation.

Step 11. Take the challenge yourself. When Jonathan was standing at a town hall meeting in his previous role, recognizing and rewarding the engineers who had progressed thanks to certification, one of the sharper sparks in the audience spoke up loudly: "If you believe so passionately in certification, when will *you* take the exam?" That stopped Jonathan pretty squarely. He hadn't taken an industry exam for a long while. But as somebody who likes to practice what he preaches, he stepped up to the plate and earned his AWS Associate Architect Certification. He could proudly stand on that stage too! Taking the exam was an excellent forcing mechanism, ensuring that Jonathan gained a broad, yet sufficiently detailed, overview of the key AWS building blocks.

Step 12. Create a unifying job family portfolio. Once the timing is right, offer your technical employees a concrete job family track.

National Australia Bank Case Study

National Australia Bank (NAB) has been helping customers with their money for almost 160 years. Today NAB has more than thirty thousand employees servicing nine million customers at over nine hundred locations in Australia, New Zealand, and around the world.

In November 2017 NAB launched an ambitious digital transformation and decided to adopt a public cloud-first strategy. Part of the transformation involved recruiting two thousand employees with new skills, such as cloud engineers, developers, and architects. They realized that in addition to bringing in new skills, they needed to invest in the development of their existing workforce. This was the catalyst that led to the creation of the NAB Cloud Guild.

As this journey began, NAB had just seven AWS Certified employees. NAB started by running a twelve-week course with focused, one-hour deep dives on the cloud. Attendance grew significantly. To meet the significant demand, NAB moved to daily deep dives with twenty-four people in each session, but then they hit a scaling limit on instructor time. They pivoted to building a practice community; instead of only AWS speaking, they had their employees present on the cloud. If you want to master something, teach it!

By March 2018, 150 employees had been trained, but only 15 were AWS Certified.

At the 2018 AWS Sydney Summit, NAB announced the launch of its Cloud Guild and its goals to train three thousand people (10 percent) and accelerate the rate of AWS certifications. Within 24 hours 1,900 employees registered for Cloud Guild training sessions; within 48 hours that number rose to 3,000.

By November 2019, more than 4,500 NAB employees had been trained on AWS, with 817 AWS Certified employees holding 1,134 certifications.

NAB's Paul Silver says:

> "If you imagine a lake and a pebble, and you drop the pebble in the lake, you'll make a splash that ripples outward across the lake's surface. That's your 10 percent, the ripple effect that continues afterward when everyone starts talking the same language...We moved from an ad-hoc cloud organization, where it was hard to move and move quickly, to one where people can clearly see the benefits and a path on how to do it. After we trained all of those people, we moved to a can-do mindset organization when it came to cloud and its potential."[64]

Verizon Communications Case Study

Verizon Communications operates reliable wireless and all-fiber networks and delivers integrated solutions to businesses worldwide. It generated $130.9 billion in 2018.[65] Its Oath subsidiary reaches about one billion people around the world with dynamic media and technology brands. To gain agility and scalability for its development teams and workloads, Verizon began exploring options for deploying cloud-native software solutions and applications on AWS.

Verizon knew that underpinning its ability to transform on the cloud would be the ability to drive a culture shift within the organization to embrace cloud development and focus on ongoing learning. So they engaged with AWS Partner A Cloud Guru to help drive the shift.

In the words of Chivas Nambiar, former Executive Director of Cloud and Platform Engineering at Verizon:

> "Our incentives were primarily focused on the ability to achieve industry-recognized certification and internal bragging rights. Certified employees were called out and employees with multiple certifications were recognized and highlighted by senior leadership. We started with very few public cloud-aware architects. While these few early adopters were enthusiastic and learned on their own, it was evident that we needed to target the larger mass of the IT organization to drive meaningful progress."[66]

Verizon set a goal to get 10 percent of all IT employees AWS Certified. It exceeded that goal; more than 1,300 IT employees received their AWS Certified Solutions Architect – Associate Certification in just seven months. Verizon also achieved a cultural shift within its engineering organization, encouraging and rewarding learning in a new and continuous way.

Final Thought

Break some glass ceilings. Engineers should be able to reach high senior levels—including director and above—without managing people. These promotions should respect technical depth, associated competency development, and technical leadership maturity.

Seeing your employees scale new heights and attain hard-earned promotions is always the most rewarding part of being a leader. Establishing VP-level individual contributors with EQ, IQ, and technical leadership skills sends a powerful message to your technology workforce. Review how you compensate your technology staff to match the market. The competition for outstanding technology talent is not slowing.

4.2 Your Interim Operating Model

If you dislike change, you're going to dislike irrelevance even more.

—GENERAL ERIC KEN SHINSEKI, FORMER CHIEF OF STAFF OF THE US ARMY

We must insert a health warning: The interim operating models we discuss will likely provoke a visceral emotional reaction. This is fine. There is no perfect operational model, and you need to do what works for your organization. The learning never stops; leaders always iterate from feedback loops and adjust accordingly. Ultimately the best operating model is one that the teams own and accept.

We're repeatedly asked what works, and we see opportunities as AWS customers migrate and try to understand their new model. Having an operating model framework congruent with keeping mission-critical technology running, meeting the needs of your business colleagues, and adopting and migrating to the cloud helps significantly.

Are current models failing? You may have seen a model that looks like Figure 9.

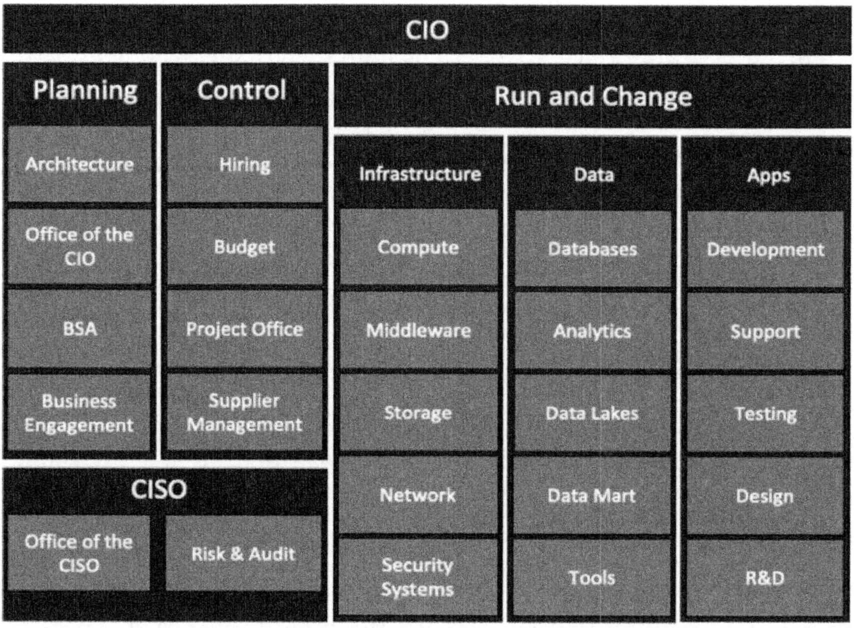

Figure 9 Traditional IT target operating model

For decades enterprises generally accepted only one operating model. And this model—waterfall—has had a cult-like following with armies of certified Project Management Professionals (PMP), ITIL folks, business solution architects, and enterprise architects (no offense if you're one of these people). We're struck by how few of these devotees actually touch the keyboard and develop real software technology solutions for their customers. But to be fair, when operating on-premises technology teams, you need teams with deep I-shaped technology skill sets. Jonathan spent several years as a Cisco engineer, and it took him many years to get remotely good at Cisco networking; he could have spent many more years getting more knowledge about that vendor's ecosystem. This changes with the AWS Cloud. The cloud equalizes skill sets across all teams; engineers become T-shaped or even Pi-shaped in their skills.

Companies have typically siloed engineers and developers into different areas and applied matrixed resourcing to slice them into too many different projects. This has led to many trade-offs, handoffs, and ever-escalating attempts to prioritize their time. Technology executives must routinely make trade-offs when deciding which engineers and developers work on which project which day, creating an ongoing source of conflict. We believe the folks who have previously been "organizers" often have underused technical skills that can find new life in a different model.

We are strongly biased against matrix resourcing (with a few exceptions we discuss later in this chapter). Escalations around matrixed resources have previously dominated our calendars in spectacularly unproductive ways. We have lost count of how many developers and engineers have complained that "It takes me hours to focus on a problem, and I've been allocated to ten projects today. What the flip!" In waterfall operating models, technical resources are typically siloed into buckets of infrastructure and applications (and siloed again into technology types) with either engineering or operations specialties.

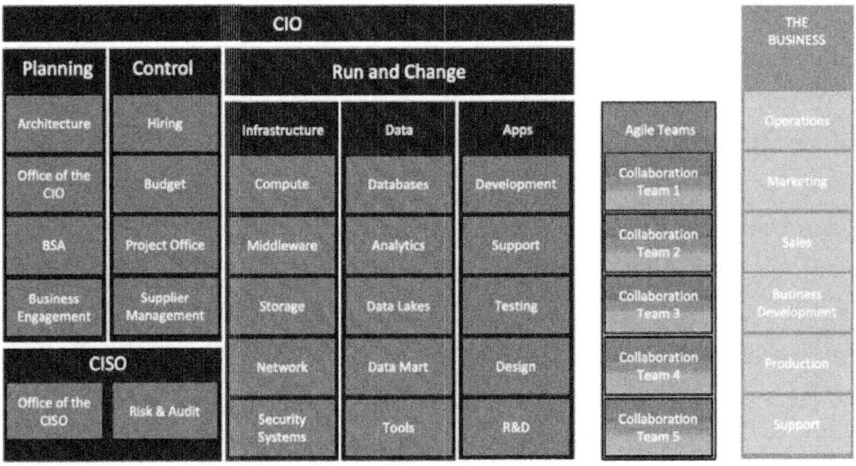

Figure 10 Traditional target operating model with collaboration teams

In a conscious move to be Agile, businesses create these "collaboration teams," or some equivalent, that sit in the middle. Alas these don't work well either as they lack autonomy and have to relentlessly engage gatekeepers. Folks from the IT and business sides end up shouting at the teams in the middle. Figure 10 shows lots of silos of command and control generating tremendous negative energy and friction everywhere. Teams should focus on achieving a high-performing flow to deliver business outcomes, which is enabled by owning their data, logic, security, etc.

As discussed in Chapter 3.2 Teams, humans have worked best in small teams dedicated to solving a task *autonomously for millennia. Spotify's engineering model, built around squads and tribes, has gained significant interest and an* intellectual following because it meets these criteria.[67] We caution AWS customers against emulating another company's culture and organization, but you can see human-driven elements that have made the Spotify model so successful.

Tech Debt and Migration Mental Models

Your operating model changes as employees come and go, but understanding the impacts that migration has on it helps you identify necessary changes to your interim operating model as you work toward your target operating model. Understanding the seven ways of migrating, including their pros and cons, provides insight into the interim possibilities for those operating model changes.

Migration is a deep topic, so Chapter 5.4 Completing a Large-Scale Migration and Modernization is dedicated to it. We've identified seven effective migration patterns for interim target operating model decisions. While there are many similar patterns, don't skip the crucial understanding of each mental model.

Relocate. The ability to extend your VMWare hypervisor into AWS and vMotion your virtual servers to run on AWS or using AWS Outposts.

Rehost. The ability to lift and shift the existing on-premises server and its host OS with installed software/database over to a new host in the cloud.

Replatform. The ability to replatform an existing application or database from the existing on-premises OS over to a new OS on the cloud.

Repurchase. The ability to move your existing workloads to software from the AWS Marketplace or a SaaS provider.

Refactor (sometimes called Rearchitect). The ability to refactor existing applications to be fully cloud-native by rearchitecting the application and data to your desired target.

Retire. Self-explanatory.

Retain. Workloads you may need to keep in place for various reasons.

Determine which investments are needed to support your strategy through thoughtful consideration of your targets for workload refactoring. The need to make and ship product changes multiple times a day and escape a waterfall or monolithic architecture should be a strong determining factor. Whatever makes your business your business—your secret sauce, as it were—directly equates to your most powerful revenue and income generators, making it the obvious target. But a word to the wise: refactoring can be way more expensive in time and money than either rehosting or replatforming, so choose wisely and recognize your teams' bandwidths.

Rehosting, replatforming, and repurchasing predominately drive interim models. Many organizations want to replatform or repurchase applications to gain the benefits of IaC, as discussed in Chapter 5.3 Resilience and Reliability. They may break out the OS and package the application for automatic deployment via a new central team or function. This path can break traditional dependencies of custom crafting the OS and having the infrastructure teams install and manage the application. In this model the application teams likely consume much of the CloudFormation, OS, and AWS account configuration from cloud operations teams. This is a common and acceptable interim model.

Many infrastructure teams try to maintain this model in perpetuity, and we understand why. Maintaining the status quo is easier for them. But problems eventually appear. The central teams providing this service become bottlenecks, and their technical expertise stretches too thin as they try to master too many technologies. This challenge is among the most common we are called upon to help with.

The (Myth of the) Full-Stack Engineer

Slowly but surely you must blend teams to have skills in application, data, and IaC experience as part of a business outcome team while fully aware of security expectations. Is this easy? No, but it is essential before the next chapter on DevOps as a target operating model. Make the folks who have previously supported your on-premises infrastructure part of the business outcome teams. They can be outsourced or insourced employees; go through the reskilling journey discussed in Chapter 4.1 Becoming Cloud-Fluent at Scale to do this. The list of full-stack engineers who can do everything— front-end and backend development, Linux kernel development, AWS Cloud engineering, and everything in between—is indeed very short. You need a team that comprises complementary skill sets, which can help you with the segregation of duty requirements. The people who ship application code can have different permissions from those who access production data in break glass procedures.

The On-Call Elephant

Let's talk about the on-call elephant. In the split, traditional enterprise waterfall delivery world of support-versus-delivery organization, we have seen more organizational and us-versus-them tension than anywhere else.

In this model the delivery team wants to throw things over the fence to the support team, who wants to add people to their team 24-7 and then blame the delivery team for software not built to *their* standards. We have some news for you: organizations with this model are doomed to be disrupted by other organizations and startups that have moved away from this legacy and, dare we say it, dysfunctional approach.

In the DevOps small team model, the team supports its own software 24-7. This can produce nothing short of outright mutiny within some organizations. We know from personal experience that dealing with critical incidents—and the mental impact they have at all levels—makes IT easily one of the most stressful roles out there.

The elephant in the room must be addressed: some engineers don't want to be on call. In the small empowered team model, there is no one else to call when your stuff breaks. The team must fix it, which means putting folks on call with a rota and having secondary on calls with escalation to team leaders and upward. There's no way of sugarcoating this—it can be a tough conversation. This is why having a leadership team with declared principles that will be followed holistically is so important. DevOps teams need to be on call. Period.

But believe us—the effort is worth it. When everyone on the team owns the result of their work 24-7, the care and fortitude with which they deliver increases. Multiple human factors come into play here, and sloppy effort is quickly called out. If your team colleague is woken up at

3:00 a.m. because you didn't enable auto scaling correctly, you will hear about it the following morning.

Exceptions to the Rule

The small team model works particularly well when dealing entirely with software configurability. This is why cloud APIs are such a cool feature; they remove previous dependency on hard skills. You now move and scale that way. Does the small team, empowered, skill-mixed, self-contained model work everywhere? For most modern organizations in a cloud-first world, it does.

But we have experienced exceptions, including:

When a team has to deal with physical hardware support and maintenance. Examples include an end user support team dealing with personal computer deployment and maintenance—this could be a large global team for large organizations. However, the third-line desktop support team likely deals entirely with software, so the small team model works well. Another example is a network team, which probably deals with tens, hundreds, or maybe thousands of network devices from corporate Wi-Fi to routers and switches. Again a mixture of a large team and perhaps third- or fourth-line engineers in smaller, software-only teams do the trick.

When dealing with a physical construction line. If you are a mature team moving an item to utility for your customers, then using lean methodology and maturing that element to the nth degree is entirely appropriate.

Certain operational processes to ensure consistent holistic monitoring and security. Keeping some teams central/divisional just makes sense. Examples include critical service teams, a central cloud operations team (responsible for OS images, preventive control exemptions, best practices, etc.), batch operations, network operations centers, security operations centers, vendor management, Agile management offices, security teams, etc. Again the model that works and is accepted is the best.

The key differentiator we see is whether or not a team can entirely use APIs to bring solutions that accomplish their work and configure their business logic to achieve their outcomes. If yes, then great—the small, decentralized DevOps model will work. (appropriate security and governance controls are mandatory.)

Aligning Teams to Outcomes

Aligning business outcome teams to an executive owner is the most effective way forward. Changing reporting lines over time —whether dotted or solid—is almost certainly the right thing to do. This creates an interesting challenge for your business partners as they now face managing development teams directly. Engineers and developers respect leaders who appreciate what they do, how they do it, and what it takes to achieve desired outcomes.

A business leader who doesn't understand that technology and business outcomes go hand in hand will not survive the disruption wave sweeping the planet. This can be very intimidating for executives not naturally inclined toward technology; when you feel threatened, your most natural reaction is fear. Yet again the leadership team—and the principles they agree to—are crucial to this changing paradigm.

How Many Teams to Support an Outcome?

Aligning teams to an outcome is empowering stuff. There are some learnings here. The question is this: How many teams can a single executive align to an outcome and manage effectively?

Just as six to twelve people is a good size for a two-pizza team; aligning six to twelve teams to an outcome is also good. If you go beyond that, keeping track of the Agile epics and the number of people involved becomes a challenge for a line of business. Keeping teams with similar interdependencies is also conducive to success.

Release Trains

The Scaled Agile Framework (SAFe) can be a useful guide when adopting Agile. However, we are always cautious of adopting things verbatim (books never have the context of your business, including this one).[68] Each organization needs to adopt specific working practices as it sees fit, but one concept we have seen work well is the cadence of sprints and release trains.

SAFe release trains typically run in three-month increments, bringing all empowered teams together with leaders to sense-check dependencies and ensure outcomes align with the executive goal. Sometimes a holistic need to align something needs to spread across all teams. Examples include aligning to publish a user interface in multiple languages, which requires all teams to work together.

In the release train model, considerable planning and forward-thinking work is required from leaders and accountable line of business (LOB) executives—it is inescapable. You will look pretty silly if you stand up at a release planning session and can't explain the business priorities and *why* behind them (as one of the authors found out the hard way, you cannot wing this bit). Engineers and developers will doubt your leadership ability, making attrition a definite risk. Ensuring team leader alignment and a deep understanding of the technical practicality of what is needed (in what ordinal sequence things could be dependent) is a modern key leadership skill and a true differentiator for modern business leaders. Whether it's a two-day quarterly offsite before the release team presentation or workshops in the office, find a leadership communication and alignment method that works for you.

The Ability to Pivot

In the release train model, sense-check that teams still drive you toward your goals every twelve weeks. If they aren't, then you need to make changes. We strongly suggest not messing with your team's two-week sprint cycles during a release train; it's a sure way to ruin their motivation.

A twelve-week sprint check-in also allows you to move certain talent skills between teams. Moving a resource from *x* to *y* is easy if you don't change the team's nucleus, and the software supporting it is safe.

Call to Action

Step 1. Review your business agility metrics. Clarify what, where, and why you want improvement, as discussed in Chapter 2.5 Measuring the Success of Your Journey.

Step 2. Understand your current operating model. Do you truly understand where the human risks are right now across your organization? Where are the skill pinch points? Where are the key service challenges right now? Doubling down on help for those areas before starting alleviates stress all around. Do you understand the entire leadership team's needs and career aspirations? Who is the right person to lead the CBO and the CCoE? Both roles are crucial.

Step 3. Identify the migration pattern that best supports your business objectives. Is *sustain, optimize,* or *grow* right for systems and parts of your organization? See Chapter 5.4 Completing a Large-Scale Migration and Modernization for a deep dive on migrations. Have you produced a straw man to map the 7 Rs to your systems? This can be incredibly insightful for identifying which teams move first and when.

Step 4. Determine your short-, medium-, and long-term resourcing plan. Do you have the right resources in every role? Of course not. We have yet to meet any enterprise with every role filled with all the skilled folks they need. But do you understand the mix of partners that can go on this journey with you? Which partners do you want to move away from? Where do you want to increase or reduce permanent headcount? Hiring for your core business and selectively using suppliers for utility is important. Have a tactical and strategic plan. We've sadly seen some organizations that have been badly advised by their incumbent providers, leading to significant discontent. We strongly encourage you to discover the AWS Partner status of any partners you work with and make an informed decision.

Step 5. Start with one team to execute in a selected target operating model. Chapter 3.5 Creating the Cloud Center of Excellence and Chapter 4.1 Becoming Cloud-Fluent at Scale discuss bringing new cloud-fluent teams together, especially if you are moving to Agile teams that will refactor or build new cloud-native applications directly. You can scale this model through a process of cellular mitosis. If you are migrating for cost reduction and opting to "optimize," you may want to leave a team as is because you will rehost an existing workload to the cloud. The team will need some training on AWS as their workloads will be on the cloud; their run books will change accordingly.

Step 6. Select the next workload and map another team to it. You're going back to Step 1. You must continually refine all workloads and their current service status, location, risk status, and technology debt, reviewing them in light of business goals and current resourcing levels. Aim to establish a flywheel of momentum for all your workloads to move with a migration plan around the 7 Rs.

4.3 Your Target Operating Model—DevOps

DevOps is not a goal but a never-ending process of continual improvement.

—JEZ HUMBLE

Atlassian, a company whose products we have both used, describes DevOps as a set of practices that automates the processes between software development and IT teams, enabling them to build, test, and release software faster and more reliably. DevOps is founded on a culture of collaboration between teams that historically functioned in relative silos.[69]

DevOps is a bit more to it than that. We think of it as an evolution to simplify software development and IT operations while driving toward higher quality, security, and compliance and removing or optimizing things that slow you down. DevOps is a philosophy based on the lean principles of continuous improvement combined with respect for people, aimed squarely at increasing velocity.

These are not new ideas, although we like to think they are. DevOps is on a continuum of principles that have emerged based on the experience of several generations of software developers, engineers, and technologists. In 1986, F. Brooks enthusiastically spoke about "growing systems organically," building on earlier work by Harlan Mills from 1971. Brooks writes:

> "Harlan Mills proposed that any software system should be grown by incremental development. That is, the system should first be made to run, even though it does nothing useful except call the proper set of dummy subprograms. Then, bit-by-bit it is fleshed out, with the subprograms in turn being developed into actions or calls to empty stubs in the level below… Much of present-day software acquisition procedure rests upon the assumption that one can specify a satisfactory system in advance, get bids for its construction, have it built, and install it. I think this assumption is fundamentally wrong, and that many software acquisition problems spring from that fallacy."[70]

1971! We are a slow lot, aren't we?

Our software development methodologies, project management approaches, and operational processes have needed improvement for decades. We are still undergoing the much-needed evolution that the automotive industry pursued in the 1980s when it adopted Toyota's principles of lean production based on Sakichi Toyoda's principle of *Jidoka* (autonomous automation) in the mid-1920s.[71]

Agile Manifesto Revisited

In 1994 seventeen software development professionals gathered to reimagine what software development (then a thirty-year-old profession) could become. At the time, the Standish Group found that only 16.2 percent of all MIS projects were completed on time and within budget according to something appropriately called the *CHAOS Report*. Another 52.7 percent were late and over budget, and 31.1 percent were outright canceled.[72]

In the past twenty-five years, the completion rate of traditionally managed projects has increased to 29 percent. While nearly double, it's certainly not something a prudent investor would bet on. Compound this with the behavior of product managers convinced that they must create new stuff to stay competitive.

Even if that is true, are you building the right stuff? According to more Standish Group research, only 40 percent of projects have high to very high value, 46 percent have average value, and 15 percent have low or very low value.[73] Projects with average value are unlikely to differentiate you from the competition, so 60 percent of projects may not be worth doing at all. Are you focused on the right things for your business?

In 1998 Ron Jeffries described a principle called You Aren't Going to Need It (YAGNI): "You save time, because you avoid writing code that you turn out not to need. Your code is better, because you avoid polluting it with 'guesses' that turn out to be more or less wrong, but stick around anyway."[74]

This brings us to DevOps. At the 2008 Agile Conference in Toronto, Andrew Schafer posted an offer to moderate an ad hoc Birds of a Feather meeting to discuss Agile infrastructure. Only one person showed up to discuss the topic: Patrick Dubois. Inspired by a video session titled, "10+ Deploys per Day: Dev and Ops Cooperation at Flickr" by John Allspaw and Paul Hammond, Dubois organized a new conference dedicated to these topics called DevOpsDays in Ghent, Belgium. With that the term was born.

Dubois and others voiced the core concern that those who write code have been organizationally and functionally separated from those who deploy and support that code. The philosophy of DevOps unites Agile, autonomous automation, TDD, continuous integration and deployment, and a culture of collaboration aimed at value creation and measured by TTV.

At its simplest, DevOps is about removing the barriers between two traditionally siloed teams: development and operations. Some organizations may not separate development and operations teams; engineers may do both. With DevOps the two teams work together to optimize the developer's productivity and operation's reliability. This bears repeating: productivity and reliability! The teams strive to communicate frequently, increase efficiencies, and improve the quality of services they provide to customers. They take full ownership of their services, often beyond where their stated roles or titles have traditionally been scoped, by thinking about the end user's needs and how they can contribute to solving them. Quality assurance and security teams may also become tightly integrated with these teams. Organizations using a DevOps model, regardless of their organizational structure, have teams that view the entire development and infrastructure lifecycle as part of their responsibilities.

These teams use practices to automate historically manual, slow processes. They use a technology stack and tooling that help them operate and evolve applications quickly and reliably. These tools also help engineers independently accomplish tasks (e.g., deploying code or provisioning infrastructure) that normally would have required waiting for other teams to complete work, further increasing team velocity. In our previous organizations, we each leveraged a centralized "platform" team to create shared resources, frameworks, and tooling to provide the development teams with continuous software integration and continuous delivery capabilities.

Let's reset for a moment.

Normally at this point, leaders say that while they understand they need to reconstitute their teams to work differently (there really should be no such thing as a single DevOps team just doing infra work for everyone else in a large enterprise), and while they want to trust their people to work in this new way, they worry about a perceived lack of control and the trade-off of empowerment needed in this model. For a leadership team used to command and control methods, this is understandable. To quote former President Ronald Reagan, you need to "trust, but verify."[75]

Verifying in DevOps comes in the form of guardrails (called controls at AWS), which allow engineers to move faster with permission as long as they stay within the defined policy. (Proactive controls are now available out of the box when using AWS Control Tower to create landing zones; see Chapter 3.5 Creating the Cloud Center of Excellence for more.)

How to Adopt a DevOps Model

Transitioning to DevOps requires a change in culture and mindset. Traditional IT service management—based on ITIL or similar frameworks—is chiefly concerned with managing risk, governance, security, and compliance. These concerns are still important, but DevOps approaches focus on speed of development, delivery, and TTM by leveraging automation to quickly iterate solutions and enable innovation. Embracing DevOps enables existing IT infrastructure, supporting migration to the cloud and operating IT in the cloud. For example, you still have a change record when new code is pushed into production, but you can automate the creation of a change ticket each time it's done.

To adopt DevOps, use scripting to identify individuals on your staff with the ability or aptitude for process improvement and automation. Look for infrastructure engineers with a background in Unix or Linux system administration or software development engineers who understand how to troubleshoot problems from the command line and are intimately familiar with infrastructure scripting (now IaC)—they quickly grasp and embrace DevOps principles. Ask your engineers what recurring processes or problems in your infrastructure are addressed manually, and then have them script solutions to automate them. This frees up time they can use to solve other problems with automation.

At the same time, have a team develop a CI/CD pipeline for and with your software development teams. Continuous integration is the practice of routinely integrating code changes into the main branch of a repository and testing the changes early and often. Continuous delivery is an approach where teams release quality products frequently and predictably from source code repository to production in an automated fashion.

Continuously improve these automations and tools.

Note that you can and should do this to support your on-premises environments as well as for your cloud workloads. DevOps is a must-have capability to truly succeed in the cloud. Be thoughtful in balancing the time required to build new cloud DevOps capability with continually optimizing the old.

You can use many excellent tools to accomplish this, including an ever-increasing suite of AWS services for DevOps.

Benefits of DevOps

Speed. Move at higher velocity so you can innovate faster for customers, better adapt to changing markets, and become more efficient at driving business results. The DevOps model enables your developers and operations teams to achieve these results. For example, microservices and continuous delivery let teams take ownership of services and then release updates to them quickly.

Rapid delivery. Increase the frequency and pace of releases to innovate and improve your product faster. The quicker you can release new features and fix bugs, the faster you can respond to your customers' needs and build a competitive advantage. CI/CD automates the software release process from build to deployment.

Reliability. Ensure the quality of application updates and infrastructure changes so you can reliably deliver more rapidly while maintaining a positive experience for end users. Use practices like CI/CD to test that each change is functional and safe. Monitoring and logging practices help you stay informed of performance in real time.

Scale. Operate and manage your infrastructure and development processes at scale. Automation and consistency help you manage complex or changing systems efficiently with reduced risk. For example, IaC helps you manage your development, testing, and production environments in a repeatable and more efficient manner.

Improved Collaboration. Build more effective teams under a DevOps cultural model, which emphasizes values like ownership and accountability. Developers and operations teams collaborate closely, share many responsibilities, and combine workflows. This reduces inefficiencies and saves time (e.g., reduced handover periods between developers and operations, writing code that considers the environment in which it is run).

Security. Move quickly while retaining control and preserving compliance. You can adopt a DevOps model without sacrificing security using automated compliance policies, fine-grained controls, and configuration management techniques. For example, using IaC and policy as code, you can define and track compliance at scale.

Business Impact

In 2018 Nicole Forsgren, Jez Humble, and Gene Kim published fascinating research about the impact of DevOps on technology companies.[76] Their research demonstrated that, compared to organizations not using DevOps, high-performing organizations using DevOps in the cloud can:

- Deploy code 46 times more frequently
- Accelerate lead time from commit to deploy 2,555 times faster
- Recover from downtime 2,604 times faster
- Make change failure rate 7 times less likely

Final Thought

What could your organization accomplish if it were one hundred or one thousand times faster? What would it mean for your business and customers to experience failures 85 percent less frequently than you do today? In our experience DevOps is rocket fuel for organizations, and we believe it is essential for yours.

PART V

ARCHITECTURE AND MIGRATIONS

5.1 Compute, Containers, and Serverless

Serverless will fundamentally change how we build business around technology and how you code.

—SIMON WARDLEY

There is a very good reason that, for the most part, humans no longer live in caves. Caves bring problems, and problems mean hard work—much of it tedious and dangerous. Caves are hard to heat, hard to secure, damp, uncomfy, and sometimes filled with bats, spiders, and other creatures. You get the picture. Most of us no longer live in caves, and our dwellings are getting better all the time with central heating, air conditioning, refrigerators, gas fireplaces, automatic lights, security alarms, etc. Amazon Alexa, anyone?

It is just the same with ever-increasing performance and abstraction in enterprise technology.

From 1952 into the late 1960s, IBM manufactured and marketed several large computer models, known as the IBM 700/7000 series. The first-generation 700s used vacuum tubes, while the second-generation 7000s used transistors.

IBM initially sold its computers without any software, expecting customers to write their own. Programs were manually initiated, one at a time. IBM later provided compilers for the newly developed, higher-level programming languages Fortran, COMTRAN, and COBOL. IBM customers wrote the first OS for IBM computers because they didn't want their very expensive machines (worth the equivalent of $2 million in today's dollars) sitting idle while operators set up jobs manually. Humans have been abstracting away and automating the layers of human-intensive technology operations ever since.

We humbly submit that, although the tech world is prone to hype cycles, no inflection point has been as transformational as the advent of the public cloud in 2006—a once-in-a-career event.

Amazon EC2

As our wise, purple-haired, tech evangelist teammate Jeff Barr pointed out to us recently, the very first public service that AWS launched in beta was the Amazon Simple Queue Service (Amazon SQS) on November 3, 2004.[77] Amazon S3 followed on March 14, 2006.[78] August 24, 2006, AWS launched Amazon EC2 in beta, and the IT world has never been the same. There are now over 750 AWS EC2 instance types, including general purpose, compute, memory, accelerated computing, storage, HPC, and even Mac.

Saying you have a lot of choice is an understatement.

Amazon EC2 is leveraged by thousands of AWS customers, including Netflix, Expedia, Airbnb, NASA JPL, General Electric, and Cathay Pacific to name a few. The ability to bring any of these compute instance types online in the Regions where they reside—on demand in minutes and billed to the second after the first minute of use—is a game changer for enterprises worldwide. You can start one, hundreds, or even thousands of instances. You can use Amazon EC2 Auto Scaling to maintain availability of your fleet, automatically scaling it up and down depending on your customers' needs and their demands on your applications. You have complete control of your instances, including root access and the ability to interact with them as you would any machine.

We have witnessed what is possible with this type of compute on our own executive journeys, where we were able to test and scale production. We've even witnessed our children benefit from this new paradigm of possibility, playing games like Fortnite, the runaway blockbuster from Epic Games. Fortnite incorporates special scheduled in-game moments where millions of players collectively experience a global, in-game synchronous event. This was simply not possible before the cloud, but it is now hosted and made possible by Amazon EC2 compute. Epic Games is breaking new ground and making history with these in-game experiences.

And these records aren't being set in gaming only. On October 19, 2017, the Children's Hospital of Philadelphia (CHOP) and Edico Genome set a new scientific world standard in rapidly processing whole human genomes into data files usable for researchers aiming to bring precision medicine into mainstream clinical practice. By deploying on one thousand Amazon EC2 F1 instances using field-programmable gate arrays (FPGAs) on the AWS Cloud, CHOP and Edico Genome processed one thousand pediatric genomes in just two hours and twenty-five minutes. They could not only analyze genomes at high throughput but also average approximately three dollars' worth of AWS compute per whole human genome analysis. The first human genome sequence cost hundreds of millions of dollars for comparison.[79]

This highly scalable compute ability to host hundreds, thousands, or tens of thousands of compute instances covering the entire spectrum—from small web servers hosted on highly horizontally scalable general purpose Amazon EC2 T3 instances to the memory-optimized instances that host intensive SAP HANA services used by the likes of Kellogg and Brooks Brothers—radically how traditional enterprises can operate.

Security, reliability, auto scaling ability, and usage-based pricing are particularly important to enterprises and startups. The speed at which you can scale compute when needed—and place your OS (AMI), patching, applications, and anything else—can become a speed bottleneck. This challenge, combined with a developer's need to package all code dependencies locally and test locally on their laptop, has led to the rise of the container.

The Rise of the Container

AWS Principal Software Development Engineer Adrian Hornsby once said during a breakout at the annual AWS London Summit, "The speed at which you can tolerate auto scaling will define what technology you should use." This comment greatly resonated with the authors.

When most enterprises start using Amazon EC2, they usually launch a new instance and use scripts to handle software configuration whenever a new instance launches. This can work extremely well, but over time the speed to auto scale the configuration "recipe" can become a bottleneck as developers ship code frequently, multiple times a day.

The next step is to create custom preconfigured AMIs (a.k.a *golden AMIs*), which enables enterprises to shift the heavy configuration setup from instance launch to an earlier "baking" time built within a CI/CD pipeline.

Finding the right balance between what is baked into an AMI and what is done at scaling time is often difficult. If you're smart with service discovery, you don't have to run or configure anything at startup time. This should be the goal; the less you have to do at startup time, the faster your scaling will be. In addition to faster scaling, the more scripts and configurations you run at startup time, the greater the chance something goes wrong.

The holy grail of the golden AMI is replacing configuration scripts with Dockerfiles. (Docker can build images automatically by reading the instructions from a Dockerfile. A Dockerfile is a text document that contains all the commands a user could call on the command line to assemble an image.)[80] This way, you don't have to maintain Ansible, Chef, or Puppet configuration scripts, which can be tricky to manage at scale. With Docker (and containers in general), isolation is done on the kernel level without needing a guest OS. Containers can be faster to develop, more efficient, and lightweight, allowing applications to become encapsulated in self-contained environments. Developers and engineers can test applications from their laptops all the way to production systems, using the same container predictably and quickly.

Enter Amazon Elastic Container Service (Amazon ECS), which was made generally available in April 2015. Amazon ECS allows you to run containerized applications in production without the manual heavy lifting of managing the container orchestration service yourself. Amazon ECS is a highly scalable, high-performance container orchestration service that supports Docker containers and allows you to run and scale containerized applications on AWS. It eliminates the need to install and operate your own container orchestration software, manage and scale a cluster of virtual machines, or schedule containers on those virtual machines. It is deeply integrated with the AWS Services you need, such as ELB, Amazon Virtual Private Cloud (Amazon VPC), AWS Identity and Access Management (AWS IAM), Amazon Elastic Container Registry (Amazon ECR), AWS Batch, Amazon CloudWatch, CloudFormation, AWS CodeStar, and AWS CloudTrail.

Like all AWS services, you can launch and stop Docker-enabled applications and query their complete state with simple API calls. The attraction of migrating Linux and Windows applications from on-premises to the cloud and running them containerized using Amazon ECS has led to the incredible growth of this service.

Along Came Kubernetes

Kubernetes, also known as K8s, is an open-source container orchestration system for automating deployment, scaling, and managing containerized applications. Google originally designed it, and it is now maintained by the Cloud Native Computing Foundation (CNCF), of which AWS is a Platinum Member. Kubernetes is incredibly popular and has a high residency on Amazon EC2. According to a survey by the CNCF, 51 percent of Kubernetes running on the cloud runs on AWS.[81]

Running Kubernetes at scale requires a lot of manual work. You need to deploy a control plane and worker nodes to create a Kubernetes cluster, and if you want high availability, you have to configure those components across multiple AZs. You also need to configure the network and have yet another credentials store that doesn't use AWS IAM.

The Amazon Elastic Container Service for Kubernetes (Amazon EKS) was released and made generally available in June 2018 to address this.[82] Amazon EKS runs the Kubernetes management infrastructure across multiple AZs, automatically detects and replaces unhealthy control plane nodes, and provides on-demand upgrades and patching. You can provision and connect worker nodes to the provided Amazon EKS endpoint. Secure and encrypted communication channels are automatically set up between your worker nodes and the managed control plane. It runs upstream Kubernetes and is certified Kubernetes conformant, so applications managed by Amazon EKS are fully compatible with applications managed by any standard Kubernetes environment. It's also integrated with AWS IAM and AWS networking.

As cool as Amazon EKS is, it's important to always abstract and look for ways to remove as much heavy lifting from the setup as possible. No container cluster is easier to manage than no cluster at all. Many engineers and developers just want to operate at container-task and task-definition levels, letting AWS manage the containers for them.

That's where AWS Fargate comes in, which was made generally available on April 24, 2018.[83] A task is the instantiation of task definition. Tasks can be run individually or as part of a service definition. Task definitions are blueprints that define what containers to use, their resource specifications like memory and CPU, the ports that need to be exposed, the volumes that will be used, permissions of containers using IAM roles, and networking details. Now you only have to think about the containers, which enables you to focus on building and operating your application. It eliminates the need to manage a cluster of Amazon EC2 instances. You no longer have to pick the instance types, manage cluster scheduling, or optimize cluster utilization. And you no longer have to worry about provisioning enough compute resources for your container applications. After you define your application requirements in the task, it manages all the scaling and infrastructure needed to run your containers in a highly available manner.

The Leap to Light Speed—Serverless

Ensuring your precious team member continually focuses on the right things is crucial. Recruiting, retaining, and continually reskilling great engineering and development talent is very hard. The unfortunate truth is that it's only going to get harder. As Marc Andreessen said in 2011, "Software is eating the world."[84]

Focusing your technology talent on business logic, data, and UX, as well as closely aligning with customer and product management differentiates you from your competitor—especially if your competitors are out there focusing on building undifferentiated infrastructure, maintaining that infrastructure for years (if not decades), and spending both CAPEX and human time for that maintenance's lifespan. As Stephan Orban says, "If enterprises or startups are going to win, they have to go faster than their competitors."[85]

So many of the conversations we had when we were AWS customers, and so many conversations we have in our current roles, revolve around an organization's quick TTM. The word "agility" comes up on average every nine minutes in our meetings! But few, if any, enterprises measure TTV (i.e., "cycle time" in the software delivery life cycle [SDLC] parlance) as part of their business agility metrics. Few enterprises or even startups have a principle to maintain or *increase* development velocity over time.

Development velocity is the speed at which you can deliver an additional unit of value to a customer. Velocity is a metric for work done and is often used in Agile software development.

Retrospectives are crucial today and have come to the fore with Agile practices. Looking back, thinking, and being very honest with ourselves are extremely useful. Where are we spending too much time? What hasn't added value? What worked? What did not?

Today's Agile software development teams are a heterogeneous mix of skill types and include software development engineers, security engineers, software quality engineers, and data scientists. The tools they use to deliver solutions, even with microservices, can be incredibly diverse. It's not just the application code you must consider; it's the surrounding elements. Identity management, telemetry tracking, logs, security groups, databases, management information systems—the list goes on. The time engineers and developers spend maintaining these tools (even when using Amazon EC2, Amazon ECS, or Amazon EKS) could be spent pulling forward and solving user problems by applying logic, data, or a better UX experience. Removing the work (and continuing to abstract higher and more efficiently) is where serverless comes in. It has a profound impact on development.

While serverless is often championed as a way to reduce costs and scale massively and on demand, there is one compelling reason above all others to adopt a serverless-first approach. Simply put, serverless is the best way to achieve maximum development velocity over time and remove vast amounts of undifferentiated heavy lifting.

The Serverless Landscape

In the same way that *cloud computing* doesn't mean server farms operate in airships at thirty-five thousand feet, *serverless* doesn't mean no servers are operating at all. There are servers; you just don't care about them—not the hardware, the hypervisor, the OS, or the software execution engine. This is all taken care of for you. So let's explore some of the serverless landscape. Serverless technologies feature automatic scaling, built-in high availability, and a pay-for-use billing model to increase agility and optimize costs. These technologies also eliminate infrastructure management tasks like capacity provisioning and patching, so you can focus on writing code that serves your customers. Serverless applications start with AWS Lambda, an event-driven compute service natively integrated with over 200 AWS services and SaaS applications.

Compute. AWS started the serverless movement in 2014 with a serverless compute platform called AWS Lambda. You can use it for nearly any application or backend service, and everything required to run and scale your application with high availability is handled for you. You pay only for the compute when a function is activated (Function as a Service)—there is no charge when your code is not running. It is an event-driven, pay-as-you-compute service that lets you run code without provisioning or managing servers. This category also includes AWS Fargate, a serverless compute engine that works with Amazon ECS and Amazon EKS.

Application integration. One of the most in-depth conversations we have with AWS customers is the complexity of application integration. AWS has a number of serverless offerings to help remove the often-chronic heavy lifting companies have to do in the critical space. Amazon EventBridge is a serverless event bus that lets you build event-driven applications at scale across AWS and existing systems. AWS Step Functions is a visual workflow orchestrator that makes it easy to sequence multiple AWS services into business-critical applications. Amazon SQS is a message queuing service enabling you to decouple and scale microservices, distributed systems, and serverless applications. Amazon Simple Notification Services (Amazon SNS) is a fully managed messaging service for both application-to-application (A2A) and application-to-person (A2P) communication. API Gateway is a fully managed service that makes creating and publishing APIs at any scale easy. AWS AppSync is a fully managed service that accelerates application development with GraphQL APIs.

Data store. The data serverless service that started it all: Amazon S3 is an object storage service designed to store and protect any amount of data. Eight more services have emerged over the last few years due to demand for serverless data offerings: Amazon Elastic File System (Amazon EFS),

Amazon DynamoDB, Amazon RDS Proxy, Amazon Aurora Serverless, Amazon Redshift Serverless, Amazon Neptune Serverless, Amazon OpenSearch Serverless, and Amazon ElastiCache Serverless.

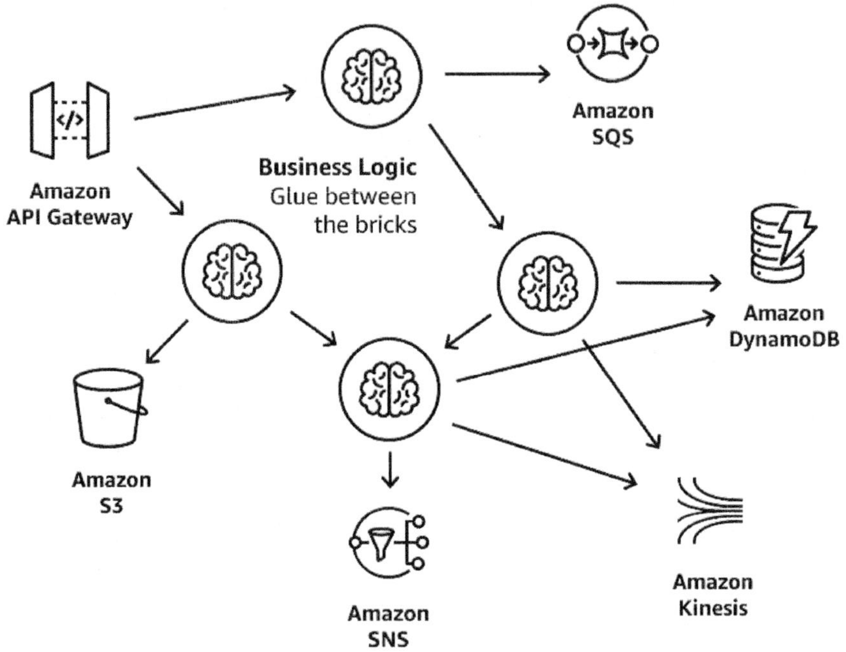

Figure 11 Business logic is all you need

The real magic is when you combine these different serverless elements to build powerful applications, change TTV for teams, and focus on the business logic.

How Much Does It Cost?

AWS Lambda is an order of magnitude cheaper than leaving a server running and waiting for code to run. AWS Lambda counts a request each time it starts executing in response to an event notification or invoke call, including test invokes from the console. You are charged for the total number of requests across all your functions. Duration is calculated from the time your code begins executing until it returns or otherwise terminates, rounded up to the nearest 100 ms. The price depends on the amount of memory you allocate to your function.

Table 1 AWS Lambda costs

Architecture	Duration	Requests
x86 Price		
First 6B GB-seconds/ month	$0.0000166667 for every GB-second	$0.20 per 1M requests
Next 9B GB-seconds/ month	$0.000015 for every GB-second	$0.20 per 1M requests
Over 15B GB-seconds/ month	$0.0000133334 for every GB-second	$0.20 per 1M requests
Arm Price		
First 7.5B GB-seconds/ month	$0.0000133334 for every GB-second	$0.20 per 1M requests
Next 11.25B GB-seconds/month	$0.0000120001 for every GB-second	$0.20 per 1M requests
Over 18.75B GB-seconds/month	$0.0000106667 for every GB-second	$0.20 per 1M requests

Food Ordering App Example

Let's break this down with an example mobile application backend. Let's assume you are a mobile app developer building a food ordering app. Customers can use the app to order food from a specific restaurant location, receive order status updates, and pick up the food when the order is ready. Because you expect high variation in demand, both by time of day and restaurant location, you build your mobile backend using serverless services, including AWS Lambda.

Given Facts

For simplicity, let's assume your application processes three million total requests per month. The average function execution duration is 120ms. You have configured your function with 1.5GB of memory on an x86-based processor. The monthly compute price is $0.0000166667 per GB-s, and the free tier provides 400,000 GB-s. The monthly request price is $0.20 per one million requests, and the free tier provides 1 million requests per month. Your charges are calculated as follows:

Monthly Compute Charge

Total compute in seconds is *total requests per month* × *average function execution duration*:

3,000,000 × 120 = 360,000 seconds

Total compute in GB-s is *total compute in seconds* × *memory*:

360,000 × 1.5 = 540,000 GB-s

Monthly billable compute in GB-s is *total compute in GB-s – free tier compute*:

540,000 – 400,000 = 140,000 GB-s

Monthly compute charge is *monthly billable compute* × *monthly compute price*:

140,000 × $0.0000166667 = $2.33

Monthly Requests Charge

Monthly billable requests is *total requests – free tier requests*:

3,000,000 – 1,000,000 = 2,000,000

Monthly requests charge is *monthly billable requests* × *monthly request price*:

2,000,000 × $0.20 = $0.40

Total Monthly Charges

Total charges is *compute charges* + *request charges*:

$$\$2.33 + \$0.40 = \$2.73 \text{ per month}$$

While users have to increase their server size if they hit a capacity constraint on Amazon EC2, AWS Lambda scales more or less infinitely to accommodate load without any manual intervention. And if an Amazon EC2 instance goes down, the developer is responsible for diagnosing the problem and getting it back online, whereas if an AWS Lambda dies, another AWS Lambda can take its place. The business logic runs on extremely cost-effective, nearly infinite scalable infrastructure, eliminating the need for servers.

Herein lies the magic of using serverless AWS components and complementing them with managed service offerings from partners like Twilio, SendGrid, and PagerDuty. Enterprises and startups alike benefit from using the providers' offerings as a strategic asset.

Serverless Principles

We should only maintain code that contains business logic. Writing any code creates debt. Write and maintain only the code you need.

We should not manage servers. There is no need to provision or maintain any servers or storage. There is no software or runtime to install, maintain, or administer.

We should have inherent flexible scaling. Your application can be scaled automatically or by adjusting its capacity by toggling the units of consumption (e.g., throughput or memory) rather than units of individual servers.

We only pay when you receive value. Pay for consistent throughput or execution duration rather than by server unit. We only want to charge you for something when you use it. If the code is there but not used, you don't pay for it.

We should leverage automated high availability. Serverless provides built-in availability and fault tolerance. You don't need to architect for these capabilities since the services running the application services provide them by default.

A 2018 CNCF survey tracked the usage of serverless technology: 41 percent of survey respondents use serverless technology, while 31 percent don't. An additional 28 percent plan to use it within the next twelve to eighteen months. Of the respondents using serverless technology, 70 percent use AWS Lambda.[86]

Call to Action

Step 1. Upskill the workforce for serverless. After the team has started using AWS and gotten a hang of the fundamentals, a serverless boot camp for application teams can be particularly useful catalysts for exploring what is possible.

Step 2. Use mapping to evaluate the applicability of serverless to new applications.

Step 3. As you migrate and refactor applications, evaluate serverless technology to remove the creation of unnecessary software and systems.

Step 4. Put principles in place to reinforce the use of serverless to remove undifferentiated heavy lifting.

Step 5. Use the AWS Well-Architected Framework to ensure best practices.

Final Thought

These services are friends, not rivals. Serverless has often been measured against containers since both technologies provide similar benefits in terms of rapid development. But serverless computing and containerization don't negate each other—they can work in tandem to build modern applications.

Leaders can mistakenly declare "We are now a serverless shop!" The reality is that in today's customer-driven world, where product managers focus on improving cycle time, security, reliability, and costs, you need to use multiple mental models: servers, containers, serverless, and the edge. The key is having the right principles to continue abstracting up the stack and encouraging and rewarding engineers, developers, and partners to do so. When they can leverage a technology like serverless, which gives them a profound ability to improve velocity, you should always evaluate and look to make the move—before your rivals do.

This can be easier said than done—even for startups.

One of the antipatterns we have seen some startups make is staying on only Amazon EC2 and believing that, because they are on AWS, they can rest on their laurels. No, you can't. The journey is never done. Always abstract up the stack and refine your technical debt to increase developer velocity.

5.2 APIs and Microservices

The whole is greater than the sum of its parts.

—ARISTOTLE

Everyone talks about microservices for development. But why? Have we been doing it wrong all these years? Well, yes and no. There are distinct benefits to monolithic applications, but TTM and development agility are not among them. The ideas behind microservices have been around for quite some time, summarized in a paper from 1978 (but arguably much older) called "UNIX Time-Sharing System." In their paper, the authors made the following observations (emphasis ours):

> "A number of maxims have gained currency among the builders and users of the UNIX system to explain and promote its characteristic style:
>
> Make each program *do one thing well.* To do a new job, build afresh rather than complicate old programs by adding new "features."

Expect the *output* of every program to become the *input to another*, as yet unknown, program. Don't clutter output with extraneous information. Avoid stringently columnar or binary input formats. Don't insist on interactive input.

Design and build software, even OSs, *to be tried early*, ideally within weeks. Don't hesitate to throw away the clumsy parts and rebuild them.

Use tools in preference to unskilled help to lighten a programming task, even if you have to detour to build the tools and expect to throw some of them out after you've finished using them."[87]

We've italicized the most important parts because these ideas directly manifest themselves in microservices and APIs:

- A microservice is a program that does one thing really well!
- Inputs and outputs are clearly defined in the API (a kind of contract).
- Microservices are small enough that they can be developed, modified, or rewritten in weeks (and in many cases, even hours or days). This aligns rather elegantly with small teams.
- Teams have the freedom to choose the best tool to address a specific problem within their microservice.

So at the risk of stating the obvious, APIs—application programming interfaces—represent a contract between a requestor (a user or a program) and a responder (a service that answers requests). API contracts should be agreed upon and become essentially immutable. Since other services expect a particular, well-defined response to a request, someone suddenly changing the contract would break the architecture. Contracts can be expanded, and the implementation details inside the service can and do change (Amazon S3 has been continually improved since its original implementation while maintaining backward compatibility). But the original API contract must not change, although new functionality can be added. An API is for life, not just for this month or this year! Luckily there is a growing body of practices, patterns, and tools that make designing APIs easier.

Microservices are small, independently managed building blocks that can be assembled in myriad and often unexpected ways to create sophisticated systems. Think of a child's building blocks. Each building block is simultaneously simple and versatile. Building blocks can be assembled into simplistic models by inexperienced parents (kids can typically create true marvels) or by experienced builders to create something as "cool" as a replica of the *Millennium Falcon*!

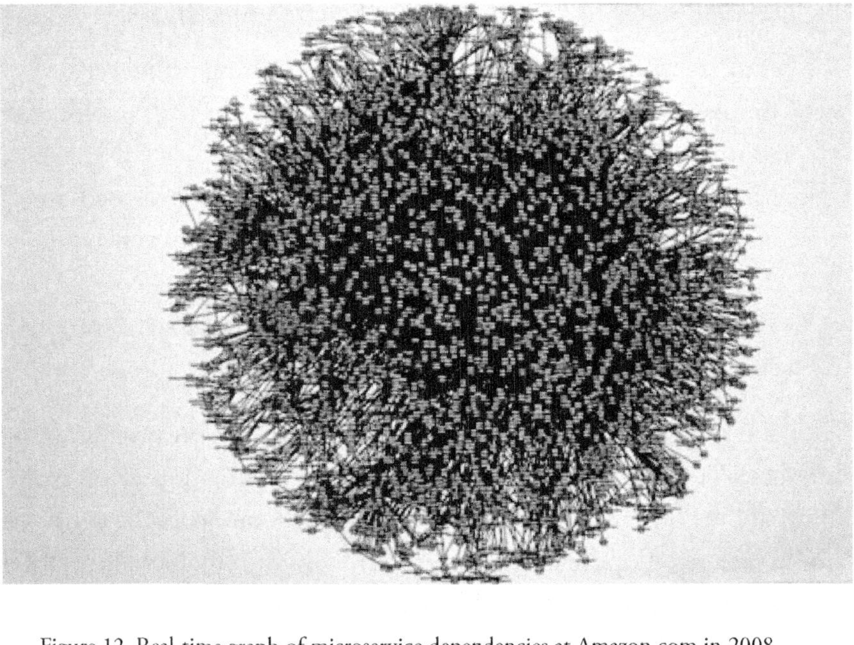

Figure 12 Real-time graph of microservice dependencies at Amazon.com in 2008

Another analogy is swarm logic, which states that intelligent-seeming behavior can emerge from complex systems composed of simple, "nonintelligent" agents. An ant has only two simple ganglia, which give it all the intelligence it needs to navigate its six legs across a truly complex environment. On one abstraction level higher, individual ants work together to make the highly complex and sophisticated ant colony thrive.

Microservices and Velocity

We believe microservices are one of the keys to increasing business velocity and improving your ability to innovate. Your product managers don't lack ideas; they lack the ability to test them without having to predict which ones will succeed. These predictions have been necessary but rarely successful to secure funding for an upfront investment. This investment used to be necessary to purchase new infrastructure capacity across multiple build, test, and production environments before starting to develop a new product, service, or thing. No wonder it takes most organizations months or years to create any new value— assuming you predicted correctly and created the right thing in the first place.

Imagine a world where your product team can try an idea in a matter of days or weeks (or, in some cases, hours) by building a simple version of the product. This minimum loveable product (MLP) interacts with your existing systems via APIs (AWS uses *loveable* instead of *valuable.*). The MLP can interact with existing services and components in a loosely coupled way to prevent a mistake from crashing your cash cow. You can try ideas—maybe one new idea per sprint (per day?)—and learn from the ones that miss the mark while scaling up the ones that hit the bullseye. If a microservice fails, applications can detect the failure and gracefully degrade rather than cause a complete outage, which is typically the case with component failures in monolithic applications.

How does AWS help with this approach?

The basic pattern of a microservice on AWS includes Application Load Balancer (ALB), Amazon ECS, AWS Auto Scaling, and a data storage service like Memcached or Redis (both part of Amazon ElastiCache) or a NoSQL service like Amazon DynamoDB. The only way to communicate with the microservice is through the API, typically a RESTful web services API, which means data from the data store is only accessible via the API!

ALB distributes incoming requests to Amazon ECS container instances running the API and business logic. Container instances are automatically added or removed depending on the number of incoming requests, which helps keep costs to the bare minimum. The data store is used to persist data needed by the microservice. Data cannot be stored on the local instance because it's ephemeral and takes your precious data to oblivion when it disappears.

This sounds fairly simple, and it is. Complexity arises in managing APIs. Important considerations include access management of APIs, throttling the request volume (to protect the backend), caching, transforming requests and responses, and managing and documenting API definitions. API Gateway helps developers create, publish, maintain, monitor, and secure APIs. It also handles the routing of requests to the nearest CloudFront Point of Presence or Regional edge caches to minimize latency.

Amazon CloudFront is a fast content delivery network (CDN) service that securely delivers data, videos, applications, and APIs globally with low latency and high transfer speeds. CloudFront can be used to secure and accelerate your WebSocket traffic as well as API calls. It supports proxy methods (POST, PUT, OPTIONS, DELETE, and PATCH) and is already integrated with API Gateway by default. With the CDN,

TLS connections with clients terminate at a nearby edge location; then Amazon CloudFront uses optimized AWS backbone network paths to securely reach your API servers.

You might further reduce the operational efforts to run, maintain, and monitor microservices by using a fully serverless architecture. When using AWS Lambda, business logic execution can be triggered by calls from API Gateway without managing any server instances whatsoever. When done properly this eliminates the architectural burden of designing for scale and high availability and the operational burden of running and monitoring the microservice's underlying infrastructure.

Challenges with Microservices

Critics argue that microservices only replace a monolith's challenges and complexity with challenges associated with cross-service and distributed systems. There are a few important things to consider when employing a microservices architecture:

Eventual consistency. With many instances of the same microservice running in parallel, achieving data consistency can be challenging. A monolithic application usually has a single, massive database where all data is stored, allowing for data consistency at all times. Let's say you have a microservice for shipping orders that needs to reduce available inventory after the order has been shipped. How do you manage consistency? Enter the world of "eventual" consistency. Your distributed application needs a little more time (we're still working in microseconds here) than a monolithic application does to ensure all associated data changes everywhere it needs to be changed.

Your data store selection for each service depends on whether your user can tolerate short-lived inconsistency. Most services work just fine with eventual consistency. The consistency, availability, and performance

(CAP) theorem states that in the presence of a network partition, one has to choose between consistency and availability. This is where the notion of eventual consistency stems from.

Service discovery. Another challenge we encountered as AWS customers was service discovery. How do you know what microservice is available? How do you know (or can a system programmatically "know") how to interact with the API? How can you know the health of a service? If it exists, is it available? Well-understood architectural patterns, namely DNS, have been around since 1985. You can also leverage ALB here since it automatically provides health checks and can be configured with path- or host-based routing. Or you can implement a solution based on Route 53.

AWS Services for Microservices

AWS offers various services that can help you develop, manage, and deploy microservices. Here are some of the most commonly used:

AWS Cloud Map. Developing a small number of microservices is straightforward. However, as you add more and more microservices to the environment, it can become challenging to manage all the dependencies and resources used by your environment.

AWS Cloud Map is a cloud resource discovery service that allows you to define custom names and maintain the updated location of dynamically changing application resources. This increases your application availability because your web service always discovers the most up-to-date locations of its resources, increasing your application availability.

Modern applications interact with various other resources, such as databases, queues, object stores, and customer-defined microservices. They need to find the location of all the infrastructure resources they depend on to function. Manual resource management becomes time-consuming and error-prone as the number of dependent infrastructure resources increases or the number of microservices scales up and down dynamically based on traffic. You can also use third-party service discovery products, but this requires installing and managing additional software and infrastructure.

Amazon SQS. Amazon SQS is a message queuing service that enables developers to decouple and scale microservices, distributed systems, and serverless applications. It eliminates the complexity and overhead associated with managing and operating message-oriented middleware, which we have both experienced. You can send, store, and receive messages between software components at any volume without losing messages or requiring other services to be available.

If your application requires queues that preserve the exact order in which messages are sent and received, then you can use FIFO (first-in-first-out) queues. FIFO queues also ensure "exactly once" processing, meaning each message is delivered once and remains available until a consumer processes and deletes it. This extra convenience comes with a slower performance, so your specific requirement determines which trade-off makes the most sense for you.

The following are common use cases for messaging:

Service-to-service communication. You have two services or systems that need to communicate with each other. Let's say a website (the front end) has to update a customer's delivery address in a customer relationship management (CRM) system (the backend). You can alternatively set up a load balancer in front of the backend CRM service and call its API actions directly from the front-end website. You can also set up a queue, have the front-end website code send messages to the queue, and have the backend CRM service consume them.

Asynchronous work item backlogs. You have a service that has to track a backlog of actions to be executed. Let's say a hotel booking system needs to cancel a booking, which takes a long time (from a few seconds to a minute). You can execute the cancellation synchronously, but then you risk annoying the customer who has to wait for the web page to load. You can also track all pending cancellations in your database and keep polling and executing cancellations. Alternatively, you can put a message into a queue and have the same hotel booking system consume messages from that queue and perform asynchronous cancellations.

State change notifications. You have a service that manages a resource and other services that receive updates about changes to that resource. Let's say it's an inventory-tracking system that tracks products stocked in a warehouse. The website must stop offering that product whenever the stock is sold out. Whenever the stock is close to being depleted, the purchasing system must place an order for more items. While those systems can keep querying the inventory system to learn about these changes, the inventory system can instead publish notifications about stock changes to a topic (better and with lower cost), and any interested program can subscribe to learn about those changes.

Amazon SNS. Publish/subscribe messaging, or pub/sub messaging, is a form of asynchronous service-to-service communication that can be used in serverless and microservices architectures. In a pub/sub model, any message published to a topic is immediately received by all subscribers. Pub/sub messaging can enable event-driven architectures or decouple applications to increase performance, reliability, and scalability.

Amazon SNS is a managed pub/sub messaging service that enables you to decouple microservices, distributed systems, and serverless applications. It provides topics for high-throughput, push-based, and many-to-many messaging. Using Amazon SNS topics, your publisher systems can fan out messages to a large number of subscriber endpoints for parallel processing, including Amazon SQS queues, AWS Lambda functions, and HTTP/S webhooks. Amazon SNS can also fan out notifications to end users using mobile push, SMS, and email.

AWS Step Functions. As in the original Unix model above, there are many occasions when microservices need to be stitched together following a particular workflow, which allows you to build and update apps quickly. Application development is simpler and more intuitive using step functions because it translates your workflow into a state machine diagram that is easy to understand, explain to others, and change. You can monitor each step of execution as it happens, which means you can identify and fix problems quickly. AWS Step Functions automatically triggers and tracks each step and retries when there are errors, so your application executes in order as expected. AWS Step Functions is, most importantly, a great tool to help you refactor (or decompose) your monolithic applications. Yelp used AWS Step Functions to do exactly that in 2017–18.

A great example of an older, more established system is their monthly subscription billing cycle. The system is core to how Yelp collects revenue and has proven technically challenging and risky to transition. The revenue engineering team knew these older systems should be moved into services, but the challenge of extracting tangled, business-critical code had proven expensive and dangerous. Luckily AWS Step Functions has made this transition a reality.

AWS AppSync. AWS AppSync lets you create a flexible API to access, manipulate, and combine data from one or more data sources. It is a managed service that uses GraphQL to make it easy for applications to get exactly the data they need. GraphQL is an open-source data query and manipulation language for APIs and a runtime for fulfilling queries with existing data.

You can use AWS AppSync to build scalable applications—including those requiring real-time updates—on a range of data sources such as NoSQL data stores, relational databases, HTTP APIs, and custom data sources with AWS Lambda. For mobile and web apps, AWS AppSync provides local data access when devices go offline and data synchronization with customizable conflict resolution when they are back online.

You can use AWS AppSync as a single interface to access and combine data from multiple microservices in your application, even if they're running in different environments such as containers in an Amazon VPC, behind a REST API on API Gateway, or behind a GraphQL API on another AWS AppSync endpoint.

Amazon EventBridge

Amazon EventBridge is a service that provides real-time access to changes in data in AWS services, your own applications, and SaaS applications without writing code. It ingests data from supported SaaS platforms and routes it to the AWS service target, so you can easily connect to and stream data from your SaaS apps without needing to write any code. This enables you to build rich integration quicker and accelerate your time to success. You can learn more about the use cases enabled by supported SaaS platforms on the AWS website.[88] Judging by the crowded rooms, it is very popular whenever an AWS engineer talks about Amazon EventBridge at any of the AWS Summits.

Final Thought

When you build anything new, you simply can't know where the stress points will be. You can have an opinion, and it will probably be wrong. Engineers can easily implement overly elaborate designs to address imaginary scaling challenges. Focus on product fit, security, and functionality early on. Then use the benefits of a loosely coupled, distributed, and highly scalable microservices architecture to see the stress points and iterate quickly. AWS continues to offer innovative services that remove many complexities of distributed architectures.

5.3 Resilience and Reliability

Failures are a given, and everything will eventually fail over time.

—DR. WERNER VOGELS

The 3:00 a.m. wake-up call that you receive as an IT leader when a critical technology system has failed is one of the perennial stresses of the job. The more senior you get, the more likely you are to become the final point of escalation for these incidents.

Dealing with these situations is not why we started a career in technology. The mean time to resolution (MTTR), wash-up, and explanations to internal and external saps time and energy and disrupts anything else you had planned. Worse, you can get caught in a continuous cycle where the events occur more and more because you can't bring the necessary resources to get to the root cause.

95 percent of what you deal with day in and day out as an executive are the decisions of yesteryear. IT systems have a habit of hanging around for decades, and you are stuck with the decisions that past leaders, who have long since moved on to other things, have "gifted" you. We always smiled

wryly when people gave us management advice on some shiny new widget that would supposedly solve all our ills. Few of those people actually lived in the real world, looking after the professional well-being of large teams, running systems 24-7, and trying to move the organization forward efficiently, all while trying to keep everyone happy with daily decisions and keeping up with the perpetual tsunami of new technology.

Attempts to break this cycle have been fought valiantly. The battle has raged between application versus infrastructure reliability elements, with seemingly ever-higher yet meaningless availability figures produced for components. These components invariably managed to fail at 3:00 a.m. for one reason or another. What? You didn't know that the vendor supplier's beta version of a patch installed a year ago would conflict with last night's emergency security patch and cause the system to fail? Sigh.

Availability	**Downtime per year**	**Categories**
95% (1-nine)	18 days 6 hours	Batch processing, data extraction, load jobs
99% (2-nines)	3 days 15 hours	Internal tools, project tracking
99.9% (3-nines)	8 hours 45 minutes	Online commerce
99.99% (4-nines)	52 minutes	Video delivery, broadcast systems
99.999% (5-nines)	5 minutes	Telecom industry (ATM Transactions)

Figure 13 The nines of availability

You may already be familiar with the perennial availability battle in Figure 13—the nines of availability.

If you want 5-nines of availability, you can only afford five minutes of downtime a year. That is a high bar.

When we ran data centers, seeing availability figures like this bandied around regularly by different hardware providers was wryly amusing.

The availability you receive from an individual component is unrelated to the mathematical reality of running data centers full of these components with different availability figures.

For example, imagine you have two components, *x* and *y*, with 99 percent and 99.99 percent availability, respectively. If you put those two components in series with one dependent on the other, the overall availability of the system declines.

This explains why you keep having failures with a single data center despite adding more and more components. Even if some components have redundancy, they are all serial—from the building to the electrical supply upward through network, storage, compute, load balancer, application, etc.

$$A = A_x A_y$$

Component	Availability	Downtime
x	99% (2-nines)	3 days 15 hours
y	99.99% (4-nines)	52 minutes
x and y combined	98.99%	3 days 16 hours 33 minutes

Figure 14 Availability math when elements are serialized

Everything Fails All the Time

One of the most important things that attracted us to AWS as customers and eventually employees is the long-term decisions AWS has made regarding security, durability, availability, speed, reliability, and recoverability. We were also impressed by the lessons they had learned as they built and scaled Amazon.com to become one of the world's largest websites. Those hard-earned lessons were poured into AWS from the beginning in 2006. And the lessons have continued. To quote Andy Jassy, "There is no compression algorithm for experience."

As Dr. Werner Vogels says in the epigraph at the start of this chapter, "Failures are a given, and everything will eventually fail over time." This is the cold, stark reality of modern technology. You might install however many 99.9999999-available pieces of hardware into your data center, but the whole lot will fail if somebody hits the "emergency power off" or any other event occurs. (If our experience is a benchmark, it absolutely does.) Murphy's law: whatever can go wrong will go wrong."

During his keynote at re:Invent 2018, Dr. Vogels shared an interesting story about his worst day at Amazon.com. On December 12, 2004—the last day Amazon retail customers could place their orders and be assured delivery of their items before Christmas—the website experienced an outage. (Murphy's law picked a great moment.) At that time Amazon was already running its system in a service-oriented architecture with three very large datasets called Orders, Items, and Customers. The Customers database ran on an Oracle RAC cluster, and a bug that controlled the logging engine occurred, causing a 12-hour outage. This outage taught Amazon an awful lot of lessons. For example, scaling up (bigger and more powerful individual compute instances) created a big operating zone when things go wrong. Amazon also learned that it had very little control or choice in the database space.

This is just one of many lessons that you can only learn as you go through various stages of significant growth and hit different elbows of the curve. Standing on the shoulders of giants and leveraging their economies of scale to learn lessons is how you reach a drastically more available place.

What Is Resiliency? And Why You Shouldn't Be Afraid of Failing

Resilient systems embrace the idea that failures are normal and that running systems in what we call partially failing is perfectly okay. When dealing with smaller systems of up to a few tens of compute instances, 100 percent operational excellence is often the normal stage, and failure is an exceptional condition. But when dealing with large-scale systems, 100 percent operational excellence is nearly impossible to achieve. The normal state of operation is partial failure.

Running in partially failing mode is a viable option for nearly all web applications, from e-commerce services like Amazon.com to video-on-demand sites like Netflix, music services like SoundCloud, and financial services institutions. We are not saying it doesn't matter if your system fails, but you should design for failure up to and including entire data center failures.

The Way Out of the Availability Trap

Building resilient architecture isn't all about software. It starts at the infrastructure layer, progresses to the network and data, influences application design, and extends to people and culture. Let's take a deep dive into some core areas. This list is by no means exhaustive, but by incorporating and establishing deployment principles around these core areas, you can see a material shift:

- Redundancy
- Auto scaling
- Infrastructure as code
- Immutable infrastructure and blue-green deployments
- Stateless applications

According to independent IDC research in February 2018, the companies interviewed experienced 95 percent less unplanned downtime when running on AWS.[89]

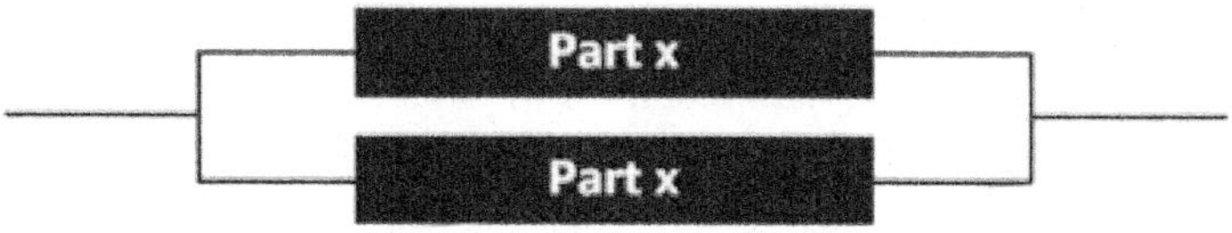

$$A = 1 - (1 - A_x)^2$$

Component	Availability	Downtime
x	99% (2-nines)	3 days 15 hours
Two x in parallel	99.99% (4-nines)	52 minutes
Three x in parallel	99.9999% (6-nines)	31 seconds

Figure 15 Availability math when components are in parallel

Redundancy

Let's consider the math when running things in parallel rather than serially.

The math suddenly becomes very different. This is part of the deep thinking behind AWS Cloud's decision to use the Region and AZ model. Component redundancy increases availability significantly.

One of the first and most important things to do when you deploy an application in the cloud is to architect it to be redundant. Redundancy is the duplication of components of a system to increase its overall availability. In the AWS Cloud, that means deploying across multiple AZs or, in some cases, multiple Regions.

While each AZ is fully independent—with redundant power, networking, and connectivity and housing in separate facilities—they are connected through links that allow for low single-digit millisecond latency between each AZ. Such a low latency allows for synchronous replications between the different AZs. This is a foundational principle for high availability and fault tolerance on AWS. If one of the AZs in a particular Region experiences intermittent issues, the other AZs continue operating independently.

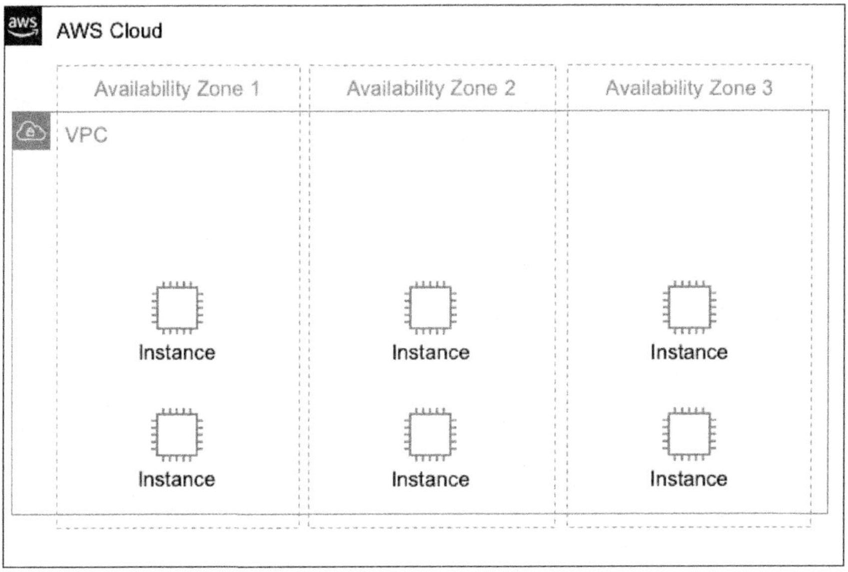

Figure 16 Amazon EC2 instances across three Availability Zones and within one Region

While each AWS SLA differs per service, we sure as heck liked having math on our side when we were AWS customers.[90]

This is why AWS always advises enterprises to leverage multi-AZ deployment (preferably using three AZs). AWS regional services such as Amazon S3, Amazon Aurora, Amazon DynamoDB, Amazon SQS, Amazon Kinesis, AWS Lambda, and ELB are built with this architecture in mind. There is some great further reading available on the Amazon Builders' Library.[91]

Auto Scaling

For many years in corporate IT, we would buy sufficient hardware and software for the most optimistic peaks we could imagine (and we usually got it wrong.) This method wasted time, effort, and money. The ability to programmatically scale technology resources to meet demand and only pay for what you use is an absolute cornerstone of the AWS Cloud tenets. This is called auto scaling.

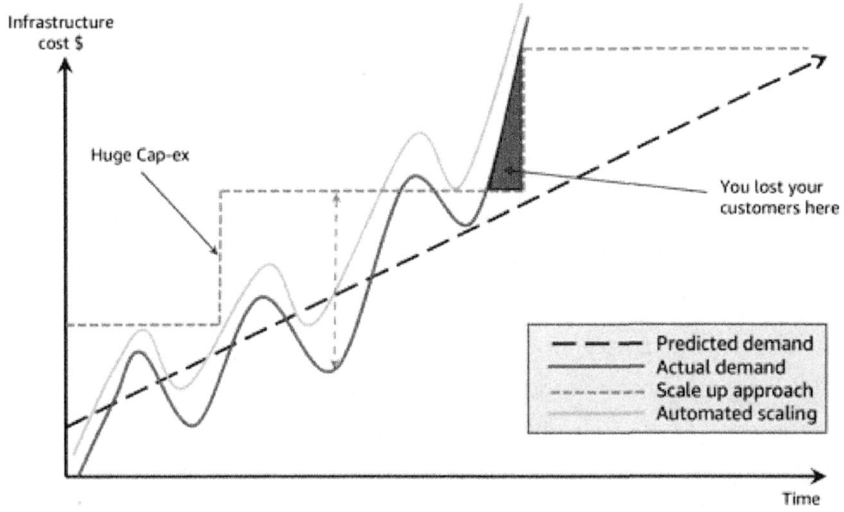

Figure 17 Traditional on-premises scaling challenge

Scaling your resources dynamically according to demand, as opposed to doing it manually, ensures your service can meet a variety of traffic patterns without needing to plan for it. Instances, containers, and functions all provide mechanisms for auto scaling—either as a feature of the service itself or as a support mechanism. Application Auto Scaling can be used to add auto scaling capabilities to services you build on AWS. This is a monumental change to how IT was traditionally delivered. Think of all the capacity projects you had to sponsor that took weeks, months, and sometimes years to mitigate risk; your best estimates were nearly always wrong. Think of the undifferentiated heavy lifting auto scaling removes.

IaC

One of IaC's essential benefits is repeatability. Let's examine the task of configuring a data center, from configuring the networking and security to deploying applications. Consider the amount of work required if you had to do that manually for multiple environments in each Region. It would be tedious, but it would most likely introduce configuration differences and drifts over time. Humans aren't great at repetitive, manual tasks with 100 percent accuracy, but machines are. Give the same template to a computer, and it will execute it ten thousand times the same way.

Now imagine your environment being compromised, suffering an outage, or even being deleted by mistake (yes, we've seen that happen). You have data backup. You have the infrastructure templates. All you have to do is rerun the template in a new AWS account, a new Amazon VPC, or even a new Region, restore the backups, and voilà, you're up and running in minutes. Doing that manually and at scale would create a nightmare scenario with a lot of sweat and tears, and worse—unhappy customers.

Another benefit of IaC is knowledge sharing. If you version control your infrastructure (and you should), you can treat that code the same way you treat application code. You can ask the teams committing code to it for improvements or changes in configuration. If that process goes through a pull request, the rest of the team can verify, challenge, and comment on that request, promoting better practices.

Immutable Infrastructure and Blue/Green Deployments

What is immutable infrastructure, and why should you, a leader, care about it?

The principle of immutable infrastructure is fairly simple: immutable components are replaced for every deployment instead of being updated in place. Anyone who has needed to apply emergency patches to live systems in place knows the rock and hard place this puts you in between. Don't patch and risk a security event or patch and risk an outage. Untested patches can often lead to outages, which is a horrible situation. Did we mention that being an IT leader is a tough job?

With immutable infrastructure, as you need to deploy a patch or any type of new software code, your IaC, via API calls, simply asks for a new Amazon EC2 node to be created in each AZ with your new AMI and the code incorporated onto it. When combined with blue/green deployments, this ability is particularly compelling.

When we used to deploy applications on-premises, we had to reuse existing infrastructure for new versions of applications. We often had to install updated applications on the same hardware; sometimes we were compelled to do risky in-place upgrades.

In the cloud you can create new infrastructure programmatically for new versions of your applications. Then you can keep the previous version running in parallel for a while before tearing it down. This technique is called blue/green deployment. It allows you to progressively switch traffic between two versions of your apps to monitor business and operational metrics on the new version and to switch traffic back to the previous version in case anything goes wrong.

This type of deployment is called canary deployment with blue/green testing. The name comes from the old British mining tradition of using canaries to detect toxic gases like carbon monoxide. To ensure mine safety, miners brought a canary along with them; if the canary died or got ill, the mine was quickly evacuated.

When you have assured yourself that your performance and experience baselines are appropriate for your new application version, simply turn the old ones off and stop paying for them. This is immutable infrastructure, and it works at compute, container, and serverless levels. Once you deploy this way, you will never, ever want to go back to any other way.

This deployment strategy supports the principle of the golden AMI, the latest version of your preferred OS with the minimum appropriately secured and hardened configuration. The application itself is often installed automatically on top of the golden AMI using perhaps Ansible, Puppet, or Chef for your automated software install. Suddenly the risk of updating underlying OS or applications can be reduced, if not eliminated, by using blue/green deployments with IaC.

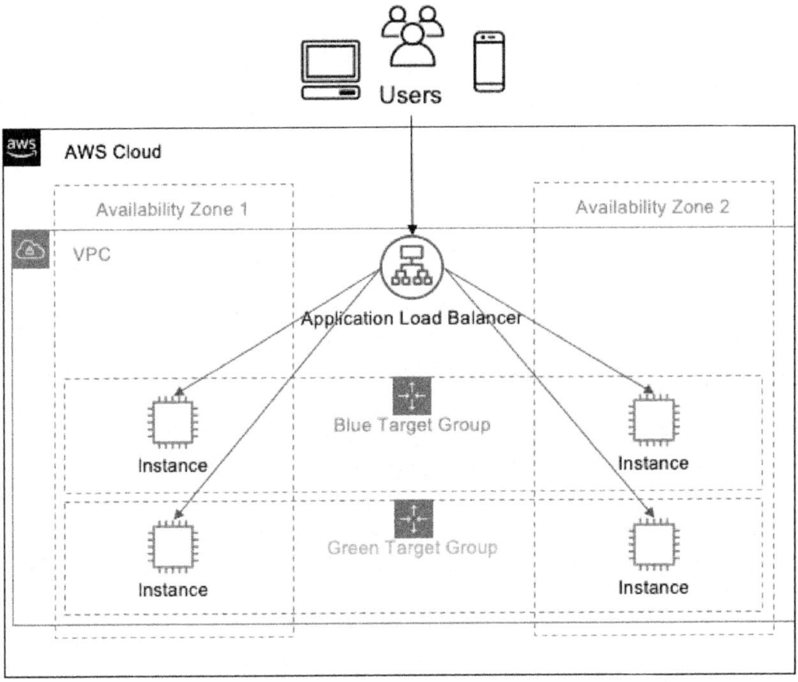

Figure 18 Blue/green deployments across two Availability Zones

No updates should ever be performed on live systems. When deploying a new patch, software update, or code of any kind, always start from a new instance of the resource being provisioned (Amazon EC2 instance, container, or AWS Lambda function). Canary deployment's benefit is the near-immediate rollback it gives you. More importantly, you get faster and safer deployments.

There are a few considerations to keep in mind during canary deployment, such as being stateless. You should not depend on any state between the old and new versions deployed. If you need stickiness, keep it to the bare minimum. Since fast rollback is a feature, your application should be able to handle it gracefully.

Managing canary deployment with database schema changes is hard—really hard. We often get asked how to do it. Unfortunately, there's no silver bullet, but there are tools that can help.[92] It depends on the changes, application, and architecture around the database.

For your serverless applications, you can also use API Gateway, which now supports canary deployments. Or you can implement canary deployments of AWS Lambda functions with alias traffic shifting.

Stateless Applications

Stateless applications are a prerequisite to auto scaling and immutable infrastructure since any request can be handled by available computing resources, regardless of whether it's Amazon EC2, a container platform, or a set of AWS Lambda functions.

Stateless Service in a Multi-AZ Setup with Auto Scaling

In a stateless service, the application must treat all client requests independent of prior requests or sessions and should never store any information on local disks or memory.

Sharing state with any resources within the AWS Auto Scaling group should be conducted using in-memory object caching systems such as Memcached, Redis, EVCache, or distributed databases like Cassandra or Amazon DynamoDB, depending on the structure of your object and performance requirements.

Putting It All Together

To have security, durability, availability, speed, reliability, recoverability, well-tested deployment, and scaling process with a fast spin-up time, you need to combine the ideas of golden AMI, IaC, immutable infrastructure, and stateless application. To do that at scale, you need to use automation. In fact, it's your only option. So "Automate all the things" is a critical foundational tenet for your teams.

Testing Your Availability

Netflix is an incredible customer for AWS. The company has been a pioneer in pushing the envelope and hasn't been shy about how much it automates and tests automation and reliability on AWS. We have benefited greatly from hearing our good friend and tech evangelist teammate, Adrian Cockcroft, talk about his journey as Director of Web Engineering and Cloud Architect at Netflix and how he handled availability and reliability testing at scale. Netflix has developed a suite of open-source tools—collectively called the Simian Army—that can generate latency, shut down compute nodes, and even shut down entire AZs to test and ensure their software is as reliable as possible. This mechanism is now collectively known as *reliability engineering* or *chaos engineering.*[93]

One way AWS has made it possible to test your own ability to withstand faults is by launching the AWS Fault Injection Service (AWS FIS). This managed service enables you to perform fault injection experiments on your AWS workloads. Fault injection is based on the principles of chaos engineering. These experiments stress an application by creating disruptive events so you can observe how your application responds. You can then use this information to improve the performance and resiliency of your applications so that they behave as expected. To use AWS FIS, set up and run experiments that help you create the real-world conditions needed to uncover application issues that can be difficult to find otherwise. AWS FIS provides templates that generate disruptions and the controls and guardrails you need to run experiments in production, such as automatically rolling back or stopping the experiment if specific conditions are met.

What does this mean for disaster recovery?

For decades in corporate IT, the words "disaster recovery" have been laden with fear, loathing, angst, and seemingly endless money spent on systems that are never ever used—let alone trusted to perform as needed—when they are needed.

With the new availability tools and methods described above, maintaining a cold/hot/primary/secondary/tertiary system that can keep up with the congruence of digital demands placed upon them for very modern hyperscale systems is like trying to put gasoline in an electric car.

The ability to test failure scenarios in real time across your application and data landscape is how you ensure you can stay online and in service. Some AWS customers have actually migrated their entire primary data centers into one AZ and their secondary data centers to a second AZ to avoid the never-ending hardware upgrade train, reduce costs, and achieve radically better infrastructure availability.

Then these AWS customers can adopt cloud-first and cloud-native principles for all new development. When you do this, you can typically still maintain the existing mechanisms you had for replication and system failover while establishing the new.

Replication and Recovery

The ability to securely replicate your data stores as you deem appropriate to other AWS Regions to hold copies of that data has fundamentally and forever changed how enterprises view disaster recovery. A comprehensive set of services to help with this includes Amazon S3's Cross-Region Replication (CRR) to securely replicate your data objects to other Regions as you deem appropriate. Amazon DynamoDB global tables give you a fully managed and multi-Region database. Amazon Aurora Global Database allows you to have a secondary, read-only version to replicate objects into AWS Regions around the world. With Amazon S3'd Glacier Deep Archive, Amazon DynamoDB global tables, and Amazon Aurora global tables, you can now achieve the backup and resiliency you've been looking for.

Final Note on AWS Backup

While leveraging all of the AWS Cloud's innate capabilities is incredibly empowering with regard to resilience and reliability, you still need to ensure your data and application logic are backed up. To help with that, you can use AWS Backup. This fully managed backup service allows you to centralize and automate data backup across AWS services in the cloud and on-premises using AWS Storage Gateway. You can centrally configure backup policies and monitor backup activity for AWS resources, such as Amazon EBS volumes, Amazon Relational Database Service (Amazon RDS) databases, Amazon DynamoDB tables, Amazon EFS file systems, and AWS Storage Gateway volumes. It automates and consolidates backup tasks previously performed service-by-service, removing the need to create custom scripts and manual processes.

We want to give a heartfelt special thanks to our good friend Adrian Hornsby, Principal System Development Engineer at AWS, for his help writing this chapter. His graphics and narrative were invaluable. More information can be found at https://medium.com/@adhorn.

5.4 Completing a Large-Scale Migration and Modernization

How emigration is actually lived—well, this depends on many factors: education, economic station, language, where one lands, and what support network is in place at the site of arrival.

—DANIEL ALARCÓN

This chapter could and probably should be its own book. Jonathan has had the privilege of presenting this at re:Invent six times since he joined AWS in 2017. (It was the third-most attended session at re:Invent 2023). This is a solid reminder for those of us who have worked with the cloud for years that the lion's share of enterprise IT workloads still reside on-premises. There is still much work to do. The AWS customers we talk with today see modernization and migration as symbiotic. Yes, you can migrate and migrate quickly. But many IT leaders carry so much operational risk and high optimization aspirations that they want to have their cake and eat it as they tackle their journeys. There are sharks there. Fear not! This chapter aims to provide an abridged and concentrated view of the critical steps and lessons learned from the now thousands of migrations we have worked on over the years and the hundreds of thousands of migrations AWS has enabled.

Start with *Why*

Does your executive committee (ExCo) or Board understand why you're moving and modernizing to the cloud? The analogy of a truck's wheels as you drive along the highway is apt. Your business cannot simply stop other changes while you migrate. While the *how* has gotten dramatically easier through tooling, mental models, and an array of AWS Partners, you better ensure your executive colleagues understand the *why* so the team can provide the resources (time, money, blocker removal, priority, understanding) in the long term. And this brings us back to the *why.* When Jonathan was refreshing the latest version of his re:Invent presentation "Completing a large-scale migration and modernization with AWS," he realized the opening slide listed eight reasons to move to the cloud: (1) Digital transformation (yes, really), (2) agility and staff productivity, (3) improved operational resilience, (4) cost reduction, (5) going global, (6) IoT and AI/ML, (7) data center consolidation, and (8) outsourcing changes.[94]

These are all valid reasons, but the list has become more nuanced, more focused, and much longer:

- Delivery speed improvement
- Time-driven data center exits
- Acquisition of another business
- Divestiture of a line of business
- Strangling technical debt
- Cost reduction
- Moving to multi-tenancy SaaS
- Licensing cost reduction
- Enabling generative AI solutions

- Removing undifferentiated lifting
- Security improvements
- Availability improvements
- Moving to data-driven business
- Changing contact center technology
- Moving to data as a product
- Durability improvements
- Sustainability improvements
- Moving to compete globally
- Scalability improvements

And many more!

We encourage you to pick a single north star for your why—not many (even though you will benefit from many), just one. It needs to be the most powerful reason for your business, one that everyone can clearly articulate, understand, and buy into. You need to ensure you build your business case around this; engaging your CFO is crucial. See Chapter 2.4 The CFO Matters. This business case needs an ExCo owner, and like it or not, that is usually the CIO/CTO.

This *why* is the mantle for the journey ahead. The journey for a very large business can take years but is so worthwhile, and you reap the benefits the date the first workload moves. Making the purpose clear to everyone gives you the sticking power to avoid "the great stall."

Putting the Right Team Together

As discussed in Chapter 3.4 Leveraging the Leadership Team, Chapter 3.5 Creating the Cloud Center of Excellence and Chapter 3.6 Creating the Cloud Business Office, instantiating teams ensures you have the right people on your journey to allocate resources and remove blockers. Continuing to scale your talent journey (discussed in Chapter 4.1

Becoming Cloud-Fluent at Scale) and engaging with the right delivery and software tooling AWS Partners to handle any specialty workloads you may have slightly before you actually need them, can make all the difference in the world.

AWS has over 150,000 Partners around the globe—that's a large number. But just over 250 have earned AWS Migration Competency for Professional Services status because AWS maintains an insanely high bar for expertise to ensure migrations can succeed. Work early to get a candidate pool of potential AWS Partners that can help and consider AWS Professional Services. Identifying the right AWS Partner is a significant indicator of success. A common mistake we see is companies working with an incumbent partner instead of someone specialized with the required competencies.

Review and assess any existing observability tooling, particularly application monitoring and orchestration tools that can provide essential metrics. When you move workloads in IT, nobody notices if performance is the same; if the performance improves, you might get a pat on the back, but if it's worse, you are sure as heck going to hear about it. You need to know your current relative baseline performance, which requires observability tooling for your existing workloads. Many tools can provide port-level metrics, showing what ports are opened and when they are used. You don't want to move a workload and find that the 3:00 a.m. query job on an operational database (that shouldn't have been created in the first place) underpins something important, and you didn't open ports for it when you moved. We highly recommend reviewing AWS Migration and Modernization tooling if you don't have this capability to ensure your tooling is ready to observe AWS Cloud workloads.[95]

When you have the right team, identifying key areas to address before charging off is important. Completing a Migration Readiness Assessment can be a useful tool for companies.[96] Completing a binary questionnaire across a range of subjects can give leadership a data-driven approach to setting up teams for success. Your approved AWS Migration Partner or AWS Professional Services organization can do this with you.

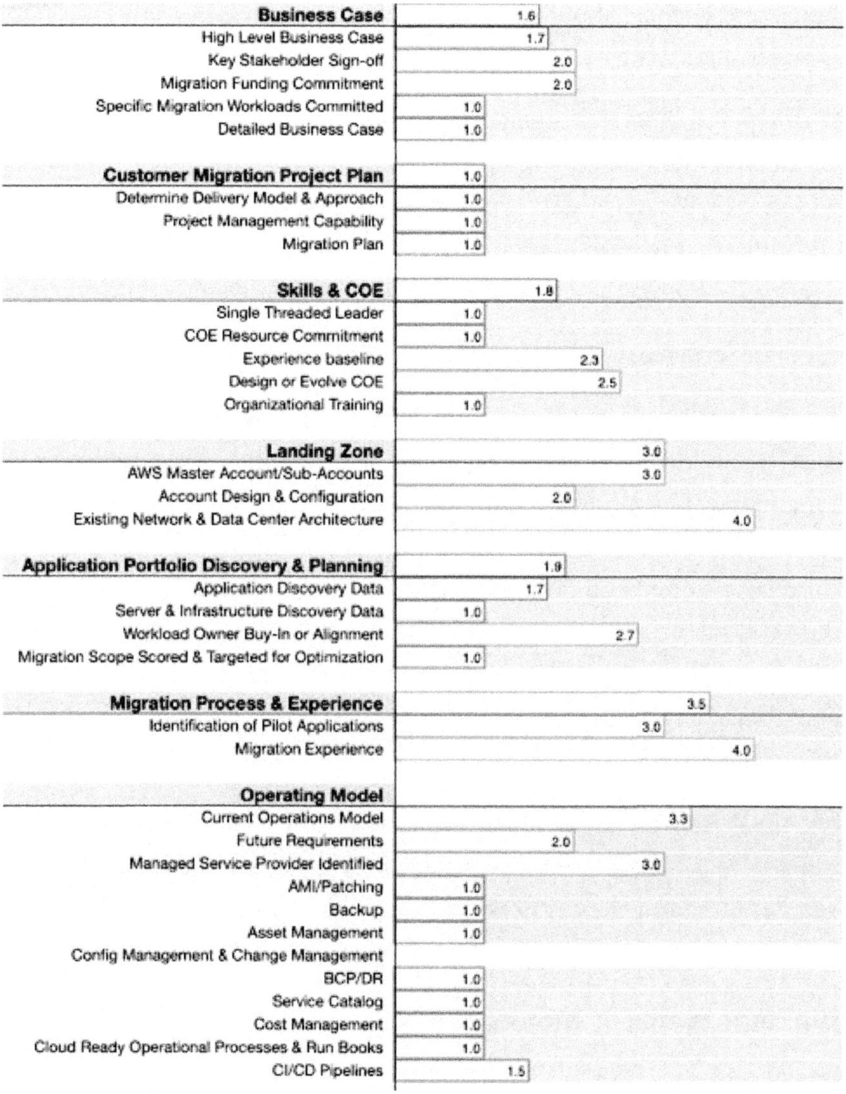

Figure 19 Migration readiness assessment example

Get Going

So you've had some early wins with your first workloads. The engineers are learning frenetically and hopefully having fun, your business customers are excited about the potential, and your CFO is now eyeing some serious savings.

At this point the CBO likely turns its focus toward migrating existing workloads. There have probably been many assumptions about which workloads will move when and where. These assumptions almost certainly bleed into timeline commitments (even though they shouldn't exist for Agile) for the new customer features you want to build.

In our experience a couple of things happen next.

The engineers and developers are initially convinced that everything must be rewritten to take advantage of the cloud. They will be passionate about this. Unless they can turn everything into CI/CD and run everything cloud-native, it just won't be right. As engineers, we can relate; we've been culpable of similar behavior. At the start of our journeys, we wanted to ensure a perfect tower of CI/CD, IaC perfection. But to paraphrase Voltaire, perfect is the enemy of good enough. The grizzled and battle-scarred leaders we have become now think a little differently.

The fiscal reality will soon hit home. Rewriting decades of intellectual property locked into your existing application suites and data stores can take decades, and the CFO would quite like those cost savings. "That data center is darn expensive—how fast can you close it?"

The Importance of Momentum

As you move production workloads on the AWS Cloud while running your existing private data centers, you officially enter hybrid mode.

This is a perfectly acceptable transitional state. It is not, as some have asserted, a valid long-term strategy unless you have workloads with specific latency or regulatory data residency requirements. Running in hybrid for many years without a clear target and removing as much undifferentiated heavy lifting as possible can present a risk to your business across people, processes, and technology. All three are left in a transitional state, and you can't get closure in any of them.

Migrate with the Correct Mental Models for Migration

As the leader, you are normally shown a tremendous amount of architectural and engineering decision points for each application—as detailed and deep as the proverbial rabbit hole can take you down. Some organizations we've worked with have had their cloud plans significantly derailed and distracted by overthinking this before starting. Using mental models allows you to break down the challenge into workable chunks. We suggest Rehost, Relocate, Repurchasing, Retain, and Retire for migration workloads. While these mental models may appear similar to other models folks have used, please note the AWS details.

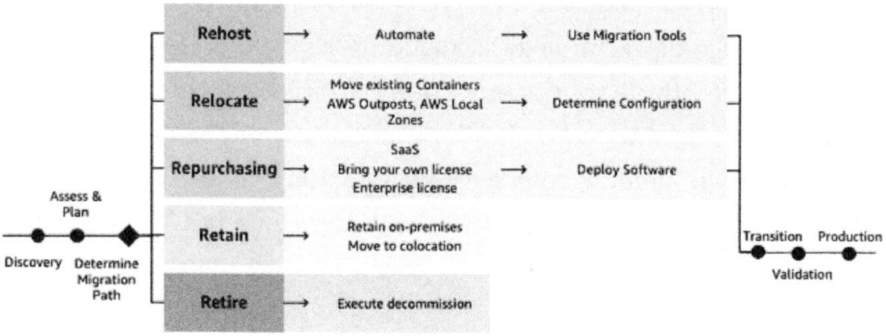

Figure 20 Migration Rs

Rehost. Take the existing OS and any applications it hosts, move it from the existing hypervisor or bare metal server instance, block copy the data, and then move the runtime components to a similarly sized Amazon EC2 instance and size-matched Amazon EBS volume. This has been done hundreds of thousands of times for AWS customers migrating to the cloud. Enel is one of the best examples in public reference. It clearly established a bold goal and migrated 5,500 instances in nine months using rehosting. That's twenty-five a day, including weekends.

Using automation to tackle this route is key. AWS Application Migration Service (AWS MGN) can largely take care of this for you. It simplifies and expedites your migration to AWS by automatically converting your source servers from physical, virtual, or cloud infrastructure to run natively on AWS. It further simplifies your migration and reduces costs by allowing you to use the same automated process for a wide range of applications without changes to applications, their architecture, or the migrated servers. You can use AWS MGN to perform nondisruptive tests prior to cutover. After testing, you can use AWS MGN to quickly migrate your applications to the cloud during a short cutover window, typically measured in minutes. It also provides very wide OS support.

Relocate. With VMware Cloud on AWS, you can use the same VMware Cloud Foundation technologies, including vSphere, vSAN, NSX, and vCenter Server, from your on-premises data centers and on the AWS Cloud without having to purchase any new or custom hardware, rewrite applications, or modify your existing operating models. The service automatically provisions infrastructure and provides full VM compatibility and workload portability between your on-premises environments and the AWS Cloud.

Another option is to move your existing Java or.NET web applications straight to a container. AWS App2Container (AWS A2C) is a command line tool for migrating and modernizing Java or .Net web applications into container format.

What if you have latency-sensitive applications, perhaps in a manufacturing environment? What if you want to stage your migrations in your own data centers first (as AWS customer Morningstar did)? AWS Outposts can help in either server or rack format. AWS Outposts servers come in a 1U or 2U form factor. They provide the same AWS infrastructure, services, APIs, and tools to on-premises and edge locations with limited space or smaller capacity requirements, such as retail stores, branch offices, healthcare provider locations, or factory floors. AWS Outposts servers provide local compute and networking services. The AWS Outposts rack is an industry-standard 42U form factor. It provides the same AWS infrastructure, services, APIs, and tools to virtually any data center or colocation space. An AWS Outposts rack provides AWS compute, storage, database, and other services locally while allowing you to access the full range of AWS services available in the Region for a consistent hybrid experience. You can scale from a single 42U rack to multiple rack deployments of up to ninety-six racks to create pools of compute and storage capacity.

AWS Local Zones are a type of infrastructure deployment that places compute, storage, database, and other select AWS services close to large population and industry centers. Use it if you are looking to run low-latency applications at the edge, simplify your hybrid cloud migrations, or need to meet stringent data residency requirements. AWS Local Zones were originally developed to help film editing in Hollywood, where filmmakers need to stage significant amounts of data and make fast edits without waiting for the round-trip time to an AWS Region. The difference between 2 ms and 20 ms is big for these types of workloads.

Repurchase. "Shop and drop." Who wants to look after email services on-site anymore, let alone legacy telephone switches, payroll, HR products, and other workplace workloads that still exist? That adds zero differentiation to your business. Many SaaS offerings—from Amazon

WorkSpaces to Workday—and numerous AWS Partner and standalone solutions are available in the AWS Marketplace. Executing migrations to get these servers out of your data center allows your technical teams to focus on the services that truly matter to your customers.

As you go through your portfolio, mark up apps and assign resources to execute their moves. If the timelines look elongated for a repurchase, go with a rehost and move them later. The goal is to keep the momentum of apps moving.

Retain. Some incumbent systems, be they AIX, Mainframe, HPUX, AS/400 (yes, many still exist), or bespoke network connections, can be impractical to refactor in an appropriate timescale to meet your target of closing data center and releasing the money spent there. There are three possible scenarios:

- Move the hardware/application to an appropriate specialist supporter of these technologies and access them remotely.
- Move the hardware/applications to one of the AWS Direct Connect Delivery Partners worldwide (e.g., Equinix). They can provide highly secure and resilient floor space with very low latency access to the AWS Regions.
- Retain a portion of minimal on-premises data center space to keep the legacy systems running.

One AWS customer we know chose to take the four-year mainframe refresh cycle, purchase and install the next new mainframe into an AWS Partner's colo to lower latency to the cloud, and physically remove it from its data center. They realized the tremendous fiscal benefit of closing the data center while giving themselves the time to deconstruct the mainframe properly.

Retire. Be careful when choosing which applications or virtual servers to move to the cloud. Unpicking systems can be hard and complex work. Retiring assets and simplifying your application portfolio can generate serious savings.

You will be utterly amazed at how much waste exists when emptying data centers. It's not unusual to find hundreds of old and expensive servers reduced to doing small copy jobs. These servers remain religiously and expensively patched, secured, and upgraded despite being orphaned as workloads were moved off. The vast array of bespoke, often poorly implemented and used monitoring tools left running to look after hardware compounds this. When teams realize double-digit percentages of workloads in a data center are no longer used, they often switch them off.

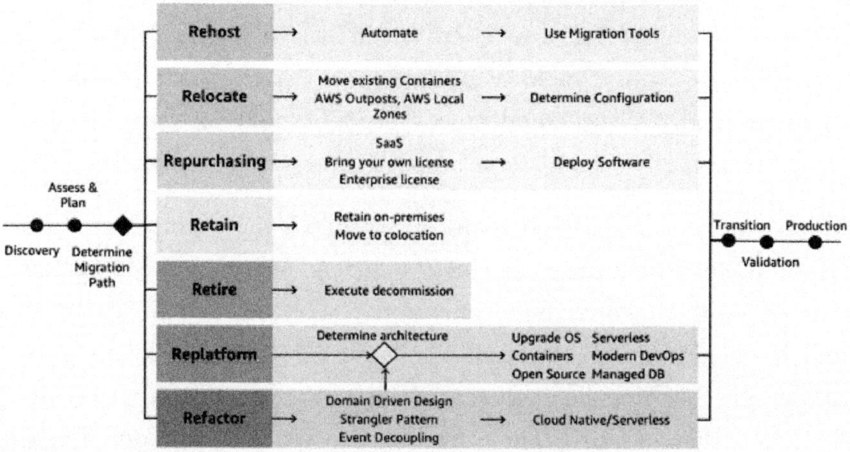

Figure 21 Migration and Modernization Rs together

The final two mental models, Replatform and Refactor (sometimes called Rearchitect), are where you modernize as you migrate. Too often engineers reach for the modernization lever early, open Pandora's box, and drown in the scope creep they take on. The north star that you set early on matters, as do the principles you put in place to enable your engineers and hold them accountable. Too much scope means you won't meet your target; too little scope means you might not get the risk reduction and optimization benefits you hoped for. We are reminded of the CTO's prayer by Josh Butts: "God, grant me engineers to build the things I can't buy, budget to buy the things I can't build, and the wisdom to know the difference." So tread carefully. What does minimum viable replatforming look like during your migration? Once you are there, a load of things becomes easier; take on too much scope before you have moved, and you might drown.

Replatform. "Lift, shift, and tinker." When you replatform, you transform and move the existing application or database. Maybe you want to move an existing application but upgrade the underlying OS from Microsoft Windows 2016 to Microsoft Windows 2022. Or maybe you want to move from Oracle WebLogic to an Apache Tomcat execution engine instead. Or you could move from a bespoke, managed database to an Amazon RDS database instance maintained by AWS.

If you go this way for your workloads, follow the example of former Edmunds.com CIO and current AWS General Manager of Marketplace, Philip Potloff: timebox your teams to two weeks to do this. As Parkinson's law suggests, "Work expands so as to fill the time available for its completion," so give the engineer teams just two weeks to replatform or else rehost the workload. The miracles, creativity, and passion engineers and developers will put in are amazing if they want to avoid a rehost.

Replatforming can be a very powerful choice. When done correctly, you get a win-win-win outcome:

- Lower running costs by hosting an Amazon EC2 compute instance from AWS, saving money. And potentially rehydrate your AMI to a set schedule by automating the installation of any application components.

- Reduce and remediate technical OS debt, reducing risk.
- Remove the need to procure or upgrade hardware for this application, saving time.

AWS MGN also allows you to modernize your OS as you move; you can convert CentOS to Rocky Linux or Convert SUSE BYOS to an AWS license instead. Extensive tooling is also available from AWS Partners like RiverMeadow, which has software on the AWS Marketplace that can automate OS upgrades in a scalable and nondisruptive way.[97] Other examples include offerings from Stromasys, which allows the movement of non-x86 workloads (e.g., Solaris or HP-UX) to cloud infrastructure without changing any data legacy code.[98]

A key part of replatforming is the ability to migrate your database. You want a tool to automate replatforming for you. The AWS Database Migration Service (AWS DMS) is a capable and mature tool. As of the time of publishing, AWS DMS has helped enterprises move more than 1,200,000 databases into AWS. It comes with schema conversion solutions that can be used to:

- Copy a database schema from a source to a target.
- Convert a database or data warehouse schema.
- Analyze a database to determine the conversion complexity.
- Determine any possible restrictions to running on Amazon RDS.
- Determine whether a license downgrade is possible.
- Convert embedded SQL code in an application or identify where manual remediation is needed.
- Migrate data warehouse data to Amazon Redshift.

AWS DMS has a free tier; you only pay for infrastructure that is instantiated to enable the migration.

Refactor. Cloud-native and cloud-first principles will likely lead you to refactoring. This path delivers the highest potential reliability and availability and typically the lowest cost. When refactoring, you can take the most appropriate AWS services available to build your apps from the ground up in a scalable and efficient way. You can leverage Amazon EC2 Auto Scaling instances and a multitude of database and file storage technologies. Leverage serverless to create a powerful fulcrum that dramatically lowers costs and removes the maximum amount of heavy lifting required. This path can take the longest time; it is best leveraged for new workloads and non-x86 architectures you may want to move to the cloud.

It is appropriate to use refactoring to be cloud-first and cloud-native as you migrate services that differentiate your business where you want the benefits.

Diving deep into refactoring is beyond the scope of this book. When AWS customers refactor, we currently see four patterns of decomposition:

- ***Event decoupling.*** Move from monolithic synchronous architecture to asynchronous architecture.
- ***The Strangler pattern.*** Martin Fowler from Thoughtworks coined this term when he noticed that the Strangler figs in Australia would seed in the upper branches of a tree and gradually work their way down until they rooted in the soil. They grew into fantastic and beautiful shapes, all the while strangling and killing their host tree. The Strangler pattern moves monolithic applications to microservices by gradually creating events and APIs for various components of the legacy application.
- ***Domain-driven design.*** In domain-driven design, the structure and language of software code (class names, class methods, class variables, etc.) should match the business domain. For example,

if a software processes loan applications, it might have classes like "loan application" and "customers" and methods like "accept offer" and "withdraw."

- ***Generative AI augmentation.*** We dive deeper into this in Chapter 6.4 Generative Artificial Intelligence.

Moving Large Amounts of Data

There are many ways to move massive amounts of data from on-premises to the AWS Cloud. We want to highlight two options. First, the AWS Snow Family offers simple management and monitoring, onboard computing, encryption, anti-tamper and tamper-evident inspection, end-to-end tracking, and secure erasure. The AWS Snow Family is incredible at moving truly massive amounts of information from on-premises to the cloud.

	Snowball Edge storage-optimized (for data transfer)	Snowball Edge storage-optimized 210 TB	Snowball Edge storage-optimized (with EC2 compute functionality)	Snowball Edge compute-optimized with AMD EPYC Gen2 and NVME	Snowball Edge compute-optimized with AMD EPYC Gen1, HDD, and optional GPU
CPU	AMD Naples, 32 cores, 3.4Ghz	AMD Rome, 64 cores, 2 GHz	AMD Naples, 32 cores, 3.4Ghz	AMD Rome, 64 cores, 2 GHz	AMD Naples, 32 cores, 3.4Ghz
vCPUs	40	104	40	104	52
Usable memory	80 GB	416 GB	80 GB	416 GB	208 GB
Security card	Yes	Yes	Yes	Yes	Yes
GPU (optional)	None	None	None	None	NVidia V100
SSD	1 TB SATA	210 TB NVMe	1 TB SATA	28 TB NVMe	7.68 TB NVMe
Usable HDD	80 TB	Not applicable	80 TB	Not applicable	39.5 TB usable
Network interfaces	2x 10 Gbit – RJ45 (one usable) 1x 25 Gbit – SFP28 1x 100 Gbit – QSFP28	2x 10 Gbit – RJ45 (one usable) 1x 25 Gbit – SFP28 1x 100 Gbit – QSFP28	2x 10 Gbit – RJ45 (one usable) 1x 25 Gbit – SFP28 1x 100 Gbit – QSFP28	2x 10 Gbit – RJ45 (one usable) 1x 25 Gbit – SFP28 1x 100 Gbit – QSFP28	2x 10 Gbit – RJ45 (one usable) 1x 25 Gbit – SFP28 1x 100 Gbit – QSFP28
Physical security features	Hidden magnetic screws Intrusion switches NFC tags Anti-tamper inserts Android app for tamper detection GPS and cellular Conformal coating	Hidden magnetic screws Intrusion switches NFC tags Anti-tamper inserts Android app for tamper detection Conformal coating	Hidden magnetic screws Intrusion switches NFC tags Anti-tamper inserts Android app for tamper detection GPS and cellular Conformal coating	Hidden magnetic screws Intrusion switches NFC tags Anti-tamper inserts Android app for tamper detection Conformal coating	Hidden magnetic screws Intrusion switches NFC tags Anti-tamper inserts Android app for tamper detection Conformal coating

Figure 22 AWS Snow Family

Second, AWS DataSync simplifies, automates, and accelerates large online data transfers to and from on-premises storage, edge locations, other cloud providers, and AWS storage services. AWS DataSync can copy data to and from:

- Network File System shares
- Server Message Block shares
- Hadoop Distributed File Systems
- Self-managed object storage
- Google Cloud Storage
- Azure Files
- Azure Blob Storage
- Azure Data Lake Storage Gen2
- Wasabi Cloud Storage
- Oracle Cloud Storage
- Cloudflare R2 Storage
- DigitalOcean Spaces
- Backblaze B2 Cloud Storage
- AWS Snowcone
- Amazon S3 compatible storage on Snow Family
- Amazon S3 buckets
- Amazon EFS file systems
- Amazon FSx for Windows File Server file systems
- Amazon FSx for Lustre file systems
- Amazon FSx for OpenZFS file systems
- Amazon FSx for NetApp ONTAP file systems

Yes, quite the list!

Creating Your Migration "Strawman" with the R Mental Models

One of the techniques we use with AWS customers—that you can apply yourself—is to take the 7 Rs and seven different colors of sticky notes, a spare meeting room with whiteboards, a drawn timeline (matched to your business goal), and a little uninterrupted time (one day is doable). Simply write each application's name in your portfolio, match it to the most appropriate sticky note, and place it in one of the R swim lanes. As a rule of thumb, you should aim to Rehost the majority, Replatform where you have to, and Repurchase when it makes sense. Refactor the key business differentiating elements that you change every day, want to reach the full potential of DevOps with CI/CD, and you are prepared to invest in getting there.

When you complete this exercise, you will end up with a contiguous timeline showing when and how an application could move. Will it be 100 percent accurate? No. Does it *need* to be 100 percent accurate? No. That is a clear assumption you should state to everyone at the outset. In our experience this initial cut is approximately 80 percent accurate, which is good enough. Remember: perfect is the enemy of good enough.

Anyone and everyone can use this annotated timeline as a point of reference. As you get more information, the timeline changes. This is fine and indeed necessary; it feeds directly into your detailed business case and migration acceleration program. Don't hide these whiteboards away—if you have a central floor or office area, place them where everyone can easily see them. There is nothing to hide here. They should be open to review and modify with new data points. These sticky note boards become a living Agile board in their own right.

Enriching Your Detailed Business Case

Now that you have categorized your entire existing application portfolio with a strawman analysis on a timeline, you can include a number of other elements to enrich and inform your detailed business case creation.

For example, you can now add all your known hardware CAPEX investments. When owning and operating your own data center, you must make a multitude of multiyear investment upgrade and maintenance decisions, including physical security, power, compute, network, storage arrays, and so on. The list is seemingly endless. These renewal dates are typically known for budgeting purposes.

One of the very big carrots/sticks that traditional on-premise hardware vendors use to encourage you to purchase new hardware is escalating maintenance costs. Imagine you place a new purchase of a storage array. In Year 1 the maintenance charge from the vendor is likely nothing. By Year 5 it will grow so much that buying a new array becomes cheaper than paying the annual maintenance bill. This "upgrade train" never ends within your own data centers and consumes exorbitant time, resources, and money to maintain. It is probably the most compelling case for undifferentiated heavy lifting that exists.

Taking the annotated application timeline and renewal data points—and any other appropriate contract of business goal inflection points—enables you to start working with either an in-house financial analyst or an AWS Cloud Economics team member who has direct experience with thousands of business cases to help you build the detailed business case you need for your CFO and key stakeholders.

AWS Migration Acceleration Program (MAP)

MAP was born from the collective learnings of thousands of migrations and is designed to help enterprises committed to a migration journey achieve a range of business benefits by migrating existing workloads to AWS. MAP provides consulting support, training, and services credits to reduce the risk of migrating to the cloud, build a strong operational foundation, and help offset the initial cost of migrations. It includes a migration methodology and tooling to automate and accelerate common migration scenarios.

MAP comprises a three-step approach for migrating to AWS.

Step 1. Migration Readiness Assessment (MRA) Phase

The MRA phase determines your readiness to migrate, identifying areas where you already have strong capabilities and where further development is needed to migrate at scale. The MRA is based on the AWS Cloud Adoption Framework (AWS CAF) and evaluates cloud readiness along seven dimensions: (1) landing zone, (2) operating model, (3) security and compliance, (4) migration process experience, (5) skills and center of excellence, (6) migration plan, and (7) business plan. Priorities and gaps identified during the assessment help define the scope for the Migration Readiness & Planning (MRP) phase. The MRA typically involves a one-day workshop conducted by AWS or an AWS MAP Partner.

Step 2. MRP Phase

During the MRP phase, you team with AWS Professional Services or an AWS MAP Partner to build the foundation for a large-scale migration while gaining experience migrating and operating several workloads on AWS. AWS and its AWS MAP Partners have developed a prescriptive methodology and approach based on best practices gleaned from hundreds of customer migration projects that significantly reduce the time to migrate while lowering cost and risk. To prepare a cloud operational foundation, follow an Agile approach with workstreams for cloud enablement engines, landing zones, target operating models, and security and compliance. AWS works with you to develop a strong migration plan and compelling business case that articulates the total cost of ownership and ROI for cloud migration. You are ready to migrate at scale at the end of this phase, which is usually completed in two to four months.

Step 3. Migration Phase

In the Migration phase, you execute the migration plan developed during the MRP phase, typically with the assistance of AWS Professional Services or an AWS MAP Partner. A key component is establishing a "migration factory" composed of teams, tools, and processes to streamline the movement of workloads from on-premises to AWS. The migration factory teams work through a prioritized backlog of workloads based on migration patterns identified in the portfolio discovery and planning process. We apply known migration and operational patterns to accelerate the movement of workloads, reduce risk, and improve the outcome where possible. With this approach you quickly achieve the business benefits of lower operating costs with increased agility and scalability. Once in the cloud, you can focus on optimizing applications, processes, operations, and costs. This phase typically takes twelve to twenty-four months to execute.

Ensuring the Right Partner and Tools for Migration

In our time at AWS, we have had to engage with a few companies that were ill-advised by their incumbent partners (not AWS Partners) on cloud adoption. Incumbent partners often want to protect and grow their on-premise revenue. In virtually every case, the migrations stalled or never even started due to bad recommendations and lack of experience from those "partners."

We were fortunate to choose "born-in-the-cloud" AWS Partners with accreditation, certified practitioners, and real work experience (always ask for references) for our journeys. Finding the right partner is like putting rocket fuel in the migration engine.

AWS Migration Competency Partners

AWS Migration Competency Partners help enterprises through every migration stage, accelerating the overall process by providing personnel, tools, and education of experienced engineers, developers, and migration professionals. Each one is continually audited and evaluated against current AWS migration best practices.

Migration Tracking

Understanding how you maintain momentum with your migrations and tracking important KPIs is crucial for the credibility and delivery of your migration.

AWS Migration Hub provides access to the tools you need to collect and inventory your existing IT assets based on actual usage, analyze application components and infrastructure dependencies, and group resources into applications. You can generate migration strategy and Amazon EC2 instance recommendations for business case and migration planning, track the progress of application migrations to AWS, and modernize applications already running on AWS. Display the hub prominently so everyone can see the journey's momentum and be inspired.

The Mainframe Question

In early 2020, when the world was shutting down due to the COVID-19 pandemic, Jonathan got some worried calls from AWS customers. Many of the mainframe workloads customers had were being asked to handle capacities and do things they hadn't done before. Examples include employment furloughed payment complexities, unemployment claims, insurance systems—the list went on and on. The mainframe million instructions per second (MIPS) usage was suddenly surging in a cost-prohibitive way, and the sheer amount of COBOL changes needed broke enterprise IT operational models.

The history of mainframe replacements is littered with failures. According to Gartner, "Rip and replace is in many cases too costly, risk and time-consuming, and has a high impact on the business. We advise organizations to instead take an iterative approach: continuous application modernization."[99]

Faced with transparent AWS customer feedback asking for more help, Jonathan and his AWS Mainframe colleagues Steve Steuart, Phil de Valence, and Neal Ardeljan, in true Amazonian style rapidly compiled these anecdotes along with a ton of personal expertise, internal findings, and external research into the first iteration of a narrative that the Services team picked up. This work went on to become AWS Mainframe Modernization, launched at re:Invent 2021.

We can't share the original narrative, but some of the external public research can, and it is fascinating. As of 2017, ninety-two of the world's top one hundred banks continue to use mainframes, and 87 percent of all credit card transactions and nearly $8 trillion in payments annually are processed on mainframes. 43 percent of US banking systems are built on COBOL. In comparison, a whopping 80 percent of in-person transactions and 95 percent of ATM interactions rely on the language, totaling 30 billion ATM transactions each year, equivalent to nearly $5 billion per day.[100] From 2008 to 2018, the aggregate installed base MIPS computing capacity across all types of mainframe processing grew by 3.5x.[101] IBM moved to Samsung for chip design and manufacturing. In August 2018, Global Foundries stopped all 7 nm chip development (the IBM z15 model was based on 14 nm architecture).[102] In December 2018, IBM signed a fifteen-year R&D agreement with Samsung to include 7 nm chip manufacturing for IBM Power Systems, IBM Z, and LinuxONE.[103]

Enterprises have compelling business reasons to modernize and migrate mainframe workloads to the AWS Cloud. However, mainframe modernization projects often require supreme patience, stoic leadership, and a robust approach to achieve the intended ROI. Based on our experience with successful AWS customer modernization projects, we have identified patterns, lessons learned, and best practices that facilitate new mainframe-to-AWS initiatives.

Enterprises have many reasons for modernizing their mainframe workloads with AWS. First, AWS customers can reduce costs by eliminating capital expenditure and MIPS, shrinking ISV license costs, and leveraging elastic pricing models. Second, AWS customers gain agility with reduced development cycles via CI/CD and virtually unlimited infrastructure resources consumed on demand. Third, AWS customers gain the advantage of leveraging mainframe data, which can contain decades of business transactions and feed data analytics or machine learning initiatives seeking competitive differentiators. Last, modernizing with AWS often resolves the mainframe retirement skill gap and attracts new talent to modernize core business workloads.

There is no one-size-fits-all approach for mainframe modernization to the AWS Cloud. Depending on the business, IT strategy, and mainframe-specific technical constraints, AWS customers select the pattern most suitable for them. If the mainframe is large enough to process multiple workloads, each workload's characteristics can favor different patterns. Workloads are more easily identified when they are program or data independent. Within one mainframe a stabilized application can follow one pattern, while an evolving application can pursue another. This ability to choose multiple strategies specific to the workload is how customers are most successful with the four drivers discussed above, specifically the business agility and skills gap.

This space is dynamic; we have conversations about mainframe modernization in every AWS customer engagement where a mainframe exists. According to GlobeNewswire, the mainframe modernization market is expected to grow at a compound annual growth rate of 16.8 percent from 2022 to 2031.[104] To dive deeper we suggest you look at the following inspiring and detailed content produced by our colleagues on the AWS Blog:

- "Modernize Your Mainframe Applications & Deploy Them in The Cloud."[105]
- "From Mainframe to AWS cloud: A comprehensive mapping guide."[106]
- "Analyzing legacy applications on-demand with AWS Mainframe Modernization and Micro Focus."[107]
- "AWS Mainframe Modernization – Refactor Legacy code base to Java using AWS Blu Insights."[108]

5.5 Leveraging the AWS Well-Architected Framework

Success is neither magical nor mysterious. Success is the natural consequence of consistently applying basic fundamentals.

—JIM ROHN

Ensuring you can use the over two hundred AWS services in a consistent, repeatable, and well-architected way gives you a sure and repeatable foundation to build upon. How do you do this? And more importantly, how do you ensure your teams can do this?

There are millions of AWS customers today. Their combined experience—and the experience of solutions architects, product owners Professional Services, and AWS Partners—has been poured into the AWS Well-Architected Framework. This is a living, documented set of best practices that is continually and relentlessly tuned and refined to provide the very best pragmatic guidance to help you build.

Creating a software system is a lot like constructing a building. If the foundation is not solid, structural problems can undermine the integrity and function of the building. In the worst case, it can unexpectedly collapse.

When architecting technology solutions on AWS, if you neglect the Six Pillars of Operational Excellence, Security, Reliability, Performance Efficiency, Cost Optimization, and Sustainability, building a system that delivers on your expectations and requirements can become challenging. Incorporating the Six Pillars into your architecture helps produce stable and efficient systems. This allows you to focus on other design aspects, such as functional requirements.

The advantages of the AWS Well-Architected Framework are fourfold:

- It allows your teams to build and deploy faster and avoid common mistakes.
- You continually and actively lower or mitigate risks.
- You make informed decisions, knowing the trade-offs if you use component *x* rather than *y*.
- Your teams continually learn current best practices, so your design patterns will continually pivot to the best they can be.

In our experience it is reassuring to have the bases covered with a Well-Architected review as you move to the cloud. You should find the right cadence that suits you when to do this. A Well-Architected review that supports your standard design review cadence or before initiating major changes can be useful in your risk management practice. The Well-Architected reviews can be conducted by Solutions Architects or AWS Well-Architected Accredited Partners.

Table 2 Operational, Security, and Resiliency Pillars

AWS Well-Architected

Operational Excellence	**Security**	**Reliability**
Organization	***Security***	***Foundation***
OPS 1-Operations priorities OPS 2-Operating model OPS 3-Organization culture	SEC 1-Secure operations	REL 1-Service quotas and constraints REL 2-Network topology
Prepare	***Identity and access management***	***Workload architecture***
OPS 4-Design for workload insights OPS 5-Development and integration OPS 6-Mitigation of deployment risks OPS 7-Operational readiness	SEC 2-Authentication SEC 3-Authorization and access control	REL 3-Service architecture REL 4-Design interactions to prevent failures REL 5-Design interactions to mitigate failures
Operate	***Detection***	***Change management***
OPS 8-Workload health OPS 9-Operations health OPS 10-Event response	SEC 4-Security events	REL 6-Resource monitoring REL 7-Demand handling REL 8-Change management

AWS Well-Architected

Operational Excellence	Security	Reliability
Evolve	***Infrastructure protection***	***Failure management***
OPS 11-Operations evolution	SEC 5-Network protection SEC 6-Compute protection	REL 9-Data backup REL 10-Fault isolation REL 11-Resiliency implementation REL 12-Reliability testing REL 13-Disaster recovery
	Data protection	
	SEC 7-Data classification SEC 8-Data protection at rest SEC 9-Data protection in transit	
	Incident response	
	SEC 10-Incident response SEC 11-Application security	

Table 3 Performance Efficiency, Cost Optimization, and Sustainability Pillars

AWS Well-Architected

Performance Efficiency	Cost Optimization	Sustainability
Selection	***Cloud financial management***	***Region selection***
PERF 1-Architecture selection PERF 2-Compute selection PERF 3-Storage selection PERF 4-Database selection PERF 5-Networking selection	COST 1-Cloud financial management	SUS 1-Region selection
Review	***Expenditure and usage awareness***	***Alignment to demand***
PERF 6-Evolving architecture	COST 2-Usage governance COST 3-Usage and cost monitoring COST 4-Resource decommissioning	SUS 2-Alignment to demand
Monitoring	***Cost-effective resources***	***Software and architecture***

AWS Well-Architected

Performance Efficiency	Cost Optimization	Sustainability
PERF 7-Monitor performance	COST 5-Service selection COST 6-Resource type, size and number COST 7-Pricing model selection COST 8-Data transfer planning	SUS 3-Software and architecture
Trade-offs	***Manage demand and supply resources***	***Data***
PERF 8-Performance trade-offs	COST 9-Manage demand and supply resource	SUS 4-Data
	Optimize over time	***Hardware and services***
	COST 10-New Service evaluation COST 11-Effort cost evaluation	SUS 5-Hardware and services
		Process and culture
		SUS 6-Process and culture

The details behind this table are constantly updated with best practices. For the scope of this book, we want to raise awareness that all of this compelling and detailed advice is available for you and your teams on the AWS website. Making the Well-Architected review part of your team's delivery cadence is the very best way to educate yourself and ensure you cover all bases when building.

PART VI

DATA AND INTELLIGENCE

6.1 Data and Data Mesh

In God we trust. All others must bring data.

—W. EDWARDS DEMING

Data is the new oil, or so the cliché goes. But data has always been valuable, and organizations have always found new ways to leverage data to create value.

Most large enterprises have preserved a quasi-archeological record of data management technology dating back to the 1960s. Thomas cut his teeth in IT on a mainframe, managing and analyzing data stored in flat files. We routinely meet with executives who want to know how to migrate their vintage AS/400s into the cloud. They were first introduced in 1988, while many of the subroutines still running on these venerable workhorses were written in COBOL, which was introduced in 1959.

The first workable version of a relational database (Oracle 2.3) was released in 1979, beating IBM to the punch, which released its first RDBMS, called SQL/DS, in 1981. DB2 soon followed in 1983, and SQL Server was introduced five years later.

The 1990s ushered in the age of the data warehouse under the intellectual leadership of Bill Inmon. In 1998 Thomas worked on one of his first transformation team projects: to implement a standard US Congressional report on the statistics of military personnel from a flat file system into an OLAP system. Around the same time, Ralph Kimball popularized the architectural patterns of star schemas and data marts, which are still prevalent in many enterprise data architectures today.

The term "big data" first appeared in a 1999 paper titled "Visually Exploring Gigabyte Datasets in Real Time," which lamented the lack of adequate compute power to analyze the amount of data that could be stored.[109] The Defense Manpower Data Center (DMDC), where Thomas worked at the time, celebrated reaching 1 TB of data stored that same year!

In software engineering multitier architecture (often referred to as n-tier architecture), or multilayered architecture, is a client–server architecture in which presentation, application processing, and data management functions are physically separated. The most widespread use of multitier architecture is the three-tier architecture.[110]

N-tier architectures used the ability to store and retrieve data from a centralized data store. This has been the predominant architectural pattern for over thirty years, and for good reason. The pattern's success is the root of the challenge that business intelligence (BI) was supposed to address. The proliferation of systems and applications with disparate data stores resulted in enterprises wanting to correlate data across these systems. Since data was stored in many different formats, and database schemas were based on divergent business rules and assumptions, correlating data became a core task for entire departments. Companies invested in big iron data warehouses and BI appliances such as IBM Netezza, Oracle Exadata, or Teradata. These required significant expertise and planning to manage the high cost, complexity, and overhead of the extract, transform, and load (ETL) processes.

With the rampant growth of new data sources and the explosion of data volumes, the appliances became too expensive to scale, and teams were forced to make tough choices about which data to load and process.

Loading and transporting data emerged as an additional challenge, with institutions moving large amounts of "batched" data across networks into systems to be processed during off hours. The continued growth of data volumes has presented these batch processes with a natural limit, where more data has to be moved and processed than can reasonably be accomplished in the available time, usually at night, when transactional volumes decline to a fraction of daytime activity.

Since 2005, new technologies have emerged to address what has become known as the "big data challenge." Approaches include MapReduce and Hadoop, data streaming, and NoSQL databases.

Data governance has also become more complex over time. Who has access to what data under which circumstance has always been a challenge. Compliance regulations (and good practice) require an understanding of data provenance. Where did the data come from, who has had access, and how has it been transformed?

Enterprises have accreted this hodgepodge of data management solutions. They are still trying to find a way to unlock the value of the "new oil" and provide better solutions to their customers.

In polyglot programming applications are written in a mix of languages because different languages are suitable for tackling different problems. In 2006 Neal Ford of Thoughtworks coined the term polyglot programming, and thought leaders began discussing polyglot database models and persistence. This means using the best tool for the job; a web cache layer is better served by Redis than an RDBMS, while a social network data store might be best implemented as a graph in Neo4J or Amazon Neptune. However, the side effect of this newer architectural pattern is a further proliferation of siloed data.

Although social media existed in nascent form with bulletin board services and AOL in the '90s, social media came to the fore in 2006 when Twitter and Facebook emerged in the public sphere. Data streams have been growing at astronomical rates ever since—and not only social media streams but also streams generated by the explosion of connected devices and sensors in every domain in the most inaccessible regions of the earth and increasingly in space.

Let's regroup for a minute. We faced some of these challenges in our previous roles. Many customer-facing applications followed the venerable n-tier design and had an underlying database that stored customer and transaction data. Every application had its schema, and business rules defined customers and their identities in subtly different ways. When the CFO wanted to know details about transaction volumes by unique customers, we were hard-pressed to furnish an answer. Worse, the CFO might get different answers depending on who analyzed the cleansed and collated data. And even when pressed, teams could not declare absolute truth with any certainty (only to the very best of their knowledge). Why? Because merging data cataloged under different underlying business rules is incredibly hard. How do you guarantee that two accounts in two different applications belong to the same person? Is it as simple as matching first and last names? What if they used two different email addresses? What if they connected from two different IP addresses? This becomes a difficult problem quickly.

Large centralized databases present the inverse challenge of many discreet databases. Monolithic applications come with large and complex databases, often with business logic buried deep within the relational database management system—typically in the form of stored procedures. Creating new applications and functionality by expanding the existing monolithic database was common procedure. This continuous accretion of tables, materialized views, stored procedures, and connection pools serving a variety of endpoints has led to database implementations as convoluted and complicated as monolithic applications. Database experts are often afraid to make changes, much less refactor or migrate these database Borg cubes. (For all our non-Star Trek fans, the Borg cube is one of the most formidable alien species and technologies known to the Federation. Its lack of identifiable function spaces—such as a bridge, engineering, or personnel quarters—reveals the hive-like Borg collective consciousness and its drones.)

These kinds of challenges exist across many business domains. We often hear that a re-architecture of these systems would cost tens of millions of dollars and take five years to complete whether the enterprise is in marketing, supply chain management, oil and gas exploration, education, or government systems. And this is only if no new requirements are added. Good luck with that! As Bernard Marr writes, "Those companies that view data as a strategic asset are the ones that will survive and thrive."[111]

Data Mesh, a Way Forward

Achieving a data-driven enterprise at scale can be challenging. The challenge is multifaceted, with complex human elements often compounded by historic technological complexity. We often hear new AWS customers say:

"Finding the data I need is too difficult."

"I just want to get access to the data I need."

"It's difficult to meet all requirements across differing business units."

"I want to focus on innovating with data, not on maintaining and administering a data lake."

"My data science team should easily find the datasets they seek and have the ability to share them with others."

"My team needs to own datasets, pipelines, and repositories that are isolated from other teams."

"Why doesn't our organization treat data as a product?"

"Current data architecture is complex, monolithic, and slow to change."

"If I share data, I've lost control."

"There is a mismatch between executive leadership goals and business line deliverables and incentives."

"Our internal policies on what can be shared is unclear, and there is lack of incentive to share."

"I need to create a model to support sharing from both producers and consumers of data."

None of these comments surprise us. We experienced the same problems in our prior roles. Much of the problem centers on the human side of the equation. One AWS customer shared an uncomfortable truth with us: "Everybody wants to be a data consumer; no one wants to be a data producer!". The statement "If I share data, I've lost control" hits home particularly hard.

Sometimes data is shared (and maybe reshared), but in an ad hoc, ungoverned way based on team connections or interpersonal relationships. This can increase the risk associated with protecting sensitive data. Organizations have been tempted to create centralized monolithic data lakes. This can work but requires exhaustive top-down leadership, management, and oversight. And it's not human-centric or compatible with the commander's intent discussed in Chapter 3.2 Teams.

Herein lies the perennial modern data challenge: You have data in many separate locations across your enterprise owned by different teams. You have externally hosted SaaS datasets, datasets you export externally, and datasets you import from external entities. You also have a tremendous and growing legal, security, and often regulatory responsibility. Enterprises want to extract value from their data but feel constrained, so how do they do it?

Big data continues to be a struggle for most enterprises. According to a NewVantage Partners Survey, only 24 percent of firms claim to have succeeded in creating a data-driven organization. A similar minority of companies claim to have successfully built a data culture within their organizations. Yet the technology is not why they are failing. Over 90 percent cite people and processes as what stands between them and transforming their organizations through data.[112]

In 2019 Zhamak Dehghani wrote a paper on moving beyond a monolithic data lake to a distributed data mesh:

> "I agree that organizations face a multi-faceted complexity in transforming to become data-driven; migrating from decades of legacy systems, resistance of legacy culture to rely on data, and ever competing business priorities. However what I would like to share with you is an architectural perspective that underpins the failure of many data platform initiatives. I demonstrate how we can adapt and apply the learnings of the past decade in building

> distributed architectures at scale, to the domain of data; and I will introduce a new enterprise data architecture that I call *data mesh.*"[113]

After Dehghani's paper Thoughtworks published a two-part series called "Data mesh: it's not just about tech, it's about ownership and communication."[114]

Why a Data Mesh?

Do you need another platform or approach? Don't think of data mesh as a platform but as a mental model with pragmatic steps. Data mesh doesn't care about or specify particular technology brands (each one has pros and cons). When done correctly, data mesh can largely preserve existing investments in data platforms, as each LOB is encouraged to treat their business data as an "independent domain." Ownership is essential; taking responsibility extends to your data. Improve data governance by pushing policy down into teams and their data domains, providing a clear mechanism for centralized data discovery while ensuring a consistent data catalog and dictionary. This enables self-service data-sharing features that allow domain owners to grant access to consumers, which allows the leadership team to measure and invest in data products based on usage and business value. Customers repeatedly tell us they have tried and failed to create a cogent data catalog many times. The advice here is simple: work backward from those de facto acronyms in your business/industry, avoid inventing new ones, avoid delegating the work to a junior architect, and instead elevate the completion of the first draft of this to an executive. Aim for a simple starting nomenclature, then develop a central location that folks can append to it in a pragmatic, bar-raising way.

We won't reproduce Zhamak Dehghani's excellent book, *Data Mesh: Delivering Data-Driven Value at Scale*, but we will explore the four primary parts of data mesh:

Domain-driven ownership. Have teams with domain knowledge. Marketing and finance departments can own the data they turn into insights and actions because they have the context that makes that data meaningful. It could be an LOB or a subgroup; you decide. The data mesh approach proposes that data management responsibility is organized around business functions or domains. Domain teams collect, transform, and provide data related to or created by their business functions. Instead of domain data flowing from data sources into a central data platform, a specific team hosts and serves its datasets in an easily consumable way. For example, a retailer could have a clothing domain with data about their clothing products and a website behavior domain that contains site visitor behavior analytics.

Data as a product. The days of churning out numbers on a report no one reads are over. Now all data you produce is treated like a product with the same lifecycle, support, iteration, and ownership as the rest of your products. Use your insights to experiment more frequently and develop a competitive advantage if you run a commercial organization or fulfill the mission if you work in the public sector. For data mesh implementation to be successful, every domain team needs to apply product thinking to the datasets they provide. They must consider their data assets as products and the rest of the organization as their customers. For the best user experience, the domain data products should be:

- Discoverable: Each data product registers itself with a centralized data catalog for easy discoverability.

- Addressable: Each data product should have a unique address that helps data consumers access it programmatically. The address typically follows the organization's standard naming conventions.
- Trustworthy: Each data product defines acceptable service level objectives around how closely it reflects the reality of the events it documents. For example, the orders domain can publish data after verifying a customer's address and phone number.
- Self-describing: Each data product has well-described syntax and semantics that follow the organization's standard naming conventions.

Self-serve functionality. Don't rely on a central BI team with an untenable backlog of demands from finance, marketing, ops, and HR. Empower teams to support their own data and subscribe to other teams' data. Different domains in a company, whether marketing, operations, or IT, should have access to the data they need to make their respective analyses and reports. Teams need to publish data pipelines to their curated datasets for other teams to access in a controlled, approved way. A distributed data architecture requires every domain to set up its own data pipeline to clean, filter, and load its data products. A data mesh introduces the concept of a self-serve data platform to avoid duplication of efforts. Data engineers set up technologies so all business units can process and store their data products. Self-serve infrastructure allows a division of responsibility. Data engineering teams manage technology while business teams manage data.

Federated governance. Data mesh architectures implement security as a shared responsibility within the organization. Leadership determines global standards and policies that you can apply across domains. At the same time, the decentralized data architecture allows a large degree of autonomy on standards and policy implementation within the domain. While there may be overarching guidelines on how to work with data in your organization, individual teams should make independent decisions with the data that affects their domain and ensure their own data quality. To clarify, drawing the line between self-serve functionality and federated governance isn't easy. But you need teams responsible for ensuring data quality and accuracy while enabling others to be autonomous without becoming a bottleneck. This looks different depending on your organization and the complexity of your data and tech stacks. We can't tell you exactly what to do, but we definitely don't want to force everyone into using the same tech stack—that leads to resentment and rejection of the goal.

Remember: have teams with domain knowledge. An organization that values a data mesh approach makes data accessible in different tools across various teams. Leaders should be able to use data to answer all performance-related questions while the BI team uses it for broader business analytics. The key benefits of data mesh are greater independence and flexibility; this aligns with the intrinsic behaviors in Chapter 3.1 Culture and Chapter 3.2 Teams. Data mesh principles align with how humans like to get stuff done. Don't fight gravity; leverage it.

It's worth mentioning that with more ownership comes greater responsibility (to quote Spiderman's Uncle Ben: "With great power, comes great responsibility"). Each team needs to be a good steward of data to ensure it remains accurate, clean, and available for the rest of the organization.

If you can shift the entire company's mindset toward this way of working, you increase each team's efficiency and output while maintaining data accuracy and integrity. Decentralizing your data management allows teams to tie their data directly to business outcomes rather than raw data because ownership lies within business domains. Instead of processing all available data, each team has context to carefully select which data needs to be processed and analyzed.

Central Data Lakes Cautionary Tale

We've seen data lakes fail because of implementation and use, not the technology itself. Success with data lakes is closely correlated to the size of your business domain. Why? If you constantly add tons and tons of information to a data lake, the human ability to understand what correlates to a particular data label, cell, row, or column starts to break. JPMorgan Chase successfully used product-specific data lakes for their mesh.[115] Data lakes have enormous value when used with the right domain size.

What Is the Difference between a Data Mesh and a Data Lake?

A data lake is a repository where you can store all your structured and unstructured data at any scale without preprocessing. In centralized data platforms, the data lake is the core technology for storing data from all possible sources.

A data mesh is a data management paradigm that uses data lakes differently. They do not form the centerpiece of the whole architecture; instead, you can use data lakes to implement data products or as part of the self-serve infrastructure.

Modern Data Architecture on AWS

Modern data architecture acknowledges that taking a one-size-fits-all approach to analytics eventually leads to compromises. Integrating a data lake with a data warehouse is not enough; integrating a data lake, a data warehouse, and purpose-built stores enables unified governance and easy data movement. Tens of thousands of organizations have successfully leveraged AWS data services to build their own data mesh by leveraging data lakes, analytics, data movement, and unified governance. To dive deeper, check out modern data architecture on AWS.[116]

Independent data mesh domains increasingly collect their data—structured and unstructured, which commonly represents 80 percent of an organization's data—in a data lake. Yes, each domain can have its own data lake. The data lake becomes a staging environment to load data into right-sized data stores, or it can be queried directly by increasingly powerful and simple-to-use tools. Migrating to the cloud can achieve cost, performance, and resilience efficiencies. Before we dive deeper, let's declare a few principles for managing and analyzing data in the cloud.

Principles for Data

Operational excellence through data. We must ensure databases are operational to support business needs. We ensure security, durability, availability, and speed in that order.

Never constrain the business. Database services are focused on enabling the organization to meet business objectives. We will never constrain the business as a result of changes in our database technologies or services.

Be a force multiplier. Enable self-service functionality whenever possible. Empower teams to leverage data without the help of the database team.

Be transparent. We will share everyone's mutual successes, failures, and lessons learned across the wider community.

Never change existing critical data. Only change derived information.

Protect the source. Maintain source data in its original form and quality and maintain data provenance.

Fix data problems at the source. We reveal data problems so they can be addressed at the source.

Use the right tool for the job. Keep it as simple as possible.

Expose data through APIs. Henceforth all teams will be exposed to their data and functionality through service interfaces.

Get the code out of the database. To aid future data movement, avoid using and removing stored procedures whenever possible.

Call to Action

Step 1. Analyze your existing data. Before building a data mesh, you must catalog your existing data and identify relevant business domains. Following certain harmonization rules is the key to effectively correlating data between domains. For example, you need to define global standards for field type formatting, metadata fields, and data product address conventions.

Step 2. Implement global data governance policies. Federated data governance requires your central IT team to identify reporting, authentication, and compliance standards for the data mesh. You can also define granular access controls that data product owners apply when hosting their datasets. While data producers define and measure data quality, central governance policies help guide their decisions.

Step 3. Build your self-service data platform. Your self-service data platform should be generic so anyone can build new domain data products on it. It should also hide underlying technical complexity and provide infrastructure components in a self-service manner. Here are some capabilities to include:

- Data encryption
- Data product schema
- Governance and access control
- Data product discovery, such as catalog registration or publishing
- Data product logging and monitoring
- Caching for improved performance

You can also build automation, such as configurations and scripts, to lower the lead time to create data products.

Step 4. Choose the right technologies. Your existing traditional storage systems, like data warehouses and data lakes, can power your data mesh. Just shift their use from monolithic systems to multiple decentralized data repositories. A data mesh also enables the adoption of cloud platforms and cloud-centered technologies. Cloud infrastructure reduces operational costs and the effort required to build a data mesh. Choose a cloud provider with rich data management services to support your data mesh architecture, and consider data integration requirements with legacy systems.

Step 5. Start an organization-wide cultural shift. You have the technology and tools required to build a data mesh with multiple data products. Unifying batch and streaming is easier than ever with tools like Amazon EMR. However, scaling your data mesh beyond small projects necessitates a paradigm shift away from the centralized data architectures of the past. It requires a new language that emphasizes the following:

- Data discovery and usage over extraction and loading
- Real-time data processing over high-volume batch processing at a later date
- Distributed data product ownership over central data platform architecture

Data technology often drives architectural decisions. A data mesh reverses this flow, putting domain data products in the center so that they drive technology decisions instead.

6.2 Machine Learning with Cloud

Don't replace people: augment them.

—TIM O'REILLY

Machine learning (ML) and artificial intelligence (AI) are hot topics in our conversations with AWS customers. ML has been somewhat of an arcane art in the past. It required specialized knowledge, massive compute power, and extremely large data sets, not to mention the need for labeled "training data."

Before we dive deeper, let's define a few terms:

- ***AI:*** software applications that exhibit human-like behavior, such as speech, natural language processing, reasoning, or intuition.
- ***ML:*** teaching machines to learn without being explicitly programmed.
- ***Deep learning:*** using neural networks to teach machines to learn from complex data where features cannot be explicitly expressed.

AWS's mission is to put ML into the hands of every developer and data scientist. AWS has put great effort into "democratizing AI" by providing all the services and tools an enterprise needs to generate value through ML and AI.

Consider C-SPAN, a nonprofit public service funded by the US cable television industry.[117] Its mission is to open Washington, DC, to the public and make government more transparent by broadcasting and archiving government proceedings, including live coverage of the US Senate and House of Representatives.

In early 2016 C-SPAN Archives developed an internal tool to tag speakers and topics of congressional proceedings with a time hack. It was relatively slow: two human indexers could use this tool, plus closed-captioning data, to index faces in about 50 percent of C-SPAN's footage at about one hour of work per hour of video.

Alan Cloutier, then a technical manager at C-SPAN, heard about Amazon Rekognition, a highly scalable image-analysis service, at the re:Invent 2016 keynote address. Within an hour he used Amazon Rekognition to search for "John McCain" and discovered that it could pick the correct face from a collection of more than one hundred thousand images with a high degree of certainty.

Within three weeks of the announcement, the C-SPAN Archives team had a working solution using Amazon Rekognition. Only one line of code is required to add an image or do a comparison, so very little development was required. The initial image collection—consisting of 97,000 known individuals—was indexed by Amazon Rekognition in less than two hours.

Why AI/ML Matters

ML can help you use historical data to make better business decisions. ML algorithms discover patterns in data and construct mathematical models using these discoveries. Then you can use these models to make predictions on future data. For example, you can use an ML model to predict how likely a customer is to purchase a particular product based on their past behavior.

ML is not really a new invention; the mathematical principles underlying it have existed for decades. In 1950 Alan Turing proposed a "learning machine" that could learn and become artificially intelligent.[118] A year later Dean Edmonds and others built the SNARC, the first neural network machine able to learn.[119]

Over the following decades, AI leaders and other researchers pronounced the imminent age of AI:

- Herbert Simon and Allen Newell (1958): "Within ten years a digital computer will be the world's chess champion."
- Herbert Simon (1965): "Machines will be capable, within twenty years, of doing any work a man can do."
- Marvin Minsky (1967): "Within a generation, the problem of creating 'artificial intelligence' will substantially be solved."
- Marvin Minsky (1970): "Within three to eight years, we will have a machine with the general intelligence of an average human being."

The first "AI Winter" came when research funding all but disappeared in the 1970s, followed by a second AI Winter beginning in 1984. In 2001 Marvin Minsky gave a talk titled "It's 2001: Where is HAL?" (a reference to the HAL Stanley Kubrick's film *2001: A Space Odyssey*, which Marvin Minsky advised on.) In this talk Minsky stated: "No program today can distinguish a dog from a cat, or recognize objects in typical rooms, or answer questions that four-year-olds can!"

Yet a mere five years later, it happened. AI—and more importantly, ML—became generally available *and* affordable. The age of AI was upon us, though in a different form than the early pioneers had predicted. So why has AI taken so long to become useful?

While scientists could run AI applications in the lab, the cost and complexity of running algorithms made them scientific curiosities rather than something with economic utility. The amount of compute power and data storage required was simply beyond the available capacity of all but the largest research institutions, and even then, only for short periods of compute time.

An important milestone was reached in December 2004, when Google released the famous MapReduce paper, which described "a programming model and an associated implementation for processing and generating large data sets."[120] Not to be outdone, Yahoo implemented the paper's ideas and released the first version of their project, Hadoop, in April 2006.[121]

With AWS's formation in early 2006, the compute and storage capacity required to enable ML at scale became available for the first time. Amazon has been using ML for over twenty years. Thousands of engineers across the company focused on AL and used ML to improve nearly every retail page, product, fulfillment technology, and store. AWS's mission has been to take ML from something only the largest, most well-funded technology companies use and put it in the hands of *every* developer. Amazon has also used ML for advances in robotics, drones, supply chain management, the family of Amazon Echo devices, and the Amazon Go store.

Jeff Bezos says, "It is a renaissance; it is a golden age. We are solving problems with machine learning and artificial intelligence that were in the realm of science fiction for the last several decades. Natural language understanding, machine vision problems—it really is an amazing renaissance."

Things really got going in late 2017, when AWS made the next generation of GPU-powered Amazon EC2 instances available for the first time. Powered by up to eight NVIDIA Tesla V100 GPUs, the Amazon EC2 P3 instances were designed to handle compute-intensive ML, deep learning, computational fluid dynamics, computational finance, seismic analysis, molecular modeling, and genomics workloads.

Jeff Barr, VP and Chief Evangelist of AWS, described the Amazon EC2 P3 instances' impact:

> "Let's go back to the dawn of the microprocessor era and consider the Intel 8080A chip that powered the MITS Altair that I bought in the summer of 1977. With a 2 MHz clock, it was able to do about 832 multiplications per second (I used this data and corrected it for the faster clock speed). The p3.16xlarge is roughly 150 billion times faster. However, just 1.2 billion seconds have gone by since that summer. In other words, I can do 100 times more calculations today in one second than my Altair could have done in the last 40 years!"[122]

The AWS suite of ML services now offers support across the full spectrum of applications—it supports dyed-in-the-wool data scientists, enables programmers and business analysts with no background in data science, and facilitates the rapid implementation of high-level applications that can be easily leveraged.

AWS ML services can be grouped by the people they serve:

- Data scientists
- Developers who need a simple integration
- Developers who have no background in ML but need to create models

When to Use ML

Humans are not good at quickly parsing through enormous piles of data to extract gems of insight. We are slow, prone to error, and easily bored. In 1996 Thomas was deployed to Bosnia as part of a NATO peacekeeping mission (IFOR). He read hundreds of pages of reports daily to extract information that might be relevant and useful to the group's peacekeeping mission. Thomas could only dream of the power and ease with which he could do this task today.

The sheer volume of available data is impossible for humans to parse and extract. Worse, finding connections or correlations in large, unstructured, often spurious datasets is impossible for most people unless they are data scientists or mathematicians.

We recommend you use ML in the following situations:

You cannot code the rules. Many human tasks, such as recognizing whether an email is spam or not, cannot be adequately solved using a simple, deterministic, rule-based solution. Many factors can influence the answer. When rules depend on too many factors, overlap, or need to be tuned very finely, it soon becomes difficult for a human to accurately code the rules. You can use ML instead.

You cannot scale. You might be able to manually recognize a few hundred emails and decide whether they are spam or not. But this task becomes tedious for millions of emails. ML solutions are effective at handling large-scale problems.

Get Started (Train Your Own Models)

You can use Amazon SageMaker to apply ML to problems that have existing examples of answers. For example, if you want to predict whether an email is spam, you need to collect example emails that are correctly labeled as spam or not spam. Then you can use SageMaker to generalize and predict how likely each new email is spam or not. This approach— learning from data labeled with the actual answer—is known as supervised ML.

You can use supervised ML approaches for these specific ML tasks: binary classification (predicting one of two possible outcomes), multiclass classification (predicting one of more than two outcomes), and regression (predicting a numeric value).

Examples of binary classification problems:

- Will the customer buy this product or not buy this product?
- Is this email spam or not spam?
- Is this product a book or a farm animal?
- Is this review written by a customer or a robot?

Examples of multiclass classification problems:

- Is this product a book, movie, or clothing?
- Is this movie a romantic comedy, documentary, or thriller?
- Which category of products is most interesting to this customer?

Examples of regression classification problems:

- What will the temperature be in Seattle tomorrow?
- How many units of this product will sell?
- How many days before this customer stops using the application?
- What price will this house sell for?

Call to Action

Building SageMaker applications is an iterative process.

Step 1. Formulate the problem. The first step in ML is deciding what you want to predict, known as the *label* or *target answer*. Imagine you want to manufacture products, but your decision depends on each product's number of potential sales. In this scenario you want to predict how many times each product will be purchased (predict number of sales). There are multiple ways to define this problem by using ML. Choosing how to define the problem depends on your use case or business need.

Step 2. Collect labeled data. Do you want to predict the number of purchases your customers will make for each product (in which case the target is numeric and you're solving a regression problem)? Or do you want to predict which products will get more than ten purchases (in which case the target is binary and you're solving a binary classification problem)? ML problems start with data—preferably *lots* of data with a known target answer, called *labeled data*. In supervised ML the algorithm teaches itself to learn from the labeled examples you provide.

Each example or observation in your data must contain two elements:

> ***The target.*** The answer you want to predict. Provide data labeled with the target (i.e., correct answer) to the ML algorithm to learn from. Then use the trained ML model to predict this answer for data with an unknown answer.
>
> ***Variables/features.*** These are examples or observation attributes used to identify patterns to predict the target answer.
>
> In the previous email classification problem, the target is a label that indicates whether an email is spam or not. Variable examples include the sender, the text in the body of the email, the text in the subject line, the time the email was sent, and the existence of previous correspondence between the sender and receiver.
>
> Data is often unavailable in labeled form. Collecting and preparing the variables and target are often the most important steps in

solving an ML problem. The example data should be representative of the data that the model uses to make a prediction. For example, if you want to predict whether an email is spam or not, you must collect both positives (spam emails) and negatives (non-spam emails) for the ML algorithm to find patterns that distinguish the two email types.

Once you have the labeled data, you might need to convert it to a format acceptable to your algorithm or software. For example, to use CSV format on Amazon SageMaker, you need to convert each data example to one row; each column contains one input variable, and the target variable is in the first column.

Step 3. Analyze your data. Avoid overcomplicating the problem and frame the simplest solution that meets your needs. Don't lose information—especially in the historical answers. Converting an actual past sales number into a binary variable of "fewer than 10" versus "fewer" would lose valuable information. Investing time in deciding which target makes the most sense for you to predict saves you from building models that don't answer your question.

Before feeding your labeled data to an ML algorithm, inspect it to identify issues and gain insights. Your model's predictive power is only as good as the data you feed it.

When analyzing your data, keep the following considerations in mind:

Variable and target data summaries. Understand the values your variables take and which are dominant in your data. You could run these summaries by a subject matter expert for the problem you want to solve. Does the data match your expectations? Does it look like you have a data collection problem? Is one class in your target more frequent than the other classes? Are there more missing values or invalid data than you expected?

Variable-target correlations. Knowing the correlation between each variable and the target class is helpful because a high correlation implies a relationship between the variable and the target class. You generally want to include highly correlated variables because they have higher predictive power (signal). Leave out variables with low correlation because they are likely irrelevant.

In Amazon SageMaker, you can analyze your data by creating a data source and reviewing the resulting data report.

Step 4. Build the model. ML's fundamental goal is to generalize beyond the data instances used to train models. You want to evaluate the model to estimate the quality of its pattern generalization for data the model has not been trained on.

You are now ready to provide the ML algorithm (that is, the *learning algorithm*) with the training data. The algorithm learns from the training data patterns that map the variables to the target and outputs a model that captures these relationships. The ML model can then be used to get predictions on new data with unknown target answers.

The goal of the ML model is to learn patterns that generalize well for unseen data instead of just memorizing the data shown during training. Once you have a model, checking if it performs well on unseen examples is important. To do this, use the model to predict the answer on the evaluation dataset (holdout data) and then compare the predicted target to the actual answer (ground truth).

Step 5. Generate predictions and inferences. Batch prediction is useful when you want to generate predictions for a set of observations all at once and then take action on a certain percentage or number of the observations. Typically you don't have a low latency requirement for such an application. If you want to decide which customers to target as part of an advertisement campaign for a product, get prediction scores for all customers, sort your model's predictions to identify which customers are most likely to purchase, and then target the top 5 percent of customers who are most likely to purchase.

Online prediction scenarios are for cases when you want to generate predictions individually for each example one by one in a low-latency environment. For example, you could use predictions to make immediate decisions about whether a particular transaction is likely fraudulent.

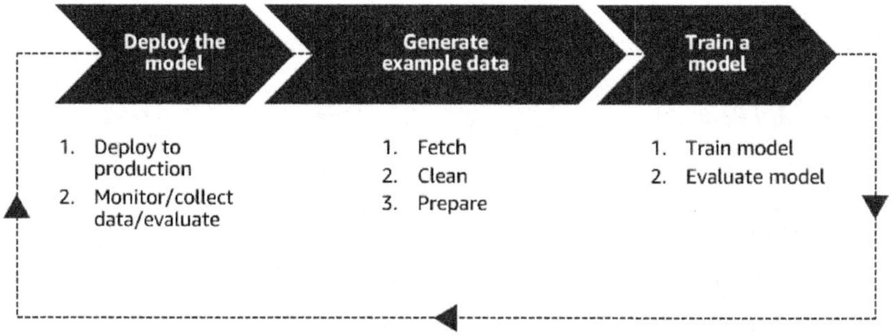

Get Started (Without the Heavy Lifting)

If you don't have the appetite (yet) to build your solutions from scratch with the help of your data scientists (you do have data scientists on your team, right?), then there is a much easier way to get started. Use Amazon SageMaker, a fully managed service that allows you to label and prepare your data, choose the appropriate algorithm, train it, and then tune and optimize it for deployment. Deployment into auto scaling production clusters can be done with a single click in the console. Once deployed, you can use the service to reliably make predictions that inform decisions and actions.

Use Amazon SageMaker Ground Truth to label data in Amazon SageMaker to reduce the time and effort required to create datasets for training. It uses ML to automatically label data in a training set based on labels applied by humans. Over time the labeling algorithm improves by continuously learning from human labelers. This allows you to apply labels to larger datasets faster and cheaper.

There is a straightforward, four-step process to develop and deploy a model that can fuel your applications and products. Although development work is involved, the team does not have to understand ML to implement an Amazon SageMaker solution:

Step 1. Create an Amazon SageMaker notebook instance.

Step 2. Train a model with a built-in algorithm and deploy it.

Step 3. Clean up.

Step 4. Integrate Amazon SageMaker endpoints into internet-facing applications.

Application developers without formal data science training have developed remarkable solutions in days or weeks rather than months or years of development time. Here are some examples:

Formula 1 Racing

In 2018 Formula 1 announced plans to move the vast majority of its infrastructure from on-premises data centers to AWS and standardize on AWS's ML and data analytics services to accelerate its cloud transformation.

Formula 1's data scientists use Amazon SageMaker to train deep learning models with more than sixty-five years of historical race data stored in both Amazon DynamoDB and Amazon S3 Glacier. With this information Formula 1 can extract critical race performance statistics to make race predictions and give fans insight into the split-second decisions and strategies adopted by teams and drivers. Pete Samara, director of innovation and digital technology at Formula 1, says:

> "For our needs, AWS outperforms all other cloud providers in speed, scalability, reliability, global reach, partner community, and breadth and depth of cloud services available. By leveraging Amazon SageMaker and AWS's machine learning services, we are now able to deliver these powerful insights and predictions to fans in real time. We are also excited that the Formula 1 Motorsports division will run High Performance Compute workloads in a scalable environment on AWS. This will significantly increase the number and quality of the simulations our aerodynamics team can run as we work to develop the new car design rules for Formula 1."[123]

Fender Guitars

Fender went all in on AWS to better engage with customers and gain supply chain efficiencies. Fender, made famous by the likes of Jimi Hendrix, runs its Fender Play, Fender Tune, and Fender Tone apps on AWS, which help customers learn to play guitar, tune their instruments, and control digital amplifiers. Ethan Kaplan, Chief Product Officer at Fender, spoke at re:Invent 2018. He described how Fender uses Amazon SageMaker to scan images of wood to find the perfect match between two pieces needed to make a guitar body. The images are fed into SageMaker and compared to thousands of others to determine the optimal wood grain.[124]

Final Thought

You don't need a specialist ML team to get started. Throughout this book, we've discussed how small, outcome-centric, product-centric, and heterogeneously skilled teams execute and deliver value quickly when the heavy lifting is removed. This is true for ML as well. Your teams can go really fast with higher-level AWS services, some of which can be used with a single API call (e.g., Amazon Rekognition).

We want to give a special shout-out to our good friend Julien Simon, for his help writing this chapter. His insight and narrative (and wit) were and continue to be invaluable. To learn more—and go much, much, much deeper into the world of AI and ML—visit him at https://medium.com/@julsimon.

6.3 Generative Artificial Intelligence

We tend to overestimate the effect of a technology in the short run and underestimate the effect in the long run.

—AMARA'S LAW

We are fascinated by the technological tipping points in history that have ignited the public's imagination—the first TV broadcast, human-crewed space flight, or video conference. Each of these events made a previously esoteric technology or concept tangible. As Amara implies in his "law," these events are preceded by false starts and inflated expectations. When (if) a tipping point is reached, it is usually accompanied by decades of unseen work described by the S-curve of innovation. Think of past promises of virtual worlds becoming commonplace. Expectations have often exceeded reality. Organizations and leaders that lean in, grounded in real-world business problems, like customer demand for more immersive customer experiences, are better prepared for change.

The most glaring current example of such an emerging technology is generative AI. To the public, generative AI has appeared from nowhere. But if you dig deeper, you'll note that the ideas underlying generative AI solutions trace their lineage back to inventions such as the Mark I Perceptron algorithm in 1958 and neural networks in the late twentieth century.

Let's first get grounded on where Gen AI has come from and how it builds on the work from the previous chapters:

- AI describes any system that can replicate tasks that mimic human intelligence.
- Most AI use cases look for a probabilistic outcome, making a prediction or decision with a high degree of certainty, similar to human judgment.
- Almost all AI systems today are created using ML, which uses large amounts of data to create decision logic in ML models.
- Deep learning is a type of ML that uses a technique known as deep neural networks.
- Generative AI is a subset of deep learning. Generative AI is powered by foundation models (FMs) trained on massive amounts of data.

The growth in availability of cost-effective, scalable compute, a massive proliferation of data, and the rapid advancement in algorithms and mathematics through the cloud have propelled this evolution, the seeds of which have existed for decades. It's led us to a truly exciting inflection point. We believe most customer experiences and applications will be reinvented with generative AI.

While generative AI is neither a silver bullet nor "just a better search engine," it is now on everyone's radar. The potential is huge. Imagine pharmaceutical companies accelerating the design of gene therapies, borrowers having rich conversational experiences with mortgage providers that quickly approve their loans, or everyone everywhere gaining opportunities through broadening access to ongoing knowledge and educational pathways.

Advancements in statistical techniques, the vast growth of publicly available data, and the power of the cloud have all been instrumental in making generative AI possible. You've likely come across two terms associated with generative AI. FMs are ML models trained on massive quantities of structured and unstructured data, which can be fine-tuned or adapted for more specific tasks. Large Language Models (LLMs) are a subset of FMs focused on understanding and generating human-like text. These models are ideal for translation, answering questions, summarizing information, and creating or identifying images and videos. These models are trained on vast quantities of unstructured, unlabeled data. To give a sense of the scale of change, the largest pre-trained model in 2019 had 330 million parameters. Now the largest models have more than 500 billion parameters. Bigger doesn't necessarily mean better, but the size of these models enables them to perform multiple tasks, unlike traditional ML models that typically focus on a narrower task.

So as a CIO, CTO, or CDO, what should you be thinking about, and how can you prepare? Here are a few topics we believe are essential.

Business Value

The potential of generative AI is incredibly exciting, with a forecasted $7 trillion increase in global GDP over the next ten years.[125] You can apply generative AI across all lines of business, including engineering, marketing, customer service, finance, and sales. Customer experience can be improved through capabilities such as chatbots, virtual assistants, intelligent contact centers, personalization, and content moderation. Employee productivity can be boosted with generative AI-powered conversational search, content creation, text summarization, and code generation. The same technology can turbocharge the production of all types of creative content, from art and music to text, images, animations, and video. Generative AI can improve business operations with intelligent document processing, maintenance assistants, quality control and visual inspection, and synthetic training data generation.

In Healthcare and Life Sciences (HCLS), one of the most promising use cases of generative AI is accelerating drug discovery and research by using models to create novel protein sequences with specific properties for designing antibodies, enzymes, vaccines, and gene therapy. HCLS companies can also use FMs to design synthetic gene sequences for synthetic biology and metabolic engineering applications, such as creating new biosynthetic pathways or optimizing gene expression for biomanufacturing purposes. They can also use FMs for agent-assist cases such as claims processing, document summarization, and personalized medical recommendations. FMs can also be used to create synthetic patient and healthcare data, which can be useful for simulating clinical trials or studying rare diseases without access to large real-world datasets.

Financial services companies can bring the power and cost-effectiveness of generative AI to serve their customers better while reducing costs. Conversational bots powered by FMs can improve customer service, gain customer loyalty, and ultimately boost profitability. Lending institutions can fast-track loan approvals for financially underserved markets. Investment firms can use the power of FMs to provide personalized financial advice to their clients at a low cost. One study estimates that these types of innovations could uplift banking productivity from $200B to $340B.[126]

In customer service integrating LLMs into a chatbot enables a meaningful conversation with a customer regardless of what they ask. It creates a more relevant experience and faster responses than many of the chatbots we've become used to. Combining AI tools like LLMs and voice technology like Amazon Polly and Amazon Comprehend enables a natural language conversation with a virtual call center agent, augmenting Amazon Connect capabilities. One company saw the application of generative AI improve issue resolution by 15 percent and reduce the time spent on issues and staff attrition. The previously intractable problem of Schedule Adherence (in real time) is now potentially alleviated!

AWS and Generative AI

AWS has been investing in and using FMs for several years in areas like search on Amazon.com and conversational experiences with Alexa. Since the launch of Amazon SageMaker in 2017, there has been a continual stream of ML and AI services broadening the reach of these tools to technologists and nontechnologists alike. Amazon Bedrock provides wide access to pretrained models. One of Amazon Bedrock's most important capabilities is how easy it makes customizing such a model. Customers simply point Amazon Bedrock at a few labeled examples in Amazon S3, and the service can fine-tune the model for a particular task without annotating large volumes of data (as few as twenty examples is enough).

Imagine a content marketing manager who works at a leading fashion retailer and needs to develop fresh, targeted ad campaign copy for an upcoming new line of handbags. They provide Amazon Bedrock with a few labeled examples of their best-performing taglines from past campaigns, along with the associated product descriptions. Amazon Bedrock makes a separate copy of the base FM accessible only to the user and trains this private copy of the model. After training, it automatically generates effective social media, display ads, and web copy for the new handbags. None of the company's data trains the original base models. Since all data is encrypted and secure in Amazon VPC, users can trust their data remains private and confidential.

Amazon SageMaker JumpStart is also available to get going quickly. It provides an ML hub where experts can discover, explore, and deploy pretrained, publicly available, and proprietary FMs. If you wish to create your own FMs, Amazon SageMaker provides managed infrastructure and tools to accelerate scalable, reliable, and secure model building, training, and deployment.

Amazon Bedrock and SageMaker JumpStart address the simple fact that one solution—or one model—is unlikely to solve every business problem you face. Contributing confidential data to public models can be costly, as some organizations have already learned.

Get Focused on Your Cloud Journey

Do you remember those TV programs you watched as children that warned "Don't try this at home"? We say, "Don't try this without the cloud." You want your teams focused on problem-solving and innovation, not on managing the underlying complexity and cost of enabling infrastructure and licenses. The cloud is the enabler for generative AI, making available cost-effective data lakes, sustainably provisioned GPUs and compute, high-speed networking, and consumption-based costing. Coupled with compute instances powered by AWS Trainium and AWS Inferentia chipsets to optimize model training and inferences, the cloud can provide lower costs, better performance, and an improved carbon footprint versus on-premises solutions (if the latter is even a realistic alternative).

Get Your Data Foundations Right—Now

The boldest house built on dodgy foundations will not last. The same is true in the world of ML. With generative AI, quality trumps the quantity of business data available.

While talking about technology debt is common, we must acknowledge that many organizations have unwittingly accumulated analogous debt with data. This typically stems from a lack of data quality, fragmented or siloed data sources, a lack of data literacy, inadequate upfront considerations of how data should be integrated into products, and a culture that talks about data but doesn't use it day-to-day. Now is the time to implement the fundamentals described in Chapter 6.1 Data and Data Mesh.

Think Beyond the Technology

The world of generative AI is incredibly exciting, but technology rarely operates in a vacuum. Face the law of unintended consequences. Start by considering your stance on ethics, transparency, data attribution, security, and privacy with AI. How can you ensure the technology is used accurately, fairly, and appropriately? Resources exist.[127] You can also read great books like Michael Kearns's *The Ethical Algorithm or our colleague Mark Schwartz's book Adaptive Ethics for Digital Transformation*, but these alone are insufficient. Do something! For example, prioritize diversity of skills and worldviews and ensure those engaged in creating and using models represent the diversity of your customers; this helps ensure relevance and the early identification of potential biases.

Train on these considerations, bake them into your governance and compliance frameworks, and even into your vendor selection processes to select partners who share your values.

Upskill Yourself and Your People

As discussed in Chapter 4.1 Becoming Cloud-Fluent at Scale, every revolution throughout history, whether agricultural, scientific, or industrial, has seen some skills become less valuable, and new skills emerge and be demanded. Agricultural employment in China went from 82 percent of all workers to 31 percent in just fifty years.[128] Many of us have jobs that didn't exist twenty years ago. Cloud architects, data scientists, and social media managers all resulted from new uses of technologies, whether due to efficiencies or the invention of new products, services, and industries. Those organizations that identified and invested in these skills early gained a sustainable advantage.

Creating momentum is critical. It provides the best opportunity to learn what works and what doesn't, to get people excited but also grounded in the technology, and to move the conversation from "what if" to "how." Finding one or two experiments you can run with generative AI aimed at meaningful business outcomes is the modern-day equivalent to Thomas Edison illuminating his first streetlamp, the spark that ignited a revolution.

AI simultaneously evokes excitement and concern. It opens a world of knowledge, innovation, and efficiency but leaves many wondering about the implications for their job security. The continued emergence of AI as a profoundly impactful tool requires considering which skills might be needed less in the future and which will be in demand. Consider the technical skills needed and how to infuse them into your organization. Programs like Machine Learning University can help, but it's important to think bigger. Skills like critical thinking and problem-solving will become even more vital. We ultimately want people, assisted by AI, to solve real business challenges and critically assess and question inferences from ML models. This is particularly important with generative

AI models that distill data rather than provide considered answers. Make the space to practice these skills incrementally and consistently eliminate low-value work—perhaps by using ML!

Start Considering Use Cases

We love the saying "Fall in love with the problem, not the solution." It reminds us that while technology is a brilliant enabler, it is just one more set of tools we can apply to real-world problems.

What time-consuming, difficult, or impossible problems could generative AI help solve? Where do you have data to help in this process? Think big about the opportunities, but start small with problems that cause day-to-day irritations, what we call "paper cuts." Can these annoyances be automated away, freeing up organizational time while improving comprehension of AI?

Developers can use Amazon Q Developer to understand generative AI's power in assisting productivity improvements while making suggestions for using unfamiliar APIs, coding more securely, and more. AWS's internal benchmarks show a remarkable 57 percent improvement in productivity while increasing the success rate of completed tasks. Amazon Q Developer is trained on billions of lines of code and can generate code suggestions ranging from snippets to full functions in real time based on your comments and existing code. It can flag or filter code suggestions that resemble open-source training data. It can identify an open-source project's repository URL and license so that you can more easily review them and add attributions. It can scan your code to detect hard-to-find vulnerabilities and get code suggestions to remediate them immediately. This is aligned with best practices for tackling security vulnerabilities, such as those outlined by Open Worldwide Application Security Project (OWASP), or those that don't meet crypto library and similar security best practices. Amazon Q Developer supports popular languages, including Python, Java, and JavaScript, and integrated development environments (IDEs), including VS Code, IntelliJ IDEA, AWS Cloud9, AWS Lambda console, JupyterLab, and Amazon SageMaker Studio. What a fantastic immediate opportunity to be a productivity hero in your organization!

Last, be excited but stay grounded. We're at an inflection point with LLMs. Sometimes it feels like the more we learn about AI, the less we know. Approach generative AI with an open, curious mind, but avoid the hype. Critically appraise what you read, and don't believe there will be a singular best model to adopt. The best approach, and one we're glad AWS has embraced with Amazon Bedrock, is recognizing that different FMs serve different needs. It democratizes access for all builders, allowing commercial and open-source FMs to be adopted. Those already experienced in AI will know this and recognize that the AWS cloud, which provides multiple models, offers a better approach than betting on a single model.

Call to Action

Step 1. Make it easy for your organization to achieve your goals by choosing the right tools and models for the job at hand. Amazon Bedrock is the easiest way to build and scale generative AI applications without worrying about the underlying infrastructure.

Step 2. Ensure you have the freedom to decide whether to build an FM or use a prebuilt one.

Step 3. Keep your data private. Organizations must ensure that generative AI services keep their data private and that they have control over who can access models. You don't want to train a publicly available model for your competitors!

Step 4. Keep it fast and cost-effective while keeping your energy footprint appropriate. This is critical whether you are running, building, or customizing models. It's one reason why AWS continues to invest in its own silicon. Between the AWS Inferentia chipsets for ML inferences and the AWS Trainium chipset for training models, the cost of ML has been reduced significantly. Inferentia can reduce the cost of inferences by up to 70 percent. As we will discuss later in Chapter 7.3 Sustainability in the Cloud, sustainability is an important boardroom topic and a critical advantage as organizations embed AI into their operations.

Final Thought

A responsible AI program must consider many attributes, almost all requiring human oversight, with AI augmenting human judgment and not replacing it. A good program goes beyond committee-based risk management by baking responsibility into your culture. Use teams with diverse backgrounds, perspectives, skills, and experiences when developing ML systems. We discussed the power of these diverse teams in organizing and delivering business value earlier, an approach AWS has used for years. AI adds urgency and dimension to this topic. If your team doesn't reflect your customer base across dimensions like gender, race, ethnicity, age, and politics, biases or toxic phrases will inevitably creep into the inferences your models make.

Center your focus on metrics that matter to your overall business strategy, maximizing the value you can deliver, not just looking at costs you can cut. A few simple ideas can start your journey of discovery. Let your developers get familiar with Amazon Q Developer. Look at how chatbots, easier access to information, or other means of automated customer engagement and recovery can be brought to life with generative AI. Or consider how an LLM trained on the information available on your intranet makes it easier to create value.

PART VII

SECURITY AND GOVERNANCE

7.1 Security Is Always Job Zero

There's so much security built into cloud computing platforms today, for us, it's our No. 1 priority—it's not even close, relative to anything else.

—ANDY JASSY

In the piece that follows, Thomas tells the story of Experian's migration to the cloud when he served as VP of emerging technologies:

When we first explored migrating to the cloud in 2014, I thought the biggest hurdle to overcome would be the executive team's natural concerns around security and compliance. At the time, there was a widespread belief among executives that Experian could never go to the cloud because of security concerns. Nevertheless, we decided to push on because we knew going to the cloud would enable our business to become nimble and fast.

Before submitting our proposal to the executive leaders and then to the funding committee, we wanted to get buy-in from our global CISO. When we met, he shared his concerns about cloud security and expressed doubt whether this was the right thing to do. I wasn't surprised by this response; in fact, I would have been surprised if he had not shared these concerns, but I was prepared to address them.

I asked him if better security might look like having more standardized hardened components and systems. I wanted to know if being able to lock down access to systems by role with a detailed audit trail might be of interest. I asked him if he thought it would be beneficial to have the ability to conduct a system audit more than once per year without incurring the ire of IT operations. I asked him how much time it took to examine and approve requests for innovation and new product ideas and whether he would like to have a way to preapprove reusable core infrastructure and software components that would allow his team to focus only on the truly novel elements of any new system. I told him that we had an opportunity to bring security thinking as a practice directly into the development teams—to create a stronger culture of security within IT.

Those are the kinds of things security professionals have wanted for a long time. They don't relish the idea of starting with "no," of being a wet blanket on innovation, or of being perceived as the brakes on the business. They also don't want to heedlessly give approvals, knowing that the security of their business, their customer and corporate data, and their personal reputation could be compromised by one careless oversight.

So I told him we could create such a future together. I asked for and received his support to start with a smallish project with his team, which was deeply involved from the beginning. I promised we would bring in world-class experts to validate our architecture and increase the number of scheduled penetration tests with an outside firm. He asked that we help create a cross-reference document to map and compare traditional security controls against new cloud-based security controls and mitigation measures.

And so our journey began. Along the way we learned that security is a shared responsibility between the customer and AWS. We learned that leveraging security capabilities offered by AWS required thoughtful architectures, and we learned that our security posture could be improved when compared to some of our established systems. Above all we learned that security doesn't have to be difficult to implement. In fact by using the tooling AWS provides, we were able to enhance security and simplify our operations. Ultimately, we were much better able to ensure the information security triad of confidentiality, integrity, and availability.

Confidentiality

In information security, confidentiality "is the property that information is not made available or disclosed to unauthorized individuals, entities, or processes."[129] This is not the same thing as privacy, although confidentiality is a prerequisite for privacy since privacy expectations, by definition, cannot be met by a system that fails to meet confidentiality requirements.

Integrity

In information security, data integrity means maintaining and assuring the accuracy and completeness of data over its entire lifecycle.[130] This means that data cannot be corrupted or accidentally deleted and cannot be modified in an unauthorized or undetected manner.

Availability

For any information system to serve its purpose, the information must be available when it is needed. Ensuring availability involves using systems resilient to unforeseen events like natural disasters that scale to meet the demands of an unexpectedly successful marketing campaign or survive denial-of-service attacks, to name just a few examples from our own experience. We've already discussed availability in Chapter 5.3 Resilience and Reliability.

AWS considers information security—not just confidentiality but also integrity and availability—as its "job zero" (a reference to developers' penchant for starting any count from *zero,* not *one.*) Security is AWS's absolute top priority. In our experience security testing and validation at most organizations is done at the end of the implementation, or very late in the lifecycle of any new initiative—as if security were this annoying and unwanted thing that one has to grudgingly deal with or something you could bolt on at the end, some kind of hardened wrapper around soft and smushy application code.

Many organizations conduct security reviews and security testing toward the end of the software development lifecycle. Many of you who read this recognize the uncomfortable moment when security audits reveal a flaw, and you have to decide whether to postpone the release or formally accept the risk in your risk register to launch on time. If you choose the latter, your very next release will likely need to contain the fix for the discovered flaw. Either way you are forced to slow down the business. Security is often seen as a necessary evil to be endured and resolved with the least effort and cost at the last (responsible) moment.

Contrast this with Otto Versand CISO Ralf Kleinfeld's conversational comment to Thomas that security is a business driver for Otto! Or the idea that security is a measure of quality! Everything should start with security, just as much as cost, performance, features, and other core design elements. New services must pass through well-defined quality gates—including security elements—not just once, but from inception and forever more, using automated security tests whenever *any* change is made.

While constantly passing through the right security gates, development can and should go very, very fast through the use of guardrails. Guardrails greatly simplify software development *and* provide automated tools to enable security by design and from the ground up.

AWS Well-Architected Framework Security Pillar

As discussed in Chapter 5.6 Leveraging the AWS Well-Architected Framework, the Well-Architected Framework helps you understand trade-offs for decisions you make while building workloads on AWS. The Security Pillar describes how to take advantage of cloud technologies to protect data, systems, and assets in a way that can improve your security posture. The paper provides in-depth best practice guidance for architecting secure workloads on AWS. We strongly encourage you to read and review the in-depth Security Pillar.[131] The paper goes deep into the seven areas that security in the cloud is composed of:

- Security foundations
- Identity and access management
- Detection
- Infrastructure protection
- Data protection
- Incident response
- Application security

For this book's scope, we focus on three areas from the paper: design principles, the Shared Responsibility Model, and governance.

Design Principles

In the cloud there are a number of principles that can help you strengthen your workload security:

Implement a strong identity foundation. Implement the principle of least privilege and enforce separation of duties with appropriate authorization for each interaction with your AWS resources. Centralize identity management and aim to eliminate reliance on long-term static credentials.

Maintain traceability: Monitor, alert, and audit actions and changes to your environment in real time. Integrate log and metric collection with systems to automatically investigate and take action.

Apply security at all layers: Apply a defense-in-depth approach with multiple security controls. Apply to all layers (e.g., edge of network, VPC, load balancing, every instance and compute service, OS, application, and code).

Automate security best practices. Automated software-based security mechanisms improve your ability to securely scale more rapidly and cost-effectively. Create secure architectures, including the implementation of controls that are defined and managed as code in version-controlled templates.

Protect data in transit and at rest. Classify your data into sensitivity levels and use mechanisms, such as encryption, tokenization, and access control where appropriate.

Keep people away from data. Use mechanisms and tools to reduce or eliminate the need for direct access or manual data processing. This reduces the risk of mishandling, modification, and human error when handling sensitive data.

Prepare for security events. Prepare for an incident by having incident management and investigation policies and processes that align with your organizational requirements. Run incident response simulations and use tools with automation to increase your speed for detection, investigation, and recovery.

Shared Responsibility

Security and Compliance is a shared responsibility between AWS and the customer. This shared model can help relieve the customer's operational burden as AWS operates, manages, and controls the components from the host OS and virtualization layer down to the physical security of the facilities where the service operates. The customer assumes responsibility for and management of the guest OS (including updates and security patches) and other associated application software in addition to the configuration of the AWS-provided security group firewall. AWS customers should carefully consider the services they choose as their responsibilities vary depending on the services used, the integration of those services into their IT environment, and applicable laws and regulations. The nature of this shared responsibility also provides the flexibility and customer control that permits deployment. As shown in Figure 24, this differentiation of responsibility is commonly referred to as Security "of" the Cloud versus Security "in" the Cloud.

AWS responsibility: "Security of the Cloud." AWS is responsible for protecting the infrastructure that runs all the services offered in the AWS Cloud. This infrastructure is composed of the hardware, software, networking, and facilities that run AWS Cloud services.

Customer responsibility: "Security in the Cloud." Customer responsibility is determined by the AWS Cloud services that a customer selects. This determines the amount of configuration work the customer must perform as part of their security responsibilities. For example, a service such as Amazon EC2 is categorized as Infrastructure as a Service (IaaS) and, as such, requires the customer to perform all of the necessary security configuration and management tasks. Customers that deploy an Amazon EC2 instance are responsible for managing the guest OS (including updates and security patches), any application software or utilities installed by the customer on the instances, and the configuration of the AWS-provided firewall (called a security group) on each instance. For abstracted services, such as Amazon S3 and Amazon DynamoDB, AWS operates the infrastructure layer, the OS, and platforms, and customers access the endpoints to store and retrieve data. AWS customers are responsible for managing their data (including encryption options), classifying their assets, and using IAM tools to apply the appropriate permissions.

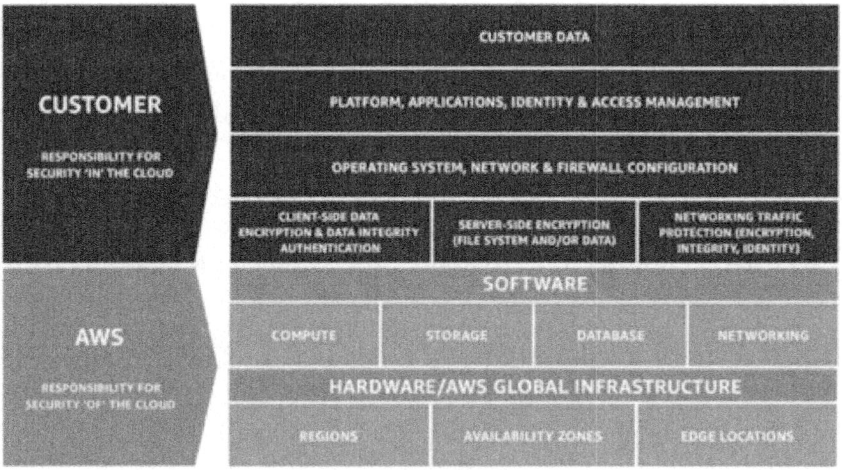

Figure 24 AWS Shared Responsibility Model

The Shared Responsibility Model also extends to IT controls. Just as AWS and its customers share the responsibility to operate the IT environment, they also share the responsibilities to manage, operate, and verify IT controls. AWS can help relieve the customer burden of operating controls by managing those controls associated with the physical infrastructure deployed in the AWS environment that the customer may have previously managed. As every customer is deployed differently in AWS, they can take advantage of shifting management of certain IT controls to AWS, which results in a (new) distributed control environment. Customers can then use the AWS control and compliance documentation available to them to perform their control evaluation and verification procedures as required. The following are examples of controls that are managed by AWS, AWS customers, or both:

Inherited controls. Controls that a customer fully inherits from AWS. Examples include physical and environmental controls.

Shared controls. Controls that apply to both the infrastructure layer and customer layers but in separate contexts or perspectives. In a shared control, AWS provides the requirements for the infrastructure, and the customer must provide their own control implementation within their use of AWS services. Examples include:

- Patch management: AWS is responsible for patching and fixing flaws within the infrastructure, but customers are responsible for patching their guest OS and applications.
- Configuration management: AWS maintains the configuration of its infrastructure devices, but customers are responsible for configuring their own guest OSs, databases, and applications.
- Awareness and training: AWS trains AWS employees, but customers must train their own employees.

Customer Specific. Controls that are solely the responsibility of the customer based on the application they are deploying within AWS services. Examples include service and communications protection or zone security, which might require AWS customers to route or zone data within specific security environments.

Governance

As a subset of the overall approach, security governance is meant to support business objectives by defining policies and control objectives to help manage risk. Achieve risk management by following a layered approach to security control objectives—each layer builds upon the previous one. Understanding the AWS Shared Responsibility Model is your foundational layer. This knowledge provides clarity on what you are responsible for on the customer side and what you inherit from AWS. A beneficial resource is AWS Artifact, which gives you on-demand access to AWS' security and compliance reports and select online agreements.

Meet most of your control objectives at the next layer. This is where the platform-wide capability lives. For example, this layer includes the AWS account vending process, integration with an identity provider such as AWS IAM Identity Center, and the common detective controls. Some of the output of the platform governance process is here too. When you want to start using a new AWS service, update service control policies (SCPs) in the AWS Organizations service to provide the guardrails for the initial use of the service. You can use other SCPs to implement common security control objectives, often referred to as security invariants. These are control objectives or configurations that you apply to multiple accounts, organization units, or the whole AWS organization. Typical examples are limiting the Regions that infrastructure runs in or preventing the deactivation of detective controls. This middle layer also contains codified policies such as config rules or checks in pipelines.

The top layer is where the product teams meet control objectives. This is because the implementation is done in the applications that the product teams control. For example, they could implement input validation in an application or ensure that identity passes between microservices correctly. Even though the product team owns the configuration, they can still inherit some capability from the middle layer.

Wherever you implement the control, the goal is the same: manage risk. A range of risk management frameworks apply to specific industries, regions, or technologies. Your main objective is to highlight the risk based on likelihood and consequence. This is the inherent risk. You can then define a control objective that reduces the likelihood, consequence, or both. Then with a control in place, you can see what the resulting risk is likely to be. This is the residual risk. Control objectives can apply to one or many workloads. The following diagram shows a typical risk matrix. The likelihood is based on the frequency of previous occurrences, and the consequence is based on the financial, reputational, and time cost of the event.

Likelihood	Risk Level				
Very Likely	Low	Medium	High	Critical	Critical
Likely	Low	Medium	Medium	High	Critical
Possible	Low	Low	Medium	Medium	High
Unlikely	Low	Low	Medium	Medium	High
Very unlikely	Low	Low		Medium	High
Consequence	Minimal	Low	Medium	High	Severe

Figure 25 Risk assessment matrix

Best Practice Areas

In the cloud there are a number of principles that can help you strengthen your system security. These principles have been well-understood in theory for many decades but were difficult to consistently implement without severely curtailing business agility in practice. AWS rigorously implements these and other security principles and thus ensures the *security of the cloud*, removing a very large burden from organizations that can instead focus their security resources on *security in the cloud*. In this shared security model, organizations can finally focus on data and application security, knowing that AWS secures the components "of the cloud."

AWS is improving the security of the cloud and advancing the field of cybersecurity by developing *automated reasoning* to create and check mathematical proofs of the correctness of systems. What is automated reasoning, you ask? It's a formal verification method that automatically generates and checks mathematical proofs, which help to prove the correctness of systems—i.e., fancy math that proves things work as expected. If you want a deeper understanding of automated reasoning, check out the re:Invent session.[132]

Culture

Throughout this book we have talked about the importance of culture and organization. Security culture is not an exception. In 2019 Thomas sat in a meeting next to Stephen Schmidt, at that time the AWS CISO (now Amazon's Chief Security Officer), as he explained one of the many ways AWS maintains security as the top priority of the business. Stephan explained that in most organizations, the CISO reports to the CIO; sometimes they report to the head of risk or the COO, but they rarely report directly to the CEO, as Stephen does. Andy Jassy convened a weekly security review with the AWS CISO, reviewing the current status across all services. Leaders (with the engineering resources) are accountable for resolving any open issues and must adhere to strict timelines for resolution.

Stephen holds routine cloud service security review meetings with all service team owners, akin to product owners with P&L responsibility. New services do not launch if there are any known security issues. Stephen has the authority to bring all resources to bear to harden AWS against new threats immediately, as was done when we were both thinking about becoming customers in 2014. The Heartbleed bug, a vulnerability of OpenSSL that could compromise TLS/SSL (and thus one of the very pillars of security on the internet), was discovered that year. AWS security engineers patched all vulnerable systems within hours of the Heartbleed bug's announcement without disrupting AWS customers!

That wasn't all they did. They began developing a new SSL implementation to address other inherent problems of OpenSSL, and in 2015 publicly released s2n.[133] This was a complete rewrite of the library that implements the TLS protocol with approximately six thousand lines of code compared to OpenSSL's approximately five hundred thousand lines. Interestingly the lines of *test* code for s2n exceed the implementation code by about ten to one! Formal verification tests for the correctness of key algorithms provided by AWS's Automated Reasoning Group are built into the automated build and integration process for s2n. Any code changes that cause the formal proofs to break are automatically rejected.

AWS also contributed back to the open-source implementations of TLS (BoringSSL and LibreSSL, both forks of OpenSSL) to assist in improving the underlying security of the internet.

In addition to making security a leadership priority, adopting the cloud is an opportunity to create a security-conscious culture throughout your organization. Developers can use automated testing—often provided by the security team—to continuously look for security defects and vulnerabilities. If such a defect is discovered, we recommend you give the developer the authority to pull the Andon cord and prevent this defect from finding its way into production. The repair cost is the lowest at this early stage, thus making it a wise upfront investment.

Training at least one engineer in every team to be a security expert (with a direct line of communication to the security team) is another good investment, as they can proactively improve the team's code, architecture, and security skills. At AWS, we do this via our Security Guardians program. Software security also benefits from peer review, as we discussed in the context of software quality and resiliency. We and AWS believe security is everyone's responsibility. At AWS everyone is expected to report security issues and be empowered to escalate security issues to the highest levels if necessary.

For decades leaders have striven to enable a culture of security—we are only as strong as our weakest link in this regard. Security will always be job zero and the area of highest investment at AWS. We do not hesitate to move engineers from new feature development to security development if we aren't satisfied with where it needs to be.

7.2 Governance, Risk Management, and Compliance

We have to conduct ourselves so when we are scrutinized, we pass with flying colors.

—JEFF BEZOS

Internal controls have existed from ancient times. In Ptolemaic Egypt, from 323 BCE to 31 BCE, there was a dual administration, with one set of bureaucrats charged with collecting taxes and another with supervising them. Internal controls are not new—they have had different names and drivers over the years.

Fast forward a few millennia.

The term *corporate governance* originated in 1960 with Richard Eells, an authority on corporate philanthropy, to denote "the structure and functioning of the corporate polity." The concept of corporate government has been around even longer, appearing in finance textbooks since the beginning of the 1900s.

Due to questionable corporate campaign practices in the mid-1970s, the US Securities and Exchange Commission (SEC) and the US Congress enacted campaign finance law reforms. In response to foreign corrupt practices, they enacted the 1977 Foreign Corrupt Practices Act (FCPA), which criminalized transnational bribery and required companies to implement internal control programs.[134] The Treadway Commission—a private sector initiative—was formed in 1985 to inspect, analyze, and make recommendations on fraudulent corporate financial reporting. As a result of their initial report, the Committee of Sponsoring Organizations (COSO) was formed.

In September 1992, COSO released the four-volume report *Internal Control-Integrated Framework*, which was later republished with minor amendments in 1994. This report presented a common definition of internal control and provided a framework against which internal control systems may be assessed and improved. It is one standard that US companies use to evaluate their compliance with the FCPA.

During this same period, concern was raised about the money spent on IT and the lack of perceived value actually received. (Erik Brynjolfsson's 1993 article "The Productivity Paradox of Information Technology: Review and Assessment" offers an interesting glimpse into the past.)[135] In a subsequent effort to bridge this gap, IT governance was born in 1993 from the concept of corporate governance—focusing on the intersection of business goals, strategic objectives, and IT management of an organization.

Regulated oversight became far more intensive during the early 2000s following a period of corporate failures at two large conglomerates. This led to the passage of the Sarbanes-Oxley Act. In February 2002 the term "governance, risk management, and compliance" (GRC) was popularized by Michael Rasmussen while at Forrester Research. According to Rasmussen, GRC is:

> "A capability to reliably achieve objectives while addressing uncertainty and acting with integrity…The reliable achievement of objectives is the governance piece, addressing uncertainty is about risk management, and acting with integrity is the compliance angle. All three of these provide a natural flow. Governance provides direction and objectives giving the context for risk management. Risk management in turn aims to comprehend uncertainty and set boundaries which then relies on compliance to ensure that we stay within those boundaries."[136]

According to a 2006 poll by *CFO,* 82 percent of respondents claimed they used COSO's framework for internal controls.[137] Other frameworks used by respondents included COBIT,[138] AS2 (Auditing Standard No. 2, PCAOB),[139] and SAS 55/78 (AICPA).[140]

We see AWS customers use both COSO and COBIT, as we did when we were customers. (See RiskOptics's article "What Are The Differences Between COBIT & COSO" for more info).[141]

COSO only responds to controls related to fiduciary duty. Primarily designed to enable Sarbanes-Oxley (SOX) 404 requirements, COSO limits itself to a certain area of an organization's IT environment. Meanwhile COBIT 5 extends beyond financial reporting to the whole environment. The two complement each other as well as the overarching GRC program.

Okay, let's reset for a moment.

While we hope that everyone appreciates a brief historical overview of primarily US corporate governance and the seriousness with which we all take it, diving deep into modern business governance is beyond the scope of this book. GRC frameworks can provoke as much debate as the three-letter term itself.

In the modern era of cloud adoption, regulated and well-managed companies utilize three main frameworks as the broad structure to govern their operations: COSO, COBIT, and the relatively newer NIST Cybersecurity Framework. The first two derive from accounting and auditing standards and the adoption of technology controls as they developed. The NIST Cybersecurity Framework focuses on the fact that every IT control is related to the secure operations in both public institutions and commercial enterprises. An overarching governance program should consider this: All three frameworks can help organizations systematize their structured approach to GRC in the cloud. Each should be evaluated to determine the best fit for the organization's objectives as it begins to utilize the cloud as part of its journey.

IT Governance, Risk Management, and Compliance

PwC identifies IT GRC objectives as follows:

> "Combining disciplines for better enterprise security. Adopting a unified IT governance, risk management, and compliance (IT GRC) approach, and managing the associated activities coherently will create efficiencies, provide a holistic view of the IT environment, and ensure accountability. Through evolution, we now find GRC programs are well established within modern enterprises."[142]

The decision-making, resource-and-portfolio management, risk management, and regulatory compliance functions included in a GRC framework aren't effective unless the organization's executive leadership is involved and supportive. (That's why we went into such detail in Chapter 3.4 Leveraging the Leadership Team.) The leadership team's early engagement and approval are crucial for any amendments to an organization's standards and policies to ensure effective and secure use of the AWS Cloud. Subsequent effective engagement with the CCoE—and eventually the CBO, when it's formed—can provide part of an inclusive oversight and engagement mechanism should holistic amendments be required.

GRC programs are sometimes looked upon as the bureaucracy getting in the way of exciting work. But a good GRC program establishes the foundation of the business's objectives. It is the proactive approach to cloud adoption that, if done well, minimizes a failure of operational controls. You always want to mitigate that unwanted 3:00 a.m. call.

Although governance, risk management, and compliance are often viewed as separate functions, they have a symbiotic relationship. Governance establishes the strategy and guardrails for meeting specific requirements that align and support the business. Risk management connects specific controls to governance and assessed risks and provides business leaders with the information they need to prioritize resources and make risk-informed decisions. Compliance is the adherence and monitoring of controls to specific governance requirements. It is also the ante required to play the game in certain industries, and with continuous monitoring, it closes the feedback loop regarding effective governance. Security architecture, engineering, and operations are built upon the GRC foundation.

For example, when forced to make investment tradeoffs and progress, does a CISO invest in a large access management practice or improve application security across their enterprise? GRC would guide this in terms of relative priority and level of investment.

Consistently agreed-upon and well-constructed principles, as discussed throughout this book, are a great mechanism for holding employees accountable to standards. Establishing a consistent set of rules and processes that all teams have to follow creates sameness across the control framework, allowing for the consistent automation of compliance evidence.

GRC requirements are key to evaluating which applications can be moved to the cloud without creating exceptions to standards and which must be redesigned to meet the control consistency that the cloud can bring.

Based on our own journeys and experience working with many AWS customers, leaders moving to the cloud often request a breakdown of each GRC element and what they should review. The following list is not exhaustive, nor will all of it apply to everyone. But it can provide you with a solid foundation to start. The key takeaways are: base governance on objectives and capabilities, include risk context in decision-making, and automate monitoring and response.

Governance

Identify Compliance Requirements

- Identify and be aware of required compliance frameworks (such as HIPAA or PCI) and any contract and agreement obligations; ensure an approach to compliance is established.
- Identify any restrictions or limitations to cloud adoption or emerging technologies. For example, is there a local regulatory or legal consideration to be taken into account?

- Identify required or chosen audit standards to implement (e.g., COSO or COBIT).

Conduct Program Assessment

- Conduct a program assessment based on industry processes such as the NIST Cyber Security Framework or ISO/IEC TR 27103:2018 to understand the capability and maturity of your current profile.[143]
- Determine the desired end-state capability and maturity—also known as a *target profile*—and ensure overall portfolio management provides a mechanism to manage desired business outcomes and track and report success.
- Document and prioritize gaps (people, processes, and technologies) for resource allocation.
- Establish a CCoE, as covered in Chapter 3.5 The Cloud Center of Excellence.
- Draft and publish a cloud strategy alongside your communications plan.
- Define and assign functions, roles, and responsibilities across the entire organization. It is critical that everyone from the development teams to internal auditors be included in developing the responsibilities required for the cloud journey.
- Ensure effective program and project management that helps you manage technology projects using methodologies that take advantage of the agility and cost-management benefits inherent to cloud services.

Update and Publish Policies, Processes, and Procedures

- Develop the overall strategy for the documentation you will use to manage your migration to the cloud. (See Chapter 5.4 Completing a Large-Scale Migration and Modernization.)

- Determine if you will add the cloud to your current documentation profiles or develop new documents that better meet the faster pace of change in the cloud. Policies, usually approved at the C-suite or board level, cannot evolve as quickly as lower-level documents, so they need to contain control elements that won't change frequently.
- The common flow of corporate governance for the cloud is usually (1) risk profile, (2) policy, (3) standard, (4) procedure, and (5) runbooks.
- Develop a cloud control framework with clear differentiation between control objectives, control implementations, and control testing. This framework will become the baseline for automation—both implementation and monitoring—and help the first, second, and third lines of defense in a regulated institution understand where their needs are met.
- In regulated entities, "lines of defense" typically oversee risk management. "In the Three Lines of Defense model, management control is the first line of defense in risk management, the various risk control and compliance oversight functions established by management are the second line of defense, and independent assurance is the third."[144]
- Update procedures to integrate cloud services and other emerging technologies. This is commonly referred to as a service adoption framework, and it creates a well-understood process to approve new service usage while defining all the necessary controls for the service across the company. A cross-functional team representing all relevant departments with control requirements that need to be met does this. At scale this is a dedicated process that enables innovation rather than slows it down.
- Establish technical governance principles that map to your overall GRC objectives.

Risk Management

*Conduct a Risk Assessment**

In our experience as leaders, the ability to make balanced, risk-based decisions thoughtfully—considering the impact, probability, and judgment to then reject, accept, or mitigate a perceived risk—is fundamental to the success of any transformation. Leaders viscerally connected to the daily standup or progress meeting establish a risk decisioning cadence to maintain progress. Areas for the leaders to consider include:

- Conducting or updating an organizational risk assessment (e.g., market, financial, reputation, legal, etc.).
- Conducting or updating a risk assessment for each business line (e.g., mission, market, products/services, financial, etc.).
- Conducting or updating a risk assessment for each asset type. This can be for the data and application types you plan to move to the cloud. This should also be done repetitively as your application portfolio in the cloud grows.
- Conducting a risk assessment for the overall utilization of cloud-based technologies to fulfill previous on-premise requirements. Cloud service providers have unique ways of delivering services, and that model must be evaluated as it changes the norms of current procurement, operational, and security models.

* Using preestablished threat models can simplify both the initial and updated risk assessment processes. However, the risk plan must incorporate feedback from all across the company; no one should be left out of the process. Everyone's voice must be heard for it to be a complete process.

Draft Risk Plans

- Conduct cross-functional reviews of all risks and develop the appropriate stance to accept, mitigate, or transfer them. Some initial risks can be retired after the team determines they are not relevant, but all documentation should be kept to demonstrate there were no biases to exclude anything from the process.

- Implement plans to mitigate, avoid, transfer, or accept risk at each tier, business line, and asset (e.g., a business continuity plan, a continuity of operations plan, and a systems security plan).
- Implement plans to mitigate any specific risk areas (such as supply chain risk or insider threat). For example, are you going to implement a two-person rule for all production changes? Or are you going to utilize a security red team to assess organizational security, often unbeknownst to client staff?
- Develop a more frequent and iterative risk review process than traditional annual reviews. Technology changes regularly, so new risks need to be developed. Mitigation plans can change with the advent of new services or features that implement compensating controls.

Authorize Systems

- Evaluate using the NIST Risk Management Framework (RMF) or other processes to authorize and track systems.
- Evaluate using NIST Special Publication 800-53 ISO ISO/IEC 27002:2013 or other control set to select, implement, and assess controls based on risk.[145]
- Implement continuous monitoring of controls and risk, employing automation to the greatest extent possible.
- Incorporate risk information into decisions.
- Link system risk to business and organizational risk.
- Automate translation of continuous system risk monitoring and status to business and organizational risk.
- Incorporate "What's the risk?" (financial, cyber, legal, reputation) into leadership decision-making.

- Be sure to carefully evaluate the risk of doing nothing into your overall decisions. In many cases the benefits of the cloud effectively mitigate or remove existing risks related to incumbent on-premises technology.

Compliance

Monitor Compliance with Policy, Standards, and Security Controls

- Automate technical control monitoring and reporting.
- Automate the workflow and validation of manual control monitoring so it can be measured with the same tooling used for automated controls. This creates a single view of your cloud control framework that is much easier to track.
- Implement manual monitoring of nontechnical controls that can't be tracked in automation (e.g., periodic review of visitor logs) and reserve special attention for any nonautomated technical controls you may have put in place.
- Evaluate the utilization of new cloud-based continuous compliance tooling that provides all lines of defense with real-time views into the status of the cloud environment to provide transparency.
- Link compliance monitoring with security information and event management (SIEM) and other tools utilized by control owners so there are no gaps in knowledge about the environment's status.

Continually Self-Assess

- Automate application security testing and vulnerability scans.
- Continuously review testing and models to keep up to date with changes to the threat landscape.
- Conduct periodic self-assessments based on sampling of controls, the entire functional area, and pen tests.

- Develop testing plans for the automation you rely on to protect your cloud environment.
- Be self-critical of assumptions, perspectives, and artifacts.
- Develop a process for conducting more frequent reviews of cloud service changes and improvements to incorporate new functionality into current control implementations.

Respond to Events and Changes to Risk

- Integrate security operations with the compliance team for response management to ensure security events don't impact control effectiveness.
- Establish standard operating procedures to respond to unintentional changes in controls.
- Mitigate impact and reset affected controls; automate as much as possible.
- Communicate events and changes to risk.
- Establish a reporting structure and thresholds for each type of incident or control deviation.
- Include general counsel in reporting.
- Ensure applicable regulatory authorities and identified stakeholders are notified when required.
- Automate where appropriate.
- Conduct regular incident management drills across the company's nontechnical aspects so teams can rely on experience when managing an event.

Going Global

One of the frequent questions we receive in our travels is, "What should the governance organizational model look like in truly large or global enterprises?" In Part 3 we discussed the CLT, CCoE, and CBO. Clearly defining these functions in an enterprise aids the establishment of your security and governance objectives. But what should you do with global or group companies? It's actually very straightforward—you establish a central CLT, CCoE, and CBO.

Each subdivision or group's single-threaded leader should have mirrored versions of this three-part structure; these single-threaded leaders (often CTO or CIO) should report back to the central CLT as required for holistic governance. Then you can choose to centralize or federate different elements of your governance framework. For example, you may choose to negotiate pricing and any contractual agreements you may enter with AWS at the central CLT level. But each division's use of the cloud can differ based on its needs.

Diving a Little Deeper

In July 2021 COSO published the guide *Enterprise Risk Management for Cloud Computing.* For those institutions using the COSO framework, this is the go-to starting place for your risk and audit functions to review when moving to the cloud.

Penultimate Thought

GRC can appear daunting to leaders who recognize the benefits of the AWS Cloud but know they need to be thoughtful about the governance adjustments they want to make when moving to the cloud.

While many organizations tend to focus on the economics or security of cloud adoption, it's critical to understand the entire GRC framework for a more holistic approach to well-managed migrations.

Failing to include the critical areas of a broader GRC framework in your initial plans will create a much slower migration path. You'll miss the opportunities to build GRC capabilities directly into your technical designs from the beginning of your program.

The most significant challenge for most organizations is admitting that they need to do things differently. No matter how well-managed you are outside of a cloud environment, the people, processes, and technology affected by your migration require an objective review of your current controls.

Enterprises need to properly consider their journey to the cloud within the concept of GRC. On the journey it is necessary to bring first-line leaders, risk leaders, and audit together—each should be aware of the others' needs regarding GRC.

Diving Even Deeper on Risk and Compliance

Many AWS customers want to dive deeper into this topic than what this chapter's space allows. We suggest having a look at the documents listed at the end of this chapter, as well as those in the bibliography, for a deeper review.

It doesn't have to be hard work, though. Going beyond the scope of this chapter, AWS Solutions Architects can offer practical advice regarding this topic. Working with AWS Professional Services or an AWS Partner, you can dive deeper and conduct an AWS CAF Governance session. This will provide you with a deeper review to ensure your cloud governance aligns with your overall corporate and technology governance targets.

For a more detailed description of risk and compliance in AWS, please see the "Amazon Web Services: Risk and Compliance" whitepaper.[146] For a more detailed description of AWS Compliance programs, please see the AWS Compliance page.[147] Thanks to Jonathan Jenkyn, Michael South, Mark Ryland, Bill Shinn, and John McDonald for some of their material and overall guidance on this chapter.

7.3 Sustainability in the Cloud

Surely we all have a responsibility to care for our blue planet.

—DAVID ATTENBOROUGH

For the second edition of this book, we have added a chapter on sustainability to the security and governance section. Why this section, you may ask? Because sustainability needs to become as normalized as security—everything you do has a sustainability trade-off. Sustainability is also a governance concern; reporting requirements are as stringent as financial disclosure requirements. EU Parliament has said, "Financial and sustainability reporting will be on an equal footing, and investors will have comparable and reliable data."[148]

What do we mean by *sustainability*? We use the UN definition: "Sustainable development meets the needs of the present without compromising the ability of future generations to meet their own needs."[149] Simple and compelling.

Thomas studied environmental studies and economic development in the 80s—too early, it turns out. For the first time in 2022, sustainability catapulted into the top ten concerns of CEOs; it's expected to become a top three concern in the near future.[150] The science is clear, and the evidence is mounting: we are responsible for climate change. In fact, "the annual rate of increase in atmospheric carbon dioxide over the past 60 years is about 100 times faster than previous natural increases, such as those that occurred at the end of the last ice age 11,000-17,000 years ago."[151] We have added more than 50 percent of carbon dioxide to the historical average of 280 ppm during the last ten thousand years— as of April 2023, the amount has reached 422 ppm. The question is no longer "Is climate change real?" The question is "What can we do about it?"

Per the *IPCC Sixth Assessment Report, 2023*:

> "Human activities, principally through emissions of greenhouse gases, have unequivocally caused global warming, with global surface temperature reaching 1.1°C above 1850–1900 in 2011–2020. Global greenhouse gas emissions have continued to increase, with unequal historical and ongoing contributions arising from unsustainable energy use, land use and land-use change, lifestyles and patterns of consumption and production across regions, between and within countries, and among individuals (high confidence)."[152]

When discussing this topic with leaders, it is clear that sustainability has become a personal issue as well as a business issue. One leader told me he had been hiking in the hills overlooking Dublin with his ten-year-old son who asked him, "Dad, will Dublin be underwater soon?" How do you even answer this question? I looked it up, and found that the recent sea level rise in Dublin is faster than expected at approximately double the rate of global sea level rise with frequent coastal flooding increasingly likely.[153] By 2100—our grandchildren's lifetimes—up to 410 million people could be at risk of experiencing coastal flooding.[154]

We don't have to wait for our grandchildren to experience this impact; climate change is already upon us. Lakes store 87 percent of Earth's liquid surface fresh water. An analysis of the world's 1,972 largest global lakes using three decades of satellite observations, climate data, and hydrologic models, demonstrates statistically significant storage declines for 53 percent of these water bodies from 1992–2020.[155] The last eight years were the warmest on record.[156] We're becoming accustomed to daily news reports about floods in Italy, droughts in Southern France, fires in California and Australia, heat waves in India, climate refugees from flooded Bangladesh, and the Sahel's desertification.

So what has the impact been in numbers?

Between 1970 and 2021, extreme weather, climate, and water-related events caused 11,778 reported disasters, resulting in just over two million deaths (90 percent in developing countries) and US$3.64 trillion in economic losses.[157] This is with only an average global temperature increase of one degree Celsius. We are on track to cross the one-and-a-half-degree Celsius threshold faster than expected, which will lead to increasingly catastrophic consequences.

The collective mismanagement of our natural resources stems from not properly accounting for "externalities," such as water, air, forests, and nature. The UK Government commissioned a report by academics led by Partha Dasgupta, Frank Ramsey Professor of Economics at the University of Cambridge and a fellow of St John's College, Cambridge. It is sobering reading:

> "Collectively, however, we have failed to manage our global portfolio of assets sustainably. Estimates show

> that between 1992 and 2014, produced capital per person doubled, and human capital per person increased by about 13% globally; but the stock of natural capital per person declined by nearly 40%. Accumulating produced and human capital at the expense of natural capital is what economic growth and development has come to mean for many people."[158]

Okay, now that everyone is thoroughly depressed, let's talk about what we can do. We are "realistic optimists" (As Winston Churchill said: "Never, never, never give up."), and we believe that technology is one of the most important tools for righting the ship. We also believe that sustainability has the potential to become the largest economic opportunity since the advent of the internet. Sustainability represents a twelve trillion dollar commercial and innovation opportunity by 2030.[159] Half of the innovations the world needs to transition to a net zero economy from 2030–2050 don't yet exist.[160] (The World Economic Forum defines net zero as "removing an equal amount of CO2 from the atmosphere as we release into it.")[161]

Amazon and AWS are doing the right things here. Amazon has committed to reaching the Paris Accord goal of net-zero carbon emissions by 2040, ten years ahead of the Paris Agreement. Amazon set a goal to become 100 percent powered by renewable energy by 2030 and has made such rapid progress that it will likely reach this goal by 2025. Amazon has invested in more than five hundred renewable energy projects. Once online, these will provide over 28 GW of renewable capacity to grids and generate more than 77,000 GWh of clean energy each year—the equivalent of powering twenty million homes in Europe.

AWS also has a goal to become water positive by 2030.[162] This means AWS will return more water to communities than it uses in direct operations. This will be accomplished by focusing relentlessly on the efficient use of water for cooling, including using AI to help optimize operations. Where possible, AWS doesn't use water for cooling at all. As of 2024 AWS has reached a water utilization efficiency (WUE) of 0.19 liters of water per kilowatt-hour of electricity used on average across AWS data centers! AWS invests in using sustainably sourced water, such as recycled water or rainwater harvesting. AWS is also developing ways to reuse water in local communities, such as providing recycled cooling water for farm irrigation. AWS also invests in water replenishment projects, restoring watersheds and bringing clean water, sanitation, and hygiene services to water-stressed communities.

AWS rated positive in Gartner's first-ever *Sustainability Assessment* in 2023, so leveraging its services is a good foundation for building your sustainability approach, or as AWS calls it, becoming "future fit."[163]

Becoming Future Fit

AWS Principal BDM of Sustainability Innovation and Transformation Hilary Tam developed the Future Fit Framework, which describes four levels of effort or complexity in sustainability. Level 1 addresses sustainable IT operations. Level 2 focuses on broad sustainable operations. Level 3 supports innovation for sustainability products, services, and business models. Level 4 includes efforts to squarely aim a business toward sustainability.

Any company's sustainability foundation is (surprise, surprise) data! Many companies still collect and report sustainability compliance data using spreadsheets and publish reports as PDFs. Here is the first opportunity to help. If you are an IT leader, you already know how to do this, so walk over to the office of the Chief Sustainability Officer or other responsible party and offer to automate their processes. If you don't want to build, many great companies, such as Persefoni or Altruistiq, offer solutions. You can track, measure, review, and forecast carbon emissions generated from your AWS usage using the Cost and Usage Report in the AWS Billing console.

Level 1

The fastest and most impactful way to decarbonize IT is migrating to the cloud if you have not already done so. We've discussed the benefits of migration earlier in the book, so now you can add sustainability to the beneficial impact ledger. AWS commissioned 451 Research, an S&P Global Market Intelligence company, to conduct a study; it found that AWS's infrastructure is 3.6 times more energy efficient than the median US enterprise data centers surveyed and up to 5 times more energy efficient than the average enterprise data center in Europe. 451 Research also found that AWS can lower customers' workload carbon footprints by nearly 80 percent compared to surveyed enterprise data centers and up to 96 percent once AWS is powered with 100 percent renewable energy. What does this mean in practical terms? According to 451 Research's calculations, by migrating the average 1 MW enterprise data center with 30 percent utilization to AWS, an organization can reduce its carbon emissions by 400 to 1000 MT per year!

Migrating what you have isn't good enough; you might migrate inefficiently designed systems or things you no longer need. So the second thing you can and should do is conduct a Well-Architected review (with or without a migration). In 2020 AWS added the Sustainability Pillar to the Well-Architected Framework, which focuses on environmental impacts, especially energy consumption and efficiency, since they are important levers to reduce resource usage.[164] The pillar describes typical trade-offs you may have to make to reach business outcomes. How much data do you need to store, and for how long? Do you need immediate access, or do you need to archive data for infrequent access? What about latency and response times? Do you need millisecond latency for every use case? Probably not. Even the choice of programming language has a measurable impact on resource usage. The most energy-efficient languages include C, Rust, Ada, and Java, while the least energy-efficient languages include PHP, Ruby, Python, and Perl.[165]

Level 2

IT operations typically don't generate most of a company's carbon footprint (exceptions include media or web-based content companies). L2 aims to reduce carbon footprint and energy requirement and optimize resource utilization. For example, the Içeçek Coca-Cola bottling plant in Turkey created a digital twin (a virtual representation of a system) of the plant, modeling the bottle-washing process from beginning to end.[166] Building the digital twin took eight weeks using AWS IoT SiteWise. The operator then simulated a variety of settings until they created an optimal configuration, which they implemented in the physical plant. The result? The process took four months and resulted in a 20 percent increase in annual energy savings, a 9 percent reduction in water consumption, and a thirty-four-day savings in processing time per year.

There are other things companies can do to optimize their operations, including finding and unlocking data to analyze, leveraging ML, implementing efficient building management systems, implementing an IoT strategy, and much more. Optimizing for environmental sustainability commonly goes hand in hand with cost reduction. No surprise since waste in any shape typically has a cost (remember the concept of Muda in the Toyota method? It was all about reducing waste!).[167]

AWS has created a set of modules called the Sustainability Insights Framework (SIF) that allows companies to quickly stitch together a solution to ingest data from multiple sources like your ERP, ERM, and utility data. This enables companies to conduct analyses to find optimization targets and report on this data in standard formats that can be included in your corporate sustainability report. In early 2023 AWS open-sourced this technology.[168] If you don't want to build your own solution, companies are beginning to offer COTS solutions using SIF or based on their own approaches.

Level 3

Level 3 aims at helping companies innovate in the sustainability sphere, using a combination of design thinking (AWS Working Backwards method) and cloud-enabled technology to invent sustainability solutions the world so desperately needs. Some analysts believe this space will be worth US$12 trillion (trillion!) in the coming years. Sustainability requires a massive global energy transformation that impacts everything we do: Companies need to invent and harness new forms of energy, such as small nuclear reactors, fusion, hydrogen, and more). A circular economy needs to be implemented, starting with reprocessing battery and e-waste minerals (rare Earth minerals, copper, gold, titanium, molybdenum, etc.) and machine and construction components and waste. Reuse and reprocess fabric instead of dumping mountains of clothing in the Atacama Desert in Chile and use agricultural waste and byproducts as raw materials or energy. Our current resource requirements are the equivalent of 1.6 Earths, so we need to get this right.[169]

ZeroNorth, a Danish technology company, provides ship captains with data to optimize routing, avoid storms, or navigate with the wind at the vessel's back to reduce fuel consumption.[170] Octopus Energy's Kraken Flex controls distributed energy assets with ML and AI, matching supply and demand designed to help the electricity grid deal with the natural volatility of renewable generation. Other companies are developing ways to leverage geospatial data from satellites to understand vegetation, water flow and availability, biodiversity across regions, soil health, and many other areas of nature-based solutions.

Level 4

Level 4 identifies and implements technology levers to help companies transform themselves into sustainable businesses. Mark Carney, governor of the Bank of Canada from 2008 to 2013 and governor of the Bank of England from 2013 to 2020, describes the source and remedy to our global management of the economy in his book *Values: An Economist's Guide to Everything That Matters.* He recommends a change (or remembrance) of values in economics, not just value (price) or what he calls "mission-oriented capitalism." Such change requires top-down leadership and bottom-up passion.

Some companies place sustainability or ESG at the core of their company mission. Signify (formerly Philips Lighting) is one such company and has placed sustainability and innovation at its core. It has been carbon neutral since 2020.[171] It will soon be a zero-waste company and has multiple ambitious goals aligned with the UN's Sustainable Development Goals (the 17 SDGs) as its strategic compass. Another example is Arup, whose stated aim is "to serve society and deliver meaningful work for a more sustainable development within the built environment."[172] Arup has committed to the 17 SGDs, prioritizing environmental regeneration, biodiversity, resource conservation, stable economic growth, and social value. We hope there will be many more companies embarking on this journey.

Emerging Topics

Biodiversity defines the richness of the natural world, including the number of species and the ecosystems in which they thrive. Loss of biodiversity is one external cost not currently captured in financial accounting methodologies. According to a Cambridge study, an estimated $44 trillion of annual economic output relies on nature.[173] Should these systems begin to fail, it would have catastrophic consequences for the global economy. The Taskforce on Nature-related Financial Disclosures (TNFD) is developing a market-led, science-based framework to enable companies and financial institutions to integrate nature into decision-making.[174] Companies are beginning to evaluate the materiality of biodiversity in their operations. Technology holds the key to making that happen, as well as understanding how to mitigate or adapt the impact on biodiversity. Tackling biodiversity loss is the next big challenge companies and governments will begin to tackle after getting a grip on carbon emissions.

The Natural History Museum (NHM) in London employs 350 scientists, one of the largest groups in the world studying and enabling research into the natural world. The NHM brings together a broad range of UK biodiversity and environmental data in one place to help these scientists build an understanding of the UK's biodiversity and environment, encourage more integrated cross-disciplinary research programs, and drive science-led nature recovery in urban spaces. The intention over time is to capture all UK biodiversity and environmental data and create a digital twin, a real-time virtual representation of the UK's biodiversity.

Final Thought

While sustainability has not traditionally been a focus for the business or IT, it is becoming an important driver and decision-making factor. Once you dive deeper into your IT and operations data, you will likely find opportunities to become more efficient while reducing carbon dioxide emissions. And while you're at it, ask yourself, "What am I leaving behind for my children and grandchildren?" Then look for ways you and your business are uniquely positioned to invent the future we need. It is the perfect problem to tackle: help the world and deliver better business outcomes simultaneously.

Call to Action

Step 1. Measure and understand your sustainability data.

Step 2. Analyze ways to optimize your operations.

Step 3. Implement the necessary changes (and rinse and repeat).

Step 4. Develop (or invent) business models, products, and services that meet the needs of the present without compromising the ability of future generations to meet their own needs.

7.4 The Multicloud Question

As Enterprise Strategists, we find multicloud topics come up in many discussions rife with confusion, false certainty, and tentativeness. Companies are bombarded with conflicting messaging; some urge them never to adopt a multicloud approach, while others insist they don't miss out because "everyone is switching to multicloud."

There are good reasons for either pursuing or avoiding multicloud strategies. This chapter focuses on eight proven practices for succeeding with multicloud, including when and where multicloud makes sense and how AWS is positioned to help enterprises succeed with their multicloud strategies.

Multicloud refers to using more than one cloud service provider (CSP) simultaneously across an organization. But first, let's clarify some terminology. Using SaaS products, such as email or project management software, alongside a CSP does not constitute a pure multicloud environment. It is a good strategy and might allow you to leverage multiple clouds, but in the context of this chapter, it is not multicloud for public clouds.

1. Pursue Multicloud Only to Fulfill Legitimate Business Needs

Although we advise AWS customers to fully realize cloud benefits by choosing a primary cloud provider, where the majority of their workloads are on a single CSP, there are valid reasons why a multicloud approach might be right for your organization. Situations that may require the complexity of a multicloud infrastructure include:

Mergers and Acquisitions

A multicloud environment can be created during an M&A transaction when the acquiring company is on one primary CSP and the acquired company is on another. Welcome to multicloud! What comes next isn't easy. As engineers, we want to say consolidate—less is more. However, it may not make sense to consolidate immediately. Your overall technology integration strategy and assessment approach should be reflected in this process; make it part of your M&A playbook. What you move from one provider to another, when you move it, and what you leave alone may vary. But establishing an integration strategy is as important as preventing multiple instances of ERP from running forever.

Desire to Leverage Long-Term Differentiated Capabilities of Another CSP

The fear of missing out drives some companies to want a bit of every cloud. We believe companies are better served by selecting a CSP that can solve the majority of their organization's challenges rather than adopting a more diffuse strategy. An 80-20 strategy is a good way of thinking about this. Indexing on the 80 percent (and not the 20 percent) can result in better efficiencies, talent retention, and value. While there may be specialized workloads that require a certain technology, those situations should be addressed case by case, where benefits and trade-offs can be considered.

Companies may think about "the right workload for the right cloud." Make sure that the analysis of what constitutes the "right cloud" extends beyond considerations for a specific workload. Ask how spreading this workload onto an additional CSP impacts overall complexity. We recommend you conduct a careful price and performance analysis of each cloud workload to ensure the value is enough to justify it.

Multicloud at the Holding Company and Primary Cloud at the Operating Company/Line of Business

For private equity organizations or large holding companies with several portfolio companies, it can make sense for each portfolio company to have its own CSP strategy (frequently driven by M&A). Focusing more of your spending on a single cloud provider might let you take advantage of its volume discounts and incentives for reserving instances. But the other shortfalls around talent, fragmented workloads, and increased risks are largely bypassed as each organization operates independently.

2. Be Mindful of Multicloud Myths

Myth 1: Everyone Is Adopting Multicloud Strategies

Advisory firms and media companies have released mixed findings on the extent that companies place their workloads in multiple clouds. Our advice is to do the right thing for your firm and make decisions based on costs and risks, regardless of how prevalent this practice may appear.

Myth 2: Multicloud Reduces the Risk of Vendor Lock-In

Some companies cite the fear of lock-in (from both contractual and technological perspectives) as a primary reason for pursuing multicloud strategies. Companies are driven to large long-term capital investments in on-premises environments, often governed by lengthy, complicated service contracts. These are big one-way door decisions (i.e., difficult and costly to reverse) for companies and necessitate a strong focus on lowering risk.

The cloud is different. Companies that run the same workload in multiple cloud providers often feel pressure to use the "lowest common denominator"—they should consider the limitations. They can sometimes avoid this problem by running different workloads with different providers.

We recommend companies work to fully understand their potential switching costs if they need to exit their existing CSP and the likelihood of that occurring. From there it's possible to define the best approach to reduce lock-in by evaluating the cost and likelihood of needing to change CSPs versus the strategic benefits of having a primary provider.

It is also important to note that the cloud is inherently more open than the traditional IT model, and we don't believe multicloud is necessary to avoid lock-in. (See Gregor Hohpe's re:Invent 2022 presentation for more).[175] Look at how AWS builds services on open-source technologies and standards, such as SQL, Linux, and containers. Customers have the choice of building on managed open-source services—such as Amazon RDS for MySQL and Amazon RDS for PostgreSQL or foundational building blocks—and they pay as they go; there is no long-term, upfront commitment. We strive to build services organizations want to use, but should a company choose to move away, AWS makes this as simple as possible. AWS provides multiple migration tools to help companies move resources from on-premises to AWS more easily and back on-premises or to other clouds if they so choose.

Myth 3: Multicloud Improves Availability

Reducing the risk of service disruption if a company's primary CSP has an outage is an increasingly rare reason for adopting a multicloud strategy. In these cases there's a belief that a company can simply and seamlessly switch its workloads to a secondary CSP.

Multicloud failover presumes that an application can be failed over to another cloud. As many companies have found, this is extremely challenging. Achieving this requires the company to maintain full portability between two CSPs, adding complexity, risk, and additional work with the belief that failover is possible.

Distinguished Gartner VP Analyst Lydia Leong summarized the problems with multicloud failover in a tweet: "Multicloud failover is complex and costly to the point of nearly almost always being impractical, and it's not an especially effective way to address cloud and resilience risks" (@cloudpundit, April 14, 2021). The problem in making failover work is all the CSP differentiators (e.g., the different network architectures and features, different storage capabilities, proprietary higher-level services, database layers, ML services, along with different security capabilities, etc.). When workloads are spread across CSPs, a failure in either CSP could cause an outage. In this case spreading workloads across CSPs actually increases risk.

We recommend companies mitigate risk by *implementing and simplifying*. Target a specific workload or application for a single cloud, migrate it, master it, remove cost and risk, and repeat. Encourage deeper learning of CSP-specific features and capabilities via training and take advantage of higher-level CSP-specific services and tooling that are already integrated. Finally, and maybe most importantly, take advantage of AWS Regions and AZs. AWS's capabilities in this area already provide AWS customers with excellent capabilities to ensure highly available and reliable solutions.

Myth 4: Multicloud Provides Better Pricing

Price competitiveness might be the weakest argument for multicloud. Organizations' experiences with complicated, expensive software or data center contracts that lock them into multi-year agreements have made them wary of procuring IT services. Traditional procurement approaches have not adapted to pay-as-you-go purchasing, volume discounts, or the reality of price competition in the cloud. (AWS has reduced prices 129 times since its inception.)

The biggest single driver of cost reduction is how well-managed and optimized a company's cloud environment is. A company may see better cost optimization by working primarily with a provider whose services offer price performance advantages (such as compute instances based on custom-designed chips like AWS Graviton) and has superior cloud financial management solutions. According to a 2021 Hackett Group study of more than one thousand organizations, infrastructure spending as a percentage of total IT spending was 20 percent lower for AWS customers than for multicloud organizations.[176]

Our experience has shown that companies don't anticipate the added cost and complexity of operating in multiple clouds, nor do they appropriately weigh it against the perceived gain in a head-to-head sourcing engagement.

3. Have a Clear Strategy and Governance to Support It

Deciding to pursue a multicloud strategy is insufficient; you must also establish a strategy for delivering on your multicloud objective, including clear governance for which workloads go where and why. Evaluation criteria should be used to optimize workloads and their dependencies. If left up to individuals, the uncoordinated sprawl across CSPs will likely erode any value the multicloud strategy sought to achieve. Evaluate CSP workload performance regularly and use your assessment as a key input to CSP selection, criteria, and future usage.

It is crucial to have comprehensive visibility into the total number of services, applications, and components used across the enterprise as part of an overall governance strategy. Integral to this is a robust tagging strategy that spans CSPs and establishes clear ownership, usage, and environment (e.g., development, QA, stage, and production) for 100 percent of deployed resources. Everything should be tagged to an owner; if it is not tagged or an owner cannot be identified, it should be removed. This codifies governance rules and automates enforcement instead of creating blocks to progress (guardrails, not gates). Cost, operations, and security must be tracked, monitored, and acted upon in the same manner with the same depth of data and transparency across CSPs. A single tool that can operate across CSPs is preferred for a given need.

4. Do Not Spread Contiguous Workloads across CSPs

We believe workflows spanning multiple CSPs introduce needless complexity, risk, and cost while complicating support, deployment, and architecture with little value added. Contiguous workloads often involve large volumes of data that need to be processed and analyzed together. When the data is distributed across multiple cloud providers, it can create challenges in data movement, synchronization, and maintaining consistency. Managing a contiguous workload across multiple CSPs can be complex and time-consuming. It requires dealing with different APIs, management interfaces, security models, and operational processes for each CSP. This complexity increases the chances of errors, increases operational overhead, and can hinder agility and scalability.

Specific criteria and guiding principles should be established when evaluating this type of design and business need.

5. Applications Should Remain with Their Transactional Data

Care should be taken when developers need to move large volumes of data between applications in different clouds, especially with compute/applications deployed in one CSP and data storage in another. Such a situation can add complexity and latency that may offset perceived benefits.

The decision criteria for determining a CSP for a workload should include a long-term view of integrating that workload with others. Will the data be needed for advanced analytics or ML beyond its current scope? Will the services provided be consumed broadly across other CSPs, or is it isolated to the workloads in that CSP? For more guidance and a decision model for deployment considerations, check out our colleague Gregor Hohpe's blog post "Multi-cloud: From Buzzword to Decision Model."[177]

6. Containers Can Help, but They Do Not Solve Every Use Case

Using containers is generally a good idea for any modern application, and they help with many elements of portability. Containers are platform-agnostic, meaning they can run on any cloud platform or infrastructure that supports containerization. This allows you to develop and package your application once and deploy it consistently across multiple cloud providers or on-premises environments without significant modifications. But be cautious as containers don't work in all cases (e.g., large monolithic applications), nor do they solve all the issues (especially data, policies, and security) around portability between CSPs.

7. Have a Single CCoE but Specialize Within

As we advise many AWS customers, you should leverage a CCoE within your organization to provide leadership, standardization, and acceleration of your cloud journey. When it comes to multicloud, we find the most successful companies have a single CCoE but specialize the skills, tools, and mechanisms particular within that CCoE to a specific CSP. We find that when AWS customers have multiple CCoEs for each CSP, it often leads to divergence, reengineering, and waste instead of a more coordinated approach through a single CCoE.

8. Make Sure Security Is Always a Top Priority

Multicloud makes security harder by increasing the risk of unauthorized access or data breaches. Multicloud forces companies to deal with multiple security models across CSPs in areas such as identity management, network security, asset management, and audit logging.

This complexity makes transparency harder and increases the burden on security teams, elevating risk. Although they are not unique to multicloud, several core security practices become more important: (1) shifting security left by automating and embedding it into delivery pipelines, cloud environments, and team priorities; and (2) encrypting data at rest and in transit within or between CSPs.

One useful approach to multicloud adoption is creating a single destination for security data (i.e., a single pane of glass). Augment this with cloud-native tools developed by every CSP to present this data so it makes sense within that environment.

Final Thought

For most organizations, a primary cloud strategy provides the most value through simplicity, focus, and risk mitigation while allowing companies to deepen their partnership and working knowledge of their primary CSP and services. This increases an organization's ability to take advantage of more sophisticated services, better attract and retain talent, and deliver value to companies faster.

A multicloud approach can make sense, but companies should ensure their decision to adopt such an approach is driven by business needs and made with a clear understanding of the trade-offs involved. In such cases, we recommend a cloud model focused on applications and business workflows that can be delivered from a single CSP, are unlikely to share data across CSPs, and have clear governance for which workload goes where.

We want to thank our colleague Tom Godden for allowing us to leverage much of his work in this space.

Afterword

"If you want to build a ship, don't drum up people together to collect wood and don't assign them tasks and work, but rather teach them to long for the endless immensity of the sea."

—ANTOINE DE SAINT-EXUPÉRY

This book was written without the specific context of how your business operates. But the common question we've found that resonates with leaders around the world is this: How can we survive the wave of disruption cascading over and around us?

Technology has become an entwined part of virtually every business. In this age of the cloud, knowing which technology to focus on and when to leverage other parts is fundamental knowledge required to survive and thrive.

We wish you the very best of luck with your cloud transformation.

Bibliography

Agile Manifesto. "Principles behind the Agile Manifesto." Last modified June 9, 2020 https://agilemanifesto.org/principles.html.

Allen, Jonathan and Oscar Rodriguez. "AWS re:Invent 2023 - Completing a large-scale migration and modernization with AWS (ENT215)." Las Vegas. Uploaded on November 30, 2023. YouTube video, 50:41. https://www.youtube.com/watch?v=iL5FJ_1vKik.

Amazon Staff. "How AWS Will Return More Water than It Uses by 2030." *About Amazon.* November 28, 2022. https://www.aboutamazon.com/news/aws/aws-water-positive-by-2030.

Anderson, David, Mark McCann, and Michael O'Reilly. *The Value Flywheel Effect: Power the Future and Accelerate Your Organization to the Modern Cloud.* Portland: IT Revolution Press, 2022.

Andreessen, Marc. "Why Software Is Eating The World." *The Wall Street Journal.* August 20, 2011. http://online.wsj.com/article/SB10001424053111903480904576512250915629460.html.

Apache Hadoop. "Apache Hadoop." Last modified March 22, 2024. https://hadoop.apache.org/.

Atlassian. "What Is DevOps?" Last modified July 23, 2024. https://www.atlassian.com/devops.

AWS. *Amazon Web Services: Risk and Compliance.* AWS Documentation, 2021. https://docs.aws.amazon.com/whitepapers/latest/aws-risk-and-compliance/welcome.html.

——— "AWS a Leader in 2023 Magic Quadrant for SCPS." Last modified July 23, 2024. https://aws.amazon.com/resources/analyst-reports/gartner/global-mq-ardm-23-magic-quadrant-for-strategic-cloud-platform-services/.

——— "AWS Classroom Training Overview." Last modified June 25, 2024. https://aws.amazon.com/training/classroom/.

——— "AWS Cloud for Finance Professionals." Last modified June 7, 2024. https://aws.amazon.com/training/classroom/aws-cloud-for-finance-professionals/.

——— *AWS Cloud Migration Readiness Guide.* AWS, 2018. https://pages.awscloud.com/rs/112-TZM-766/images/a-practical-guide-for-cloud-migration-readiness.pdf.

——— "AWS Compliance." Last modified July 9, 2024. https://aws.amazon.com/compliance/.

——— "AWS Fargate Available in Ohio, Oregon, and Ireland Regions." News release, April 26, 2018. https://aws.amazon.com/about-aws/whats-new/2018/04/aws-fargate-now-available-in-ohio-oregon–and-ireland-regions/.

——— "AWS re:Invent 2018: Fender Uses AWS to Bring Music to More Customers." Last modified June 7, 2024. https://aws.amazon.com/solutions/case-studies/fender/.

——— "AWS Service Level Agreements (SLAs)." Last modified July 5, 2024. https://aws.amazon.com/legal/service-level-agreements/.

———"AWS-Solutions-Library-Samples/Guidance-for-AWS-Sustainability-Insights-Framework." GitHub. https://github.com/aws-solutions-library-samples/guidance-for-aws-sustainability-insights-framework.

———"aws/s2n-tls." GitHub. Last modified July 19, 2024. https://github.com/aws/s2n-tls.

——— "AWS Well-Architected." Last modified June 7, 2024. https://aws.amazon.com/architecture/well-architected/.

——— "Best practices for building AMIs." In *AWS Marketplace Seller Guide,* 145–147. AWS Documentation, 2024. https://docs.aws.amazon.com/marketplace/latest/userguide/best-practices-for-building-your-amis.html.

———"C-SPAN Case Study." Last modified June 7, 2024. https://aws.amazon.com/solutions/case-studies/cspan/.

——— "Coca-Cola İçecek Improves Operational Performance Using AWS IoT SiteWise." Last modified June 7, 2024. https://aws.amazon.com/solutions/case-studies/coca-cola-iot-sitewise/.

———"Database Schema Changes." In *Practicing Continuous Integration and Continuous Delivery on AWS,* 42. AWS Documentation, 2024. https://docs.aws.amazon.com/whitepapers/latest/practicing-continuous-integration-continuous-delivery/database-schema-changes.html.

———"Introducing the Amazon Simple Queue Service." News release, November 3, 2004. https://aws.amazon.com/about-aws/whats-new/2004/11/03/introducing-the-amazon-simple-queue-service/.

———"Linux Bastion Hosts on AWS." Last modified June 7, 2024. https://aws.amazon.com/solutions/implementations/linux-bastion/.

———"McDonald's Home Delivery Case Study." Last modified June 7, 2024. https://aws.amazon.com/solutions/case-studies/mcdonalds-home-delivery/.

———"Modern data architecture on AWS." In *Modern Data Architecture Rationales on AWS*, 5–8. AWS, 2022. https://docs.aws.amazon.com/whitepapers/latest/modern-data-architecture-rationales-on-aws/modern-data-architecture-on-aws.html.

———"Netflix Case Study." Last modified June 7, 2024. https://aws.amazon.com/solutions/case-studies/netflix-case-study/.

———"SaaS Partner Event Sources." Amazon EventBridge. Last modified June 7, 2024. https://aws.amazon.com/eventbridge/integrations/.

———*Security Pillar - AWS Well-Architected Framework*. AWS Documentation, 2024. https://docs.aws.amazon.com/pdfs/wellarchitected/latest/security-pillar/wellarchitected-security-pillar.pdf#welcome.

———*Sustainability Pillar - AWS Well-Architected Framework.* AWS, 2023. https://docs.aws.amazon.com/wellarchitected/latest/sustainability-pillar/sustainability-pillar.html.

———"Transform Responsible AI from Theory into Practice." Last modified July 23, 2024. https://aws.amazon.com/machine-learning/responsible-ai/.

———*Verizon Builds a Cloud-Fluent Organization with the Help of A Cloud Guru on AWS.* AWS. https://d1.awsstatic.com/case-studies/partner-case-studies/verizon-a-cloud-guru-case-study.pdf.

AWS Integration and Automation. "aws-ia/terraform-aws-contol_tower_account_factory." GitHub. Accessed July 26, 2024. https://github.com/aws-ia/terraform-aws-control_tower_account_factory.

AWS Partner Network. "Engage with AWS Partners." Last modified June 13, 2024. https://partners.amazonaws.com/.

AWS Training and Certification. "AWS Skill Builder." Accessed July 23, 2024. https://skillbuilder.aws/.

Azhar, Azeem. "To Reach True Net-Zero, We Need Tech That Doesn't Yet Exist." *Wired,* January 19, 2021. https://www.wired.co.uk/article/net-zero-innovation-business.

Banta, Elizabeth. "IBM Unveils Z15 With Industry-First Data Privacy Capabilities." *IBM Newsroom,* September 12, 2019. https://newsroom.ibm.com/2019-09-12-IBM-Unveils-z15-With-Industry-First-Data-Privacy-Capabilities.

Barnard, Kaitlyn. "CNCF Survey: Use of Cloud Native Technologies in Production Has Grown over 200%." *Cloud Native Computing Foundation* (blog), August 29, 2018. https://www.cncf.io/blog/2018/08/29/cncf-survey-use-of-cloud-native-technologies-in-production-has-grown-over-200-percent/.

Barr, Jeff, "Adventures in Scaling in Changing Times." *AWS News Blog,* May 14, 2020. https://aws.amazon.com/blogs/aws/adventures-in-scaling-in-changing-times/.

———"Amazon EKS – Now Generally Available." *AWS News Blog,* June 5, 2018. https://aws.amazon.com/blogs/aws/amazon-eks-now-generally-available/.

———"Amazon S3." *AWS News Blog,* March 14, 2006. https://aws.amazon.com/blogs/aws/amazon_s3/.

———"New – Amazon EC2 Instances with Up to 8 NVIDIA Tesla V100 GPUS (P3)." *AWS News Blog,* October 25, 2017. https://aws.amazon.com/blogs/aws/new-amazon-ec2-instances-with-up-to8-nvidia-tesla-v100-gpus-p3/.

Beckers, Kristian. *Pattern and Security Requirements: Engineering-Based Establishment of Security Standards.* New York: Springer, 2015.

Bezos, Jeff. "2018 Letter to Shareholders." *Amazon News,* April 11, 2019. https://www.aboutamazon.com/news/company-news/2018-letter-to-shareholders.

Bizo, Daniel. *The Carbon Reduction Opportunity of Moving to Amazon Web Services.* (451 Research, 2019). https://sustainability.aboutamazon.com/carbon-reduction-aws.pdf.

Bland, Rob, Anna Granskog, and Tomas Nauclér. "Accelerating toward Net Zero: The Green Business Building Opportunity." *McKinsey Sustainability,* June 14, 2022. https://www.mckinsey.com/capabilities/sustainability/our-insights/accelerating-toward-net-zero-the-green-business-building-opportunity.

Boritz, J. Efrim. "IS Practitioners' Views on Core Concepts of Information Integrity." *International Journal of Accounting Information Systems* 6, no. 4 (December 2005): 260–79. https://doi.org/10.1016/j.accinf.2005.07.001.

Brooks, Frederick P. "No Silver Bullet Essence and Accidents of Software Engineering." *Computer* 20, no. 4 (April 1987): 10–19. https://doi.org/10.1109/mc.1987.1663532;

Brynjolfsson, Erik. "The Productivity Paradox of Information Technology." *Communications of the ACM* 36, no. 12 (December 1993): 66–77. https://doi.org/10.1145/163298.163309.

Bryson, Steve, David Kenwright, Michael Cox, David Ellsworth, Robert Haimes. "Visually exploring gigabyte data sets in real time." *Communications of the ACM* 42, no. 8 (August 1999): 82–90. https://doi.org/10.1145/310930.310977.

BSI. *PD ISO/IEC TR 27103:2018: Information Technology. Security Techniques. Cybersecurity and ISO and IEC Standards,* (London: BSI, 2018). https://doi.org/10.3403/30362593.

Carvalho, Larry and Matthew Marden. *Fostering Business and Organizational Transformation to Generate Business Value with Amazon Web Services,* (Framingham, MA: IDC, 2018). https://pages.awscloud.com/rs/112-TZM-766/images/AWS-BV%20IDC%202018.pdf?aliId=1614258770.

Chui, Michael et al., *The economic potential of generative AI: The next productivity frontier*, (McKinsey & Company, 2023). https://www.mckinsey.com/capabilities/mckinsey-digital/our-insights/the-economic-potential-of-generative-AI-the-next-productivity-frontier#industry-impacts.

Cockcroft, Adrian. "Adrian Cockcroft on Mapping Your Stack." YouTube video, 08:26, https://www.youtube.com/watch?v=mzIdKGCOf1g.

Cook, Bryan. "AWS re:Invent 2016: Automated Formal Reasoning About AWS Systems (SEC401)." Las Vegas. Uploaded on December 1, 2016. YouTube video, 45:56, https://youtu.be/U40bWY6oVtU?si=jjT00R237ArW4Bx5.

Coutinho, Paulo, Sanjukta Mukherjee, and Sunil Divvela. "From Mainframe to AWS Cloud: A Comprehensive Mapping Guide," *AWS Cloud Operations & Migrations Blog*, June 28, 2023. https://aws.amazon.com/blogs/mt/from-mainframe-to-aws-cloud-a-comprehensive-mapping-guide/.

Custodio, Ernesto. "Agile vs. Waterfall: Comparing Success Rates in Project Management," *Agile Gensis,* January 30, 2024. https://www.agilegenesis.com/post/agile-vs-waterfall-comparing-success-rates-in-project-management.

Cutress. Ian and Anton Shilov. "GlobalFoundries Stops All 7nm Development: Opts To Focus on Specialized Processes." *AnandTechRSS,* August 27, 2018. https://www.anandtech.com/show/13277/globalfoundries-stops-all-7nm-development.

Dalio, Ray. *Principles: Life and Work*. New York: Simon and Schuster, 2017.

Dasgupta, Partha. *The Economics of Biodiversity: The Dasgupta Review*. (London: HM Treasury, 2021). https://assets.publishing.service.gov.uk/media/602e92b2e90e07660f807b47/The_Economics_of_Biodiversity_The_Dasgupta_Review_Full_Report.pdf.

Dean, Jeffrey and Sanjay Ghemawat. "MapReduce: Simplified Data Processing on Large Clusters." Paper presented at the Sixth Symposium on Operating System Design and Implementation, San Francisco, CA. December 2004. https://research.google/pubs/mapreduce-simplified-data-processing-on-large-clusters/.

Dehghani, Zhamak. "How to Move Beyond a Monolithic Data Lake to a Distributed Data Mesh." *Martin Fowler,* May 20, 2019. https://martinfowler.com/articles/data-monolith-to-mesh.html.

Department of the Army. *ADP 6-0, Mission Command: Command and Control of Army Forces.* (Washington, DC: Department of the Army, 2019). https://armypubs.army.mil/epubs/DR_pubs/DR_a/ARN34403-ADP_6-0-000-WEB-3.pdf.

Derek DeBellis et al., *Accelerate State of DevOps 2023* (DORA Publications, October 5, 2023). https://cloud.google.com/devops/state-of-devops.

Docker Docs. "Dockerfile Reference." Last modified July 23, 2024. https://docs.docker.com/engine/reference/builder/.

Doerr, John. *Measure What Matters: How Google, Bono, and the Gates Foundation Rock the World with OKRs*, 16. New York: Portfolio, 2018.

Elmalak, Sam and Ben Woodward. "AWS re:Invent 2017: Architecting Security and Governance Across a Multi-Account Strategy." Las Vegas. Uploaded on November 28, 2017. YouTube video, 1:01:57, https://www.youtube.com/watch?v=71fD8Oenwxc.

European Parliament. "Sustainable Economy: Parliament Adopts New Reporting Rules for Multinationals," news release, October 11, 2022. https://www.europarl.europa.eu/news/en/press-room/20221107IPR49611/sustainable-economy-parliament-adopts-new-reporting-rules-for-multinationals.

Formula 1. "Formula 1 Selects AWS as Official Cloud and Machine Learning Provider." *Formula 1,* June 29, 2018. https://www.formula1.com/

en/latest/article.formula-1-selects-aws-as-official-cloud-and-machine-learning-provider.3thFUei8926UA28csUs0EQ.html.

Felipe, Jesus, Connie Dacuycuy, and Matteo Lanzafame. *The Declining Share of Agricultural Employment in the People's Republic of China: How Fast?* Mandaluyong: Asian Development Bank, 2014. https://www.adb.org/sites/default/files/publication/149676/ewp-419.pdf.

Forsgren, Nicole, Jez Humble, and Gene Kim. *Accelerate: State of DevOps 2018: Strategies for a New Economy.* Mountain View, CA: Google Cloud, 2018. https://services.google.com/fh/files/misc/state-of-devops-2018.pdf.

———*Accelerate: The Science of Lean Software and DevOps: Building and Scaling High Performing Technology Organizations.* Portland: IT Revolution, 2018.

Frost & Sullivan. *Why Business Agility Matters.* Cambridge: PEGA, 2018. https://www.pega.com/why-business-agility-matters.

Gartner. "Gartner Survey Reveals Significant Shifts in CEO Thinking on Sustainability, Workforce Issues and Inflation in 2022," news release, May 18, 2022. https://www.gartner.com/en/newsroom/press-releases/2022-05-18-gartner-survey-reveals-significant-shifts-in-ceo-thinking-on-sustainability-workforce-issues-and-inflation-in-2022.

Gartner Research. *Sustainability Assessment: Amazon.* Stamford: Gartner, 2023. https://www.gartner.com/en/documents/4378699.

Giner, Pablo et al., "Data Mesh: It's Not Just about Tech, It's about Ownership and Communication (Part 2)." *Thoughtworks* (blog), December 19, 2022. https://www.thoughtworks.com/en-gb/insights/blog/data-engineering/data-mesh-its-not-just-about-tech-its-about-ownership-and-communication2.

Githens, Greg. "Pillars of Strategic Initiative Success." *Leading Strategic Initiatives* (blog), August 11, 2011, https://leadingstrategicinitiatives.com/2011/08/11/pillars-of-strategic-initiative-success/.

Glenn, Marie *Organizational Agility: How business can survive and thrive.* London: Economist Intelligence Unit, 2009, https://graphics.eiu.com/marketing/pdf/EMC_OrganisationalAgility.pdf.

Hamilton, James. "AWS re:Invent 2016: Amazon Global Network Overview with James Hamilton." Las Vegas. Uploaded on June 27, 2017. YouTube video, 33:35. https://www.youtube.com/watch?v=uj7Ting6Ckk.

Hastings, Reed and Erin Meyer. *No Rules Rules: Netflix and the Culture of Reinvention.* New York: Penguin Press, 2020.

Hennesey, Chris. "Making dollars and sense out of FinOps." Las Vegas. Uploaded on November 29, 2023. YouTube video, 52:57. https://www.youtube.com/watch?v=hI9Jg6n_Ku0.

Hofstede, Geert and Gert Jan Hofstede. *Cultures and Organizations: Software for the Mind.* New York: McGraw Hill, 2004.

Hohpe, Gregor. "AWS re:Invent 2022 - Modern cloud applications: Do they lock you in? (ARC207)." Las Vegas. Uploaded on December 5, 2022. YouTube video, 58:29. https://youtu.be/Ud9h1hJgoKk.

——— "Multi-Cloud: From Buzzword to Decision Model." *The Architect Elevator* (blog), April 20, 2022. https://architectelevator.com/cloud/multi-cloud-decision-model/.

Holder, L. D. "Concept of the Operations: See Ops Overlay." *Military Review* (August 1990): 28, quoted in Richard Dempsey and Jonathan M. Chavous. "Commander's Intent and Concept of Operations." *Military Review* November-December 2013: 58-66. https://www.armyupress.army.mil/Portals/7/military-review/Archives/English/MilitaryReview_20131231_art001.pdf.

IBM. "IBM Expands Strategic Partnership with Samsung to Include 7nm Chip Manufacturing." *PR Newswire,* December 20, 2018. https://www.prnewswire.com/news-releases/ibm-expands-strategic-partnership-with-samsung-to-include-7nm-chip-manufacturing-300769471.html.

Info-Tech Research Group. "Manage and Improve Core IT Processes." Accessed July 25, 2025. https://www.infotech.com/browse/management-and-governance.

The Institute of Internal Auditors. *The IIA's Three Lines Model: An Update of the Three Lines of Defense.* Lake Mary, FL: The Institute of Internal Auditors, 2020. https://www.theiia.org/globalassets/documents/resources/the-iias-three-lines-model-an-update-of-the-three-lines-of-defense-july-2020/three-lines-model-updated-english.pdf.

ISO. *ISO/IEC 27002:2013(En) Information Technology — Security Techniques — Code of Practice for Information Security Controls.* Geneva: ISO, 2013. https://www.iso.org/obp/ui/#iso:std:iso-iec:27002:ed-2:v1:en.

Izrailevsky, Yury, Stevan Vlaovic, and Ruslan Meshenberg, "Completing the Netflix Cloud Migration." *Netflix,* February 11, 2016. https://about.netflix.com/en/news/completing-the-netflix-cloud-migration.

Jain, Anu. "How JPMorgan Chase Built a Data Mesh Architecture to Drive Significant Value to Enhance Their Enterprise Data Platform." *AWS Big Data Blog,* May 5, 2021. https://aws.amazon.com/blogs/big-data/how-jpmorgan-chase-built-a-data-mesh-architecture-to-drive-significant-value-to-enhance-their-enterprise-data-platform/.

Jeffries, Ron. "YAGNI, yes. Skimping, no. Technical Dept? Not even." *Ron Jeffries,* April 2, 2019. https://ronjeffries.com/articles/019-01ff/iter-yagni-skimp/.

Johnson, Jim. *CHAOS Report: Beyond Infinity.* Boston: The Standish Group, 2020. https://standishgroup.myshopify.com/.

Kearns, Michael and Aaron Roth. *The Ethical Algorithm: The Science of Socially Aware Algorithm Design.* New York: Oxford University Press, 2019.

Khanna, Prachi, Didier Durand, and Phil de Valence. "Analyzing Legacy Applications On-Demand with AWS Mainframe Modernization and Micro Focus." *AWS Cloud Operations & Migrations Blog,* July 27, 2022. https://aws.amazon.com/blogs/mt/analyzing-legacy-applications-on-demand-with-aws-mainframe-modernization-and-micro-focus/.

Kim, Gene. Kevin Behr, and George Spafford. *The Phoenix Project: A Novel about IT, DevOps, and Helping Your Business Win, 5th ed.* Portland: IT Revolution Press, 2018.

Klinect, Thomas and Stefan Van Der Zijden. *Use Continuous Modernization to Build Digital Platforms from Legacy Applications.* Stamford: Gartner, 2018. https://www.gartner.com/en/documents/3846764.

Kniberg, Henrik. "Spotify Engineering Culture – Part 1 (aka the 'Spotify Model')." Uploaded on July 30, 2019. YouTube video, 13:12. https://www.youtube.com/watch?v=Yvfz4HGtoPc.

——— "Spotify Engineering Culture (Part 1)." *Spotify R&D Engineering* (blog), March 27, 2014, https://engineering.atspotify.com/2014/03/spotify-engineering-culture-part-1/.

Lean Enterprise Institute. "7 Wastes." Lean Enterprise Institute. Accessed July 25, 2024. https://www.lean.org/lexicon-terms/seven-wastes/.

Lee, Hoesung, Katherine Calvin, Dipak Dasgupta, Gerhard Krinner, Aditi Mukherji, Peter Thorne, Christopher Trisos, Jose Romero, Paulina Aldunce, Ko Barrett, et al. *Synthesis Report of the IPCC Sixth Assessment Report (AR6).* Geneva: Intergovernmental Panel on Climate Change, 2023. https://report.ipcc.ch/ar6syr/pdf/IPCC_AR6_SYR_SPM.pdf.

Lindsey, Rebecca. "Climate Change: Atmospheric Carbon Dioxide." *NOAA Climate,* May 12, 2023. https://www.climate.gov/news-features/understanding-climate/climate-change-atmospheric-carbon-dioxide.

Malhotra, Ankit and Morteza Zijerdi. "Five things you should do to create an accurate on premises vs cloud comparison model." *AWS*

Cloud Financial Management (blog), April 28, 2022. https://aws.amazon.com/blogs/aws-cloud-financial-management/five-things-you-should-do-to-create-an-accurate-on-premises-vs-cloud-comparison-model/.

Marr, Bernard. "What is Big Data?" Bernard Marr & Co. Last modified July 25, 2024. https://bernardmarr.com/what-is-big-data/.

Marquet, L. David. *Turn the Ship Around!: A True Story of Turning Followers into Leaders*. New York: Portfolio/Penguin, 2013.

Megginson, Leon C. "Lessons from Europe for American Business," *Southwestern Social Science Quarterly* 44, no. 1 (June 1, 1963): 4.

Mills, Harlan D. "Top Down Programming in Large Systems." *Software Productivity*. Boston: Little, Brown and Company, 1983.

Morgan, Timothy Prickett. "New System Z15 Mainframe Takes the Heat Off Power Systems." *The Four Hundred,* September 16, 2019. https://www.itjungle.com/2019/09/16/new-system-z15-mainframe-takes-the-heat-off-power-systems/.

Moses, CJ. "How AWS Manages Security at Massive Scale: Fireside Chat with CJ Moses, Deputy CISO AWS." Washington D.C. Uploaded on July 25, 2017. YouTube video, 52:47. https://www.youtube.com/watch?v=qXO5j1xomAM.

Nasdaq. "Verizon Communications Inc. Common Stock (VZ)." https://www.nasdaq.com/market-activity/stocks/vz/financials.

The National Association of Clothiers. *The Clothier and Furnisher* 78 (July 1911): 86. https://babel.hathitrust.org/cgi/pt?id=nyp.33433090813787.

National Human Genome Research Institute. "The Cost of Sequencing a Human Genome." National Human Genome Research Institute. Last modified November 1, 2021. https://www.genome.gov/about-genomics/fact-sheets/Sequencing-Human-Genome-cost.

Nejad, Amin Shoari, Andrew C. Parnell, Alice Greene, Peter Thorne, Brian P. Kelleher, Robert J. N. Devoy, and Gerard McCarthy. "A Newly Reconciled Dataset for Identifying Sea Level Rise and Variability in Dublin Bay." *Ocean Science* 18, no. 2 (April 22, 2022): 511–22. https://doi.org/10.5194/os-18-511-2022.

Netflix Technology Blog. "The Netflix Simian Army." *Medium,* July 19, 2011. https://netflixtechblog.com/the-netflix-simian-army-16e57fbab116.

NewVantage Partners. *Big Data and AI Executive Survey 2021.* Boston: NewVantage Partners LLC, 2021. https://c6abb8db-514c-4f5b-b5a1-fc710f1e464e.filesusr.com/ugd/e5361a_76709448ddc6490981f0c-bea42d51508.pdf.

NIST. "Cybersecurity Framework." Last modified July 25, 2024. https://www.nist.gov/cyberframework.

——— *NIST SP 800-53 Rev. 5: Security and Privacy Controls for Information Systems and Organizations.* Gaithersburg: NIST, September 23, 2020. https://doi.org/10.6028/NIST.SP.800-53r5.

O'Reilly, Barry. *Unlearn: Let Go of Past Success to Achieve Extraordinary Results.* New York: McGraw Hill, 2018.

Orban, Stephan. *Ahead in the Cloud: Best Practices for Navigating the Future of Enterprise IT.* North Charleston: CreateSpace Independent Publishing Platform, 2018.

———"Today's IT Executive is a Chief Change Management Officer." *AWS Cloud Enterprise Strategy Blog,* September 30, 2015. https://aws.amazon.com/blogs/enterprise-strategy/todays-it-executive-is-a-chief-change-management-officer/

———"What Makes Good Leaders Great?" *LinkedIn Pulse,* October 23, 2015. https://www.linkedin.com/pulse/what-makes-good-leaders-great-stephen-orban/

———"You Already Have the People You Need to Succeed with the Cloud." *AWS Cloud Enterprise Strategy Blog*, November 18, 2015. https://aws.amazon.com/blogs/enterprise-strategy/you-already-have-the-people-you-need-to-succeed-with-the-cloud/.

Paredes, Divina. "Amazon CTO: Stop spending money on 'undifferentiated heavy lifting.'" *CIO New Zealand*, June 9, 2013.

Pastore, Richard, Michael Fuller, and Justin Gillespie. *The Business Value of Migration to Amazon Web Services.* Atlanta: The Hackett Group, 2022. https://pages.awscloud.com/rs/112-TZM-766/images/hackett-group-the-business-value-of-migration-to-aws-012022.pdf.

Pereira, Rui, Marco Couto, Francisco Ribeiro, Rui Rua, Jácome Cunha, João Paulo Fernandes, João Saraiva. "Energy Efficiency across Programming Languages: How Do Energy, Time, and Memory Relate?" *Proceedings of the 10th ACM SIGPLAN International Conference on Software Language Engineering*. October 2017, 256–67. https://doi.org/10.1145/3136014.3136031.

Philips. *Carbon Reduction Plan*. Amsterdam: Phillips, 2023. https://www.philips.com/c-dam/b2bhc/master/services/upgrading-services/carbon-reduction-plan-philips.pdf.

Pink, Daniel H. *Drive: The Surprising Truth About What Motivates Us*. New York: Riverhead Books, 2009.

PwC. "IT Governance, Risk and Compliance (IT GRC)." Accessed July 25, 2024. https://www.pwc.com/la/en/risk-assurance/it-grc.html.

——— *PwC 2023 Cloud Business Survey.* London: PwC, 2023. https://www.pwc.com/us/en/tech-effect/cloud/cloud-business-survey.html.

Rasmussen, Michael. "GRC 3.0 – A History of GRC." *The GRC Pundit Blog,* April 16, 2013. https://grc2020.com/2013/04/16/11grc-3-0-a-history-of-grc/.

Reuters Graphics. "COBOL Blues." Last modified November 30, 2022. http://fingfx.thomsonreuters.com/gfx/rngs/USA-BANKS-COBOL/010040KH18J/index.html.

RiskOptics. "What Are The Differences Between COBIT & COSO." *ZenGRC,* May 1, 2018. https://reciprocity.com/what-are-the-differences-between-cobit-coso/.

RiverMeadow. "Modernize Your Operating Systems," Last modified July 25, 2024. https://www.rivermeadow.com/automated-os-upgrade.

Rudgley, Grant and Nina Seega. *Biodiversity Loss and Land Degradation: An Overview of the Financial Materiality.* Cambridge: University of Cambridge Instittue for Sustainability Leadership, 2020. https://www.cisl.cam.ac.uk/system/files/documents/biodiversity-loss-and-land-degradation-overview.pdf.

Rumelt, Richard. *Good Strategy/Bad Strategy: The Difference and Why It Matters.* London: Profile Books, 2017.

Rustin, Randall. *Debugging techniques in large systems.* Hoboken: Prentice-Hall, 1971.

SAFe Studio. "Agile Release Train." Last modified October 24, 2022. https://scaledagileframework.com/agile-release-train/.

Schwartz, Mark. *Adaptive Ethics for Digital Transformation: A New Approach for Enterprise Leaders (Featuring Frankenstein vs the Gingerbread Man).* Portland: IT Revolution Press, 2023.

——— "The Frozen Middle—Part One: Understanding," *AWS Cloud Enterprise Strategy Blog,* June 6, 2019. https://aws.amazon.com/blogs/enterprise-strategy/the-frozen-middle-part-one-understanding/.

——— *War and Peace and IT: Business Leadership, Technology, and Success in the Digital Age.* Portland: IT Revolution Press, 2019.

Shaw, Helen. "The Trouble with COSO." *CFO,* March 15, 2006. https://www.cfo.com/news/the-trouble-with-coso/677100/.

Silver, Paul and Jonathan Allen. "AWS re:Invent 2019: How to go from zero to hundreds of certified AWS engineers (ENT231)," Las Vegas, YouTube video, 53:57. https://www.youtube.com/watch?v=yHzJw007oO8.

Sethi, Karandeep Singh, Prachi Khanna, and Youssef Ridene. "AWS Mainframe Modernization – Refactor Legacy Code Base to Java Using AWS Blu Insights." *AWS Cloud Operations & Migrations Blog,* April 18, 2023. https://aws.amazon.com/blogs/mt/aws-mainframe-modernization-refactor-legacy-code-base-to-java-using-aws-blu-insights/.

Sethi, Vive. "3M Hackathon: Machine learning for every developer." *AWS for Industries* (blog), September 24, 2020. https://aws.amazon.com/blogs/industries/3m-hackathon-ml-for-every-developer/.

Splunk. *The State of Observability 2023.* San Francisco: Splunk, 2023. https://www.splunk.com/en_us/campaigns/state-of-observability.html.

Stein, Steven J and Howard E. Book. *The EQ Edge: Emotional Intelligence and Your Success.* Mississauga: Jossey-Bass, 2011.

Stevens, Rob. "Gravity appoints Arup as Digital Master Planners." *Gravity Smart Campus News,* July 31, 2020. https://thisisgravity.co.uk/tag/arup/.

Stormacq, Sébastien. "Modernize Your Mainframe Applications & Deploy Them In The Cloud." *AWS News Blog,* June 8, 2022. https://aws.amazon.com/blogs/aws/modernize-your-mainframe-applications-deploy-them-in-the-cloud/.

Stromasys. "Seamless Virtualization & Emulation for Legacy Hardware." Accessed July 25, 2024. https://www.stromasys.com/.

Taskforce on Nature-Related Financial Disclosures. "The Taskforce on Nature-Related Financial Disclosures." Accessed July 25, 2024. https://tnfd.global/.

Thompson, K. "UNIX Time-Sharing System." *Bell System Technical Journal* 57, no. 6 (July 1978): 1931–46. https://doi.org/10.1002/j.1538-7305.1978.tb02137.x.

Transparency Market Research. "Mainframe Modernization Services Market is estimated to grow from US$ 23.5 Billion in 2021 to US$ 108.9 Billion by 2031 end at a Steady CAGR, TMR Study." News release, GlobalNewswire. November 10, 2022. https://www.globenewswire.com/news-release/2022/11/10/2552914/0/en/Mainframe-Modernization-Services-Market-is-estimated-to-grow-from-US-23-5-Billion-in-2021-to-US-108-9-Billion-by-2031-end-at-a-Steady-CAGR-TMR-Study.html.

United Nations. "Sustainability." United Nations Academic Impact. Last modified July 25, 2024. https://www.un.org/en/academic-impact/sustainability.

United Nations Environment Programme. *Ecosystem Restoration for People, Nature and Climate: Becoming #GenerationRestoration.* New York: United Nations, 2021. https://doi.org/10.18356/9789280738643.

United States Office of Strategic Services. *Simple Sabotage Field Manual.* Arlington: United States War Department Strategic Services Unit, 1944.

Uzzi, Brian and Jarrett Spiro. "Collaboration and Creativity: The Small World Problem," *American Journal of Sociology* 111, no. 2 (September 2005): 447–504, https://doi.org/10.1086/432782.

Wardley, Simon. "A quick and easy guide to measurement." *LinkedIn Pulse,* February 9, 2024, https://www.linkedin.com/pulse/quick-easy-guide-measurement-simon-wardley-25mrc.

———"On Being Lost." *Bits or pieces* (blog), August 8, 2016, http://blog.gardeviance.org/2016/08/on-being-lost.html.

Weill, Peter. "The Agility Paradox." Slides presented at MIT CIO Summit, Boston, MA, June 2006.

Weiss, Becky and Mike Furr. "Static stability using Availability Zones." Amazon Builders' Library. Last modified July 25, 2024. https://aws.amazon.com/builders-library/static-stability-using-availability-zones/.

Whiting, Kate. "8 Ways the World Is Adapting to Rising Sea Levels." *World Economic Forum Agenda*, August 22, 2022. https://www.weforum.org/agenda/2022/08/rising-sea-levels-global-adaptation/.

Willink, Jocko and Leif Babin. *Extreme Ownership: How U.S. Navy SEALs Lead and Win (New Edition)*. New York: St. Martin's Press, 2017.

Wilson, Glenn. *DevSecOps: A leader's guide to producing secure software without compromising flow, feedback and continuous improvement.* Norwich: Rethink Press, 2020.

Wood, Johnny. "What does net-zero emissions means and how can we get there?" *World Economic Forum Agenda,* November 9, 2021. https://www.weforum.org/agenda/2021/11/net-zero-emissions-cop26-climate-change/.

World Meteorological Organization. "Past eight years confirmed to be the eight warmest on record." News release, January 12, 2023. https://wmo.int/news/media-centre/past-eight-years-confirmed-be-eight-warmest-record.

———"Rising Risks." World Meteorological Organization. Last modified July 26, 2024. https://wmo.int/about-us/world-meteorological-day/wmd-2022/rising-risks.

Xie, J., S. Sreenivasan, G. Korniss, W. Zhang, C. Lim, and B. K. Szymanski. "Social Consensus through the Influence of Committed Minorities." *Physical Review* E 84, no. 1 (July 2011). https://doi.org/10.1103/physreve.84.011130.

Yao, Fangfang, Ben Livneh, Balaji Rajagopalan, Jida Wang, Jean-François Crétaux, Yoshihide Wada, and Muriel Berge-Nguyen. "Satellites Reveal Widespread Decline in Global Lake Water Storage." *Science*

380, no. 6646 (May 19, 2023): 743–49. https://doi.org/10.1126/science.abo2812.

ZeroNorth. "ZeroNorth Onboard." Accessed July 26, 2024. https://zeronorth.com/zeronorth-onboard.

Author Biographies

–JONATHAN ALLEN

Jonathan joined AWS as an enterprise strategist in 2017. In this role, he works with enterprise technology executives around the globe to share experiences and strategies for how the cloud can help them increase speed and agility while devoting more of their resources to their customers.

He has worked with over 1,200 enterprises, helping them successfully complete migrations, transition their organizations, and realize the benefits of AWS Cloud aligned to their business. Aside from working with many of the world's leading brands, Jonathan is a frequent speaker. He has covered over 350 events in his tenure at AWS and writes frequently on the AWS Cloud Enterprise Strategy Blog.

Prior to joining AWS, Jonathan spent seventeen years working as a leader at Capital One Financial Corporation, including roles as senior director and divisional CTO. He was part of the technology leadership team that selected AWS as Capital One's predominant cloud partner in 2014. He was accountable for architecting and engineering the UK division's AWS Cloud strategy using an Agile DevOps execution of the technical build-out and system migrations in partnership with the US divisions.

Prior to his time at Capital One, Jonathan was a software and systems engineer working for multiple independent systems houses.

In 2012 he was awarded IT Manager of the Year by The Chartered Institute for IT. He holds a diploma in computer studies from Loughborough College, a CIO MBA from Boston University, and is a certified AWS Solutions Architect. He has previously held Cisco and Microsoft advanced accreditations and can still program in Cobol(!), although Python is his language of choice today.

twitter.com/jonatallen

linkedin.com/in/jonatallen

–THOMAS BLOOD

Thomas joined AWS in October 2016 as an enterprise evangelist and strategist and now leads AWS Digital Innovation for Europe, the Middle East, and Africa (EMEA).

Thomas has worked with more than four hundred enterprise technology customers to share experiences and strategies for how AWS can help them increase speed and agility to innovate on behalf of their customers. Thomas is a frequent speaker, having covered over one hundred events in his tenure at AWS.

Prior to joining AWS, Thomas was VP of Emerging Technologies at Experian Consumer Services, where he led an effort to re-architect the technology platform using a cloud-native approach in AWS. This transformation has changed how the business develops software, systems, and solutions. It has caused a ripple effect throughout the global enterprise, with multiple business units pursuing their own journey to the cloud.

Over the previous twenty years, Thomas worked in diverse technical leadership roles at Edmunds, the Department of Defense, the Naval

Postgraduate School, as well as two technology startups. He spent a number of years in the US Army, serving as an intelligence analyst in Europe and the Middle East.

Thomas earned his master's degree in interdisciplinary studies from California State University at Monterey Bay and a bachelor's in economic development and environmental studies. He studied intermediate Arabic at the American University in Cairo and completed postgraduate courses in biometrics and identity management at the Naval Postgraduate School in Monterey. He speaks German, English, Spanish, and some Arabic and French.

twitter.com/groberstiefel

linkedin.com/in/thomasblood

ENDNOTES

1. Bezos, "2018 Letter to Shareholders."
2. AWS, "McDonald's Home Delivery."
3. Sethi, "3M Hackathon."
4. Forsgren, Humble, and Kim, Accelerate: The Science of Lean.
5. DeBellis et al., Accelerate State of DevOps 2023.
6. Megginson, "Lessons from Europe."
7. Izrailevsky, Vlaovic, and Meshenberg. "Completing the Netflix Cloud Migration."
8. Paredes, "Amazon CTO."
9. Pastore, Fuller, and Gillespie, Business Value of Migration.
10. Barr, "Amazon S3."
11. AWS, "AWS a Leader in 2023."
12. Barr, "Adventures in Scaling."
13. Bizo, The Carbon Reduction Opportunity.
14. Malhotra and Zijerdi, "Five things."
15. Hamilton, "AWS re:Invent 2016."
16. Kim, Behr, and Spafford. The Phoenix Project.
17. Schwartz, War and Peace and IT.
18. Dalio, Principles: Life and Work.

19. Hastings and Meyer. No Rules Rules.
20. National Association of Clothiers, The Clothier and Furnisher.
21. Rumelt, Good Strategy/Bad Strategy.
22. Orban, "Today's IT Executive."
23. Orban, "What Makes Good Leaders Great?"
24. AWS, "Netflix Case Study."
25. Githens, "Pillars of Strategic Initiative Success."
26. Wardley, "On Being Lost."
27. Wardley, "On Being Lost."
28. Cockroft, "Aidan Cockcroft on Mapping."
29. Anderson et al., Value Flywheel Effect.
30. PwC, PwC 2023 Cloud Business Survey.
31. Schwartz, War and Peace and IT.
32. Agile Manifesto, "Principles Behind the Agile Manifesto."
33. Hennesey, "Making dollars and sense."
34. AWS, "AWS Cloud for Finance."
35. Wikipedia, s.v. "Campbell's Law," last modified February 27, 2024, https://en.wikipedia.org/wiki/Campbell%27s_law.
36. Forsgren, Humble, and Kim, Accelerate: The Science of Lean.
37. Wardley, "Quick and easy guide."
38. Hofstede and Hofstede, Cultures and Organizations.
39. Schwartz, "The Frozen Middle."
40. Department of the Army, ADP 6-0, Mission Command.
41. Holder, "Concept of the Operations."
42. Marquet, Turn the Ship Around!
43. Wikipedia, s.v., "Metcalfe's law," last modified March 27, 2024, https://en.wikipedia.org/wiki/Metcalfe%27s_law.
44. Willink and Babin, Extreme Ownership.
45. Kniberg, "Spotify Engineering Culture (Part 1)."
46. Wilson, DevSecOps: A leader's guide.
47. Uzzi and Spiro, "Collaboration and Creativity."

48. Stein and Book, The EQ Edge.
49. Moses, "How AWS Manages Security."
50. AWS, "Best Practices for Building AMIs."
51. Splunk, The State of Observability 2023.
52. AWS Integration and Automation, "aws-ia/terraform."
53. AWS, "Linux Bastion Hosts on AWS."
54. AWS, "AWS Well-Architected."
55. Wikipedia, s.v. "OODA loop," last modified January 12, 2024, https://en.wikipedia.org/wiki/OODA_loop.
56. O'Reilly, Unlearn.
57. Pink, Drive.
58. Forsgren, Humble, and Kim, Accelerate: State of DevOps 2018.
59. Orban, "You Already Have the People You Need."
60. AWS, "AWS Classroom Training Overview."
61. AWS Training and Certification, "AWS Skill Builder."
62. Elmalak and Woodward, "AWS re:Invent 2017."
63. J. Xie et al., "Social Consensus."
64. Silver and Allen, "AWS re:Invent 2019."
65. Nasdaq, "Verizon Communications Inc."
66. AWS, Verizon Builds a Cloud-Fluent Organization.
67. Kniberg, "Spotify Engineering Culture – Part 1."
68. SAFe Studio, "Agile Release Train."
69. Atlassian, "What Is DevOps?"
70. Brooks, "No Silver Bullet Essence"; Mills, "Top Down Programming"; Rustin, Debugging techniques in large systems.
71. Wikipedia, s.v. "Autonomation," last modified March 7, 2024, https://en.wikipedia.org/wiki/Autonomation.
72. Johnson, CHAOS Report: Beyond Infinity.
73. Custodio, "Agile vs. Waterfall."
74. Jeffries, "YAGNI, yes. Skimping, no."

75. Wikipedia, s.v. "Trust, but verify," last modified February 20, 2024, 05:23, https://en.wikipedia.org/wiki/Trust,_but_verify.
76. Forsgren, Kim, and Humble, Accelerate: State of DevOps 2018.
77. AWS, "Introducing the Amazon Simple Queue Service."
78. Barr, "Amazon S3."
79. National Human Genome Research Institute, "The Cost of Sequencing."
80. Docker Docs, "Dockerfile Reference."
81. Barnard, "CNCF Survey."
82. Barr, "Amazon EKS."
83. AWS, "AWS Fargate Available."
84. Andreessen, "Why Software Is Eating The World."
85. Orban, Ahead in the Cloud.
86. Barnard, "CNCF Survey."
87. Thompson, "UNIX Time-Sharing System."
88. AWS, "SaaS Partner Event Sources."
89. Carvalho and Marden, Fostering Business.
90. AWS, "AWS Service Level Agreements (SLAs)."
91. Weiss and Furr, "Static stability using Availability Zones."
92. AWS, "Database Schema Changes."
93. Netflix Technology Blog, "The Netflix Simian Army."
94. Allen and Rodriguez, "AWS re:Invent 2023."
95. AWS Partner Network, "Engage with AWS Partners."
96. AWS, AWS Cloud Migration Readiness Guide.
97. RiverMeadow, "Modernize Your Operating Systems."
98. Stromasys, "Seamless Virtualization & Emulation."
99. Klinect and Van Der Zijden, Use Continuous Modernization.
100. Reuters Graphics, "COBOL Blues."
101. Morgan, "New System Z15 Mainframe."
102. Cutress and Shilov, "GlobalFoundries Stops."
103. IBM, "IBM Expands Strategic Partnership."

104. Transparency Market Research, "Mainframe Modernization."
105. Stormacq, "Modernize Your Mainframe Applications."
106. Coutinho, Mukherjee, and Divvela, "From Mainframe to AWS Cloud."
107. Khanna, Durand, and de Valence, "Analyzing Legacy Applications."
108. Sethi, Khanna, and Ridene, "AWS Mainframe Modernization."
109. Bryson et al., "Visually exploring gigabyte data sets."
110. Wikipedia, s.v. "Multitier architecture," last modified January 6, 2024, 23:04, https://en.wikipedia.org/wiki/Multitier_architecture.
111. Marr, "What is Big Data?"
112. NewVantage Partners, Big Data and AI Executive Survey 2021.
113. Dehghani, "How to Move Beyond a Monolithic Data Lake."
114. Giner et al., "Data Mesh."
115. Jain, "How JPMorgan Chase Built a Data Mesh Architecture."
116. AWS, "Modern data architecture on AWS."
117. AWS, "C-SPAN Case Study."
118. Wikipedia, s.v. "Alan Turing," last modified April 1, 2024, 05:56, https://en.wikipedia.org/wiki/Alan_Turing.
119. Wikipedia, s.v. "Stochastic Neural Analog Reinforcement Calculator," last modified March 27, 2024, 22:44, https://en.wikipedia.org/wiki/Stochastic_Neural_Analog_Reinforcement_Calculator.
120. Dean and Ghemawat, "MapReduce."
121. Apache Hadoop, "Apache Hadoop."
122. Barr, "New – Amazon EC2 Instances."
123. Formula 1, "Formula 1 Selects AWS."
124. AWS, "AWS re:Invent 2018."
125. Chui et al., The Economic Potential of Generative AI.
126. Chui et al., The Economic Potential of Generative AI.
127. AWS, "Transform Responsible AI from Theory into Practice."
128. Felipe et al., The Declining Share.
129. Beckers, Pattern and Security Requirements.
130. Boritz, "IS Practitioners' Views."

131. AWS, Security Pillar.
132. Cook, "AWS re:Invent 2016."
133. AWS, "aws/s2n-tls."
134. Wikipedia, s.v. "Foreign Corrupt Practices Act," last modified February 19, 2024, 03:04, https://en.wikipedia.org/wiki/Foreign_Corrupt_Practices_Act.
135. Brynjolfsson, "The Productivity Paradox."
136. Rasmussen, "GRC 3.0."
137. Shaw, "The Trouble with COSO."
138. Wikipedia, s.v. "COBIT," last modified November 14, 2023, 01:18, https://en.wikipedia.org/wiki/COBIT.
139. Wikipedia, s.v. "Public Company Accounting Oversight Board," last modified December 1, 2023, 05:34, https://en.wikipedia.org/wiki/Public_Company_Accounting_Oversight_Board.
140. Wikipedia, s.v. "Committee of Sponsoring Organizations of the Treadway Commission," Last modified March 26, 2024, 18:27, https://en.wikipedia.org/wiki/Committee_of_Sponsoring_Organizations_of_the_Treadway_Commission#cite_note-3.
141. RiskOptics, "What Are The Differences Between COBIT & COSO."
142. PwC, "IT Governance, Risk and Compliance."
143. NIST, "Cybersecurity Framework"; BSI, PD ISO/IEC TR 27103:2018.
144. The Institute of Internal Auditors, "IIA's Three Lines Model."
145. NIST, NIST SP 800-53 Rev. 5.; ISO, ISO/IEC 27002:2013(En).
146. AWS, Amazon Web Services: Risk and Compliance.
147. AWS, "AWS Compliance."
148. European Parliament, "Sustainable Economy."
149. United Nations, "Sustainability."
150. Gartner, "Gartner Survey Reveals Significant Shifts."
151. Lindsey, "Climate Change."
152. Lee et al., Synthesis Report.
153. Nejad et al., "A Newly Reconciled Dataset."

154. Whiting, "8 Ways."
155. Yao et al., "Satellites Reveal Widespread Decline."
156. World Meteorological Organization, "Past eight years."
157. World Meteorological Organization, "Rising Risks."
158. Dasgupta, The Economics of Biodiversity.
159. Bland, Granskog, and Nauclér, "Accelerating toward Net Zero."
160. Azeem, "To Reach True Net-Zero."
161. Wood "What does net-zero emissions mean."
162. Amazon Staff, "How AWS Will Return More Water."
163. Gartner Research, Sustainability Assessment: Amazon.
164. AWS, Sustainability Pillar.
165. Pereira et al., "Energy Efficiency across Programming Languages."
166. AWS, "Coca-Cola İçecek Improves Operational Performance."
167. Lean Enterprise Institute, "7 Wastes."
168. AWS, "AWS-Solutions-Library."
169. United Nations Environment Programme, Ecosystem Restoration.
170. ZeroNorth, "ZeroNorth Onboard."
171. Philips, Carbon Reduction Plan.
172. Stevens, "Gravity appoints Arup."
173. Rudgley and Seega, Biodiversity Loss and Land Degradation.
174. Taskforce on Nature-related Financial Disclosures, "Taskforce."
175. Hohpe, "AWS re:Invent 2022."
176. Pastore, Fuller, and Gillespie, Business Value of Migration.
177. Hohpe, "Multi-Cloud: From Buzzword to Decision Model."

Printed in Great Britain
by Amazon

55067592R00215